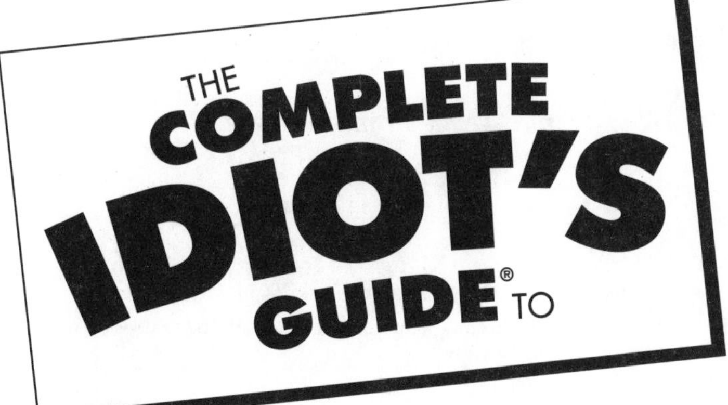

Altered Art

Illustrated

by Allyson Bright Meyer

A member of Penguin Group (USA) Inc.

For Daniel, because I just love you.

ALPHA BOOKS

Published by the Penguin Group

Penguin Group (USA) Inc., 375 Hudson Street, New York, New York 10014, U.S.A.

Penguin Group (Canada), 10 Alcorn Avenue, Toronto, Ontario, Canada M4V 3B2 (a division of Pearson Penguin Canada Inc.)

Penguin Books Ltd, 80 Strand, London WC2R 0RL, England

Penguin Ireland, 25 St Stephen's Green, Dublin 2, Ireland (a division of Penguin Books Ltd)

Penguin Group (Australia), 250 Camberwell Road, Camberwell, Victoria 3124, Australia (a division of Pearson Australia Group Pty Ltd)

Penguin Books India Pvt Ltd, 11 Community Centre, Panchsheel Park, New Delhi—10 017, India

Penguin Group (NZ), cnr Airborne and Rosedale Roads, Albany, Auckland 1310, New Zealand (a division of Pearson New Zealand Ltd)

Penguin Books (South Africa) (Pty) Ltd, 24 Sturdee Avenue, Rosebank, Johannesburg 2196, South Africa

Penguin Books Ltd, Registered Offices: 80 Strand, London WC2R 0RL, England

International Standard Book Number: 978-1-59257-606-7
Library of Congress Catalog Card Number: 2006936703

09 08 07 8 7 6 5 4 3 2 1

Interpretation of the printing code: The rightmost number of the first series of numbers is the year of the book's printing; the rightmost number of the second series of numbers is the number of the book's printing. For example, a printing code of 07-1 shows that the first printing occurred in 2007.

Printed in the United States of America

Publisher: *Marie Butler-Knight*
Editorial Director: *Mike Sanders*
Managing Editor: *Billy Fields*
Executive Editor: *Randy Ladenheim-Gil*
Senior Development Editor: *Christy Wagner*
Production Editor: *Megan Douglass*
Copy Editor: *Emily Garner*
Cartoonist: *Richard King*
Cover Designer: *Kurt Owens*
Book Designer: *Trina Wurst*
Indexer: *Heather McNeill*
Layout: *Chad Dressler*
Proofreader: *Mary Hunt*

Contents at a Glance

Contents

Appendixes

Introduction

Altered art confuses some people. When I mention to others that I enjoy creating altered books, I'm often met with a blank stare. After a short explanation, the inevitable question follows: "But why would anyone want to do that?" The reasons are many and are explored in detail in Chapter 1. But first and foremost, I create altered art because it's fun.

Creating altered art enables you to work with art forms and mediums you've likely never explored. If you're coming to altered art from the world of scrapbooking, you'll enjoy the possibilities and freedom that breaking out of the traditional album format allows. If you're currently a rubber stamper, you'll discover new surface techniques and ideas for using your stash of stamps. And if you've never created art of any kind before, fasten your seat belt. You're in for a real treat.

No matter what your current level of artistic experience, this book helps you dive into the world of altered books and projects with confidence and enthusiasm. You can turn outdated, throwaway books and objects into works of art and celebrate your memories, your personality, and your artistic self. Best of all, there are no rules when it comes to creating altered art.

Before creating your first project, it's a good idea to have a basic knowledge of tools, techniques, and skills at your fingertips—that's where this book comes in. After reading this book and creating some of the many projects contained in these pages, the sky's the limit. Whether you plan to create art for yourself or to share, remember to enjoy the process.

Above all, this book is for you. If you're completely new to the world of altered art, I recommend that you start at the beginning. By the end of the first chapter, you'll have your first project primed and ready to go. If you're an experienced crafter, take the time to flip through the different sections of the book and find a project that most appeals to you. The simple instructions for each project enable you to work in almost any order. Remember that although supply lists are provided for most of the projects in this book, you can always substitute items you already own for those listed. Altered art is all about you—feel free to adapt any of the projects to meet your own needs.

Most of the techniques and ideas in this book can be combined to create your own unique effects. Want to create a book made from envelopes to hold your favorite photographs? Read Chapters 4 and 14. Want to add pockets to an altered book to hold hand-drawn treasures? Try Chapters 7 and 10. The possibilities are endless.

How to Use This Book

This book is divided into five parts:

Part 1, "Foundations," introduces you to the world of altered art and helps you prepare your first book for creation. You also learn a variety of basic background techniques for your pages and discover how to add a decorative cover to your completed book. If you're brand new to the world of altered art, start here to gain a basic understanding of the skills and techniques you need to get started.

Part 2, "Creative Imagery," helps you add flair to your altered book pages by introducing you to the basics of working with photographs, vintage and antique images, rubber stamps, and even your own drawings. You also discover unique image transfer techniques in Part 2.

Part 3, "Fun Additions," teaches you how to take your altered books from good to fabulous by adding texture, extra pages and pull-outs, and unique structures. After you've tried a few of the projects in Part 2, or if you're an intermediate altered artist looking for something more, be sure to check out Part 3.

Part 4, "Unique Book Structures," helps you deal with some of the structural challenges that certain types of books and albums present. Learn how to alter a child's board book as well as a record collector's album—plus—make your own books from simple office supplies.

Part 5, "Beyond the Book," provides projects and instructions for those artists looking to move past the world of altered books and create altered art for the home. You discover artist trading cards, as well as special and unique home décor projects. These are great for the beginning or experienced crafter looking for something more.

Finally, you'll find a set of appendixes. Appendix A contains a complete glossary of all the new terms and techniques I introduce throughout the book. Appendix B introduces you to the book's team of creative designers, who all contributed artwork to this book. Appendix C helps you find the exact product you need to replicate any of the projects in this book. And Appendix D helps you find more information, both in books and online, about many of the techniques and projects presented in this book.

Be sure not to miss the color insert! These 8 pages of full color feature some of the best projects throughout the book and allow you to see them as they were meant to be seen—in true, living color.

Whatever you choose to create, I applaud you. Just remember to have fun and let your creative spirit be your guide!

Extras

Throughout this book, you'll encounter four types of boxes that provide you with extra help or information as you read:

Picture This

Look here for fun ideas and special tips to make creating your projects easier and more exciting.

Transforming Talk

In these boxes, I explain new or difficult terms specifically related to the craft of altered art.

Altered Alert

Check these boxes for warnings as you're reading about and working on projects. They can help you avoid frustrating errors!

UNALTERABLE FACT

These boxes offer fun facts and useful information about altered art.

Acknowledgments

Writing this book has been a truly rewarding experience. It would simply have been impossible without the help of so many people. I would like to thank with immense gratitude:

The entire Alpha Books team—I have loved working with you to create the best book possible. In particular, thank you to Randy Ladenheim-Gil for your guidance and support of this manuscript, and for your leadership as I learn the ropes of the publishing world. Thank you also to Christy Wagner for your enthusiasm, encouragement, and assistance throughout the process of writing this book—I couldn't have done it without you!

Jacky Sach of BookEnds, LLC—once again, I appreciate all the time and effort you provide to help make my writing career a lasting success. Thank you.

The many companies who provided product and industry expertise—100 Proof Press, Altered Pages, Beacon Adhesives, Carolee's Creations, Daylab, Enchanted Ink, Fiber Scraps, Jacquard, Lazar StudioWERX, Leisure Arts, Masquepen, Michael Miller Memories, Microfleur, Sakura, Stampbord, Stewart Superior, Strano Designs, Technique Tuesday, Victorian Scrapworks, Violette Stickers, and Walnut Hollow. An additional thank you to Daylab for providing instruction and guidance with image transfer.

Daniel J. Meyer—for providing wonderful photographs of projects and techniques.

Thank you to all the amazing artists who allowed their work to be included in this book.

An extra-special thank you to Kate Schaefer for enduring tight deadlines, artistic specifications, and photography requirements with a smile. Your friendship means the world to me.

Finally, my family and friends—thank you for being so supportive of this project amidst wedding plans, moving, and more. It's amazing to have such wonderful people in my life.

Trademarks

In This Part

Part 1

Foundations

The world of altered art can seem intimidating and complex. Really, though, it's quite simple. In Part 1, we explore the foundations of altered art. I give you a brief history of the evolution of the craft and provide you with the direction you need to get started. You'll be able to select basic supplies and learn how to choose the perfect book for your first altered project. A detailed walkthrough of basic background techniques helps you create fabulous altered pages, regardless of your theme or skill level. Finally, you learn how to cover a book and add finishing touches to your altered art projects.

Whether you're a complete beginner, an experienced crafter, or an artist like Andy Warhol, Part 1 provides you with the background you need to gain a solid understanding of altered art. Let's get started altering!

In This Chapter

- A short history of altered art
- Understanding the components of altered art
- Creating a sampler and working with themes
- Preparing your book for alteration

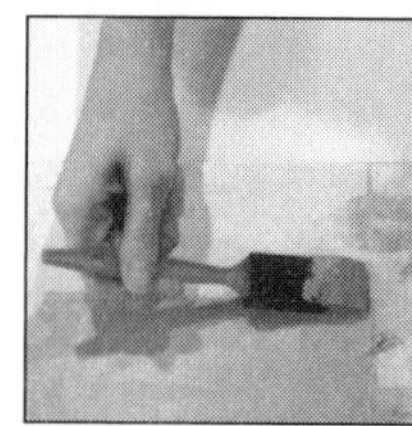

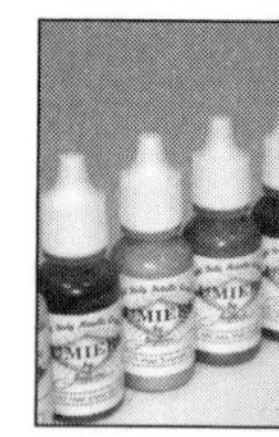

Chapter 1

Getting Started

So you've decided to become an altered artist, and you've told a few of your friends. Chances are, when you said, "I'm thinking about creating an altered book," you got a funny look and the very typical response: "Huh?" Then you had to explain what exactly altered art is and why you've chosen to create it.

Creating *altered art* can seem intimidating at first, especially to those who have never worked with some of the craft's more popular tools and mediums, such as ink and acrylic paint. In all reality, creating altered art is much simpler than you think! One of the most wonderful things about altered art is that there really are no rules. You can create whatever you want, for any reason you want. It's just that simple.

Transforming Talk

Altered art is the craft of taking a secondhand item, such as a book or old wooden box, and using creative techniques and tools to alter and change the item, giving it a new purpose and artistic meaning.

Ancient History

Altered art is hardly a new art form. Artists, scribes, and thrifty people have been working with this art form for centuries. Sometimes, altered art is simply the process of reusing an item in a new and different way. Artists such as Leonardo da Vinci would paint over an existing painting to reuse the canvas. During the Great Depression, many families were forced to think outside of the box when it came to obtaining new things. Many families even created clothing out of brightly colored flour sacks. That's not quite altered art, but it was coming close. Items that would otherwise have been discarded were finding new life and new purposes. This is one of the key themes of altered art creation.

The idea of altering books was first seen in the early 1900s. Many individuals who lived during this time created scrapbooks containing their photographs, mail, and all sorts of other memorabilia. While some people chose to collect their items in scrapbooks containing blank pages, others—perhaps those simply looking for yet another way to reuse an item they already owned—chose to paste items directly onto the pages of printed books.

Today, altered books and other forms of altered art are rapidly increasing in popularity. This can largely be attributed to a British artist named Tom Phillips, who many believe is the father of the modern altered book. In 1970, Phillips published a work titled *A Humument*, which was his altered art take on the 1892 novel *A Human Document*. The book quickly became a modern cult classic, particularly in the art world. Phillips has continually worked to revise and alter the pages with subsequent editions, eventually altering each and every page of the book.

Maps, travel brochures, mail, art postcards, and handwritten notes were just a few of the items many individuals chose to paste into scrapbooks like this one.

A Humument has served as an inspiration to so many other artists and crafters who now create their own works of altered art. While Phillips has completed many other projects and artistic works, *A Humument* is the one that has so dramatically shaped the world of altered art as we know it today.

UNALTERABLE FACT

A Humument is widely available in print. View the entire first edition online at www.humument.com or check out the fourth edition in book form (released in April 2005 by Thames & Hudson).

Altered art is now growing into a mainstream art form, and the unique creations of altered artists are gaining widespread attention. The International Society of Altered Book Artists works diligently to promote the art form through exhibitions, newsletters, and more. Many crafters are finding their way to altered art from other mainstream crafts—scrapbooking and rubber stamping in particular. No matter what your experience, or why you've decided to create altered art, there's something in this art form just for you.

The Parts of Altered Art

Altered art requires two basic pieces:

- The object you want to alter
- The unique additions you add to make the art your own

The heart of altered art requires changing an existing item, and that item can be almost anything at all. Before you go to toss something in the trash, ask yourself if it can be altered. In all likelihood, the answer is yes. Books, cigar boxes, food containers, cans, and tins—these are just a few of the items that can be altered with dazzling results.

The easiest and most common way to enter the world of altered art is to begin by altering books. Books are a very forgiving medium. If you make an error, you can simply rip out the page and begin again. In general, purchasing books to alter isn't very expensive. Old hardcovers can be found at garage sales, resale shops, and perhaps even in your own basement. Plus the text and images found inside printed books provide an amazing base for your work.

UNALTERABLE FACT

I focus primarily on altered books throughout this *Idiot's Guide*. If you're already hungry for different project ideas, turn to Part 5 for all sorts of fun and unique out-of-the-book techniques.

Altered art is unique because no two pieces are alike. Adding paint, images, and some of your own text enables you to create a piece of art that is uniquely yours.

Throughout this book, I show you hundreds of different ways to add your own special touch to your books and creations.

What's the Point?

Why would someone bother to create altered art in the first place? There are as many different reasons to create altered art as there are people who practice the craft, but I believe there are four basic reasons that can apply to almost everyone.

Altered Alert

When it comes to altered art, some people just aren't going to get it. These are the same people who insist on living life in the same way, day after day. Do not let their unwillingness to think outside the box impact your creative enthusiasm!

Self-Expression

First and foremost, creating altered art provides a way to express yourself artistically as almost no other craft can. Because there are no real rules to creating altered art, the sky truly is the limit. You can create whatever you want, for your own purposes.

Many people choose to use altered books as a basis for creating personal journals. Store-bought blank books create lovely vehicles for writing, but sometimes it's just not enough—especially if you'd like to add more than just text to your journals. An altered book provides a unique journaling surface with unlimited possibilities—without breaking your pocketbook.

These altered book pages were created using a vintage greeting card image, some Victorian scraps, and a bit of old lace.

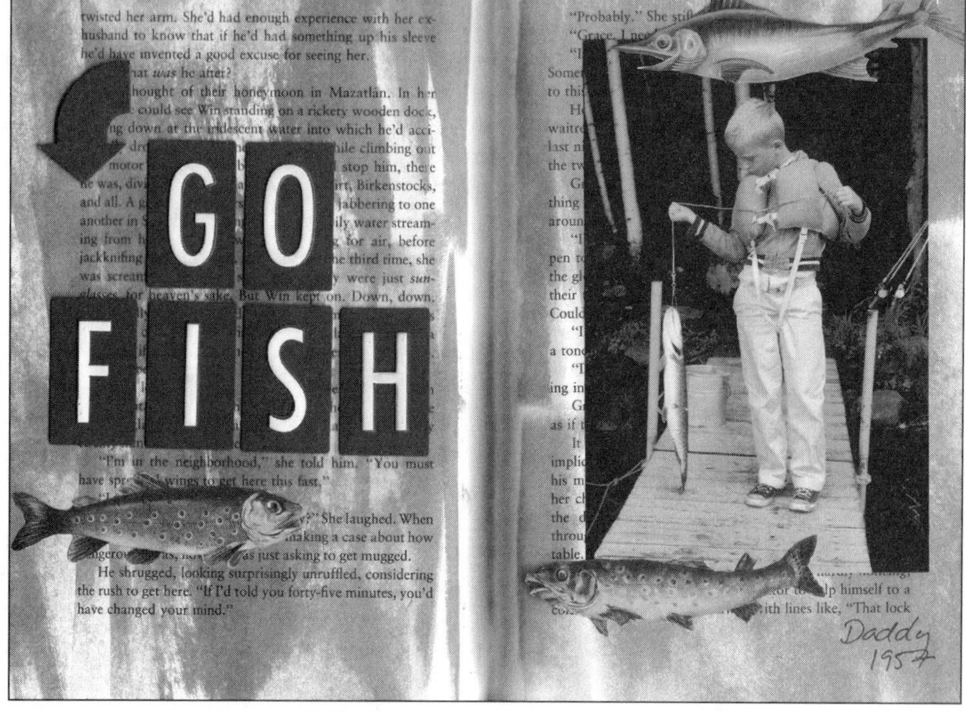

I love this photo of my father as a young boy. Creating these altered book pages was a fun way to connect with the things I love about my dad as well as work with a new artistic theme.

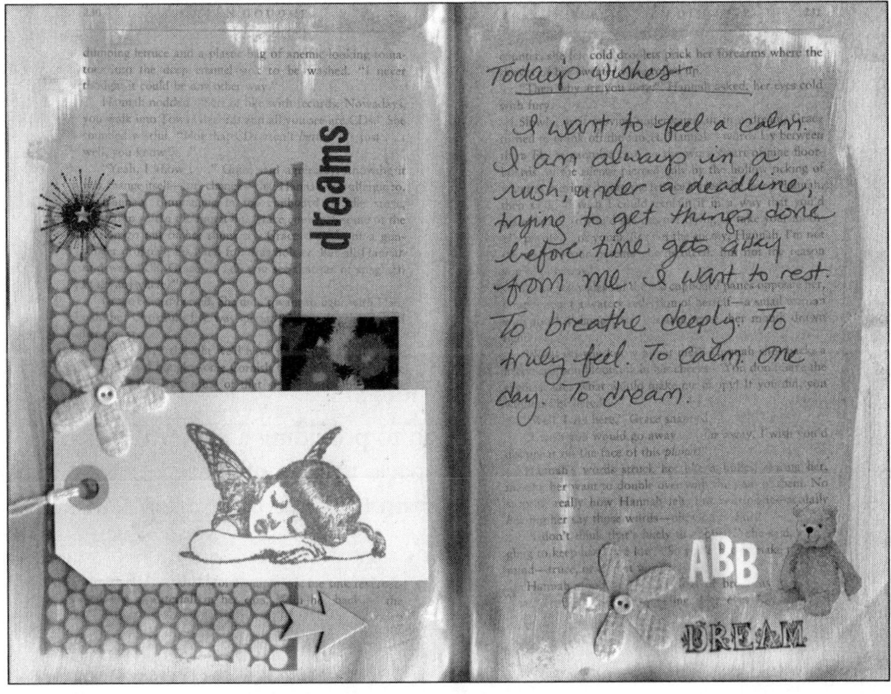

This art journal spread creatively conveys my feelings about dreams and rest.

Artistic journal entries enable the artist to really sit back and reflect on the topic at hand, and these pages provide the artist a more unusual way to express his or her feelings. Take a look again at the previous photo. Could I have simply written this text in a blank book? Yes. But by creating my art journal spread in an altered book, it allowed me to dive into my emotions and express my feelings in more than just words. This method of self-expression can be beneficial and fun for almost anyone. In particular, it works quite well for those who want to journal but enjoy visual art more than writing.

Memory Preservation

Altered art is often used as a vehicle to preserve your memories and photographs. Altered books can allow more creative and artistic options than traditional scrapbooks. They also allow the artist to explore ideas and memories in ways that more standard options do not.

For example, if you're like most people, you probably have hundreds of photographs lying around. Maybe some of them have found their way into photo albums and scrapbooks, but lots of them probably haven't. Altered books are a great way to use some of those photos that haven't found their way into homes yet.

Whether you choose to work with age-old family photos or yesterday's snapshots from a walk to the park, including your photos in your altered books is fun and easy. Preserving your memories in altered books is a great way to relive the moment and really connect with the subject of your photograph.

Altered Alert

When adding photographs to your altered books, it's a good idea to use copies instead of originals. Altered books aren't acid-free, and you don't want to risk ruining your only copy of an important family photograph.

Connecting with Others

Giving a piece of altered art as a gift is like giving the recipient a piece of you. Whether you've created a special book project for a friend or a set of altered coasters for your father, the art contains your own special and unique touch. Many of the project ideas throughout this book are fantastic for gift giving.

Over the last several years, one trend in altered art has emerged that allows you to connect with others in a way no other art form has allowed: artist trading cards (ATCs). ATCs are small pieces of art that can be traded with other artists, shared with friends, or kept in your own collection. Much like standard baseball cards, ATCs allow individuals all over the world to connect through the mutual love of a hobby. All that's missing is a stick of gum!

To learn how to create ATCs, as well as ways you can connect with other artists, turn to Chapter 15.

Home Décor

I believe altered art creations are a unique decorative addition to almost any space. Many items you alter will, all on their own, create fabulous pieces of home décor. Whether you choose to alter a photo frame, mirror, or something else entirely, you have endless possibilities for showcasing altered items in your home. You can also use altered art techniques to work directly on stretched canvas, to create one-of-a-kind wall art for your home.

In addition to providing a personal touch to your living space, the use of altered art as décor is almost certain to be a conversation starter in your home.

Try displaying one of your altered books in a prominent place in your home, and see what happens the next time you have company over.

"What's that?" they'll ask.

"An altered book," you'll reply.

"Huh?" they'll say, implying all sorts of questions with that one small word. Now you finally have the answers.

These artist trading cards (ATCs) are fun, funky, and artistic.

(Cards by Belinda Spiwak)

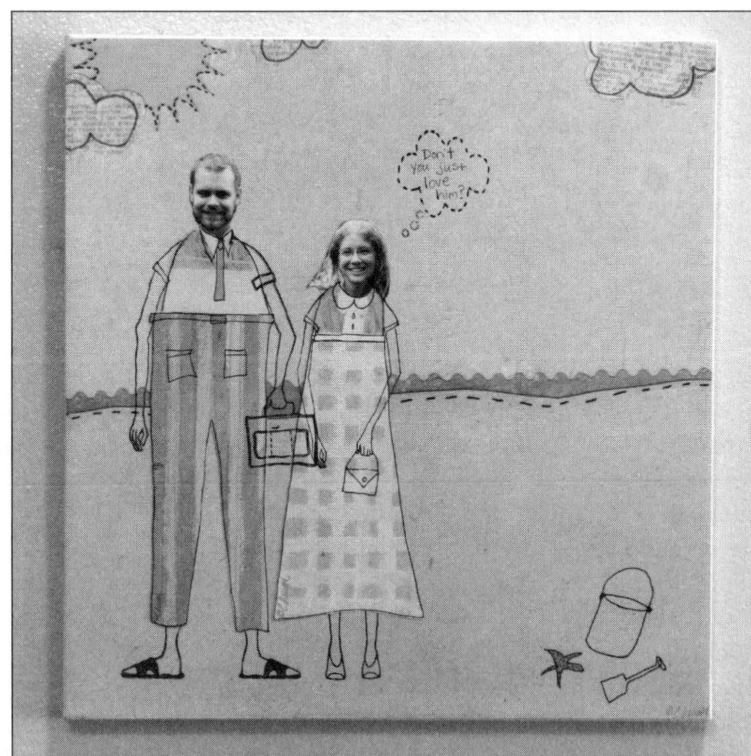

I created this wall hanging to display my love for both the beach and my husband.

(Poppets craft products designed by Claudine Hellmuth, a product of Lazar StudioWERX)

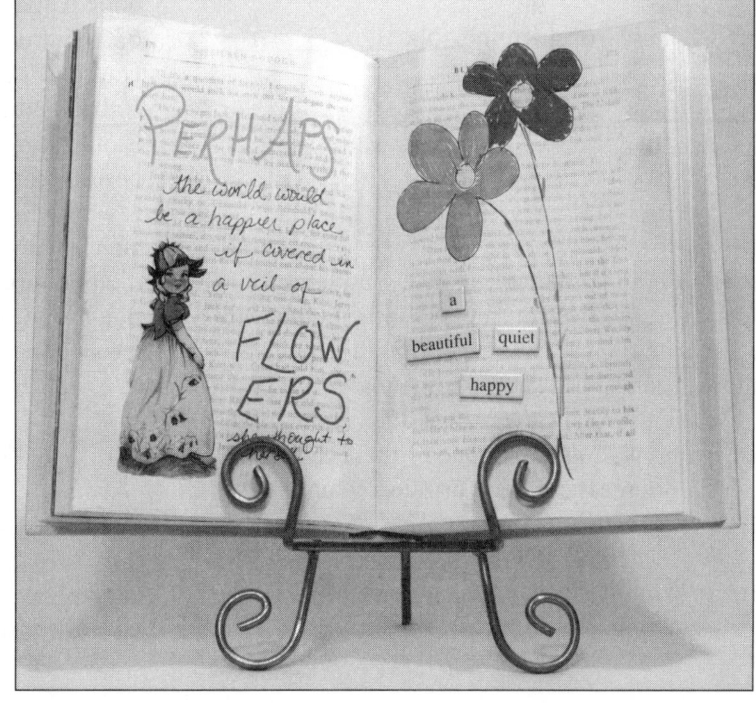

Altered books can serve as décor items simply by displaying them on a small easel or stand.

Selecting a Book

The first step in making an altered book is locating a book to alter. Because the book is the foundation of your art, it's important to give careful consideration to many factors when choosing your book.

Deciding on a Theme (or Not)

First, you'll want to decide if your altered book is going to have a theme or if you'd like to create a *sampler.* Creating a sampler is a great first project for beginning altered artists. You're not limited to working with a specific theme or medium, so you can get lots of practice creating different types of altered art pages and designs. I recommend working in a sampler as you perfect the techniques and ideas throughout the book. Then, when you feel comfortable, try creating one of the more specialized projects or design your own.

> **Transforming Talk**
>
> A **sampler** is an altered book that contains pages and spreads decorated in all sorts of ways, without any real regard to whether or not they go together.

If you don't want to create a sampler, or if you already have, consider creating a book with a favorite theme. When working in a themed book, each spread should somehow relate to that subject. You can create a book about almost anything you want. Try one of these theme ideas for an easy project, or select your own:

- A favorite color
- Wildlife or a favorite animal
- Childhood toys
- A relative or significant other
- Magic
- Spirituality
- Travel
- Food
- Music

If you're creating a sampler, look for a book that appeals to you in some way or another. Perhaps the title catches your eye, or maybe you simply like the binding style. Anything goes! If you're creating a book based on a theme, look for a book that matches that theme. For example, an old Audubon Society field guide would make an excellent base for an altered book about nature.

The Binding

Once you know what type of book you're looking for, you next need to look at a few physical concerns. First, it's important to use a hardcover book. Paperback books won't hold up to lots of alteration and will likely rip and fall apart as you're working. Next—and most important—is the condition of the book's binding. A book is only as good as its binding. It might have beautiful art and text inside, but if the binding is weak, the book will fall apart when you try to alter it, leaving you with much frustration and disappointment. Look for a book with a sewn binding in good condition. Be sure the binding feels strong and tight.

> **Picture This**
>
> If a book you love has a weak binding, consider purchasing it anyway. It won't work well as a complete altered book, but you can rip out the pages and use them for other altered art projects.

Basic Supplies

Now that you've found a book to alter, you only need a few more things to get started. Regardless of which altering techniques you choose to use in your book, it's important to have a few basic tools on hand. Start by gathering the following:

- A ruler
- A pair of scissors
- A craft knife

You'll use these basic tools regularly, so be sure to keep them easily accessible.

You'll also want to purchase a rubber *brayer*, which you'll use for paint and ink application, as well as to spread your adhesive evenly when gluing book pages together.

Transforming Talk

Much like a miniature paint roller, a **brayer** is a small roller with a handle that's used to evenly apply ink and paint to paper and other surfaces.

Finally, you'll want to purchase a variety of adhesives. Adhesives are one of the most important tools to have on hand when creating altered art, and all adhesives are not created equal. At the very least, you need a strong, acid-free glue stick to create your pages and prepare your book. As you try new techniques, you'll likely also need a few specialty adhesives. Refer to the specific instructions for each technique for more information on adhesives.

Preparing Your Pages

With your book and a few basic supplies on hand, you're ready to prepare your book for creation. Two basic procedures will, once complete, leave your book ready and waiting for your artistic touch.

Thinning Out

Book bindings are designed for flat, thin pages. When the book is closed, the covers lie flat and even. When you add art and three-dimensional accents to a book, the pages no longer lie flat on top of each other when closed, making it nearly impossible for your book to close evenly—or in some cases, for your book to close at all. For this reason, you should *thin out* your book before you begin altering it.

Transforming Talk

Thinning out your book is the process of removing pages from your book to allow it to close evenly after you add some artwork.

To thin out your book, you need to remove pages to allow for extra room for your art and embellishments. I recommend ripping out every fifth page through the entire book, from beginning to end. This process might seem tedious at first, but it can go rather quickly, and it's really important to do this to enable your book to close evenly and preserve your binding.

Follow these simple steps to remove a page from your book:

1. Using a ruler, mark a space at the top of your page about 3/4 inch from the inside binding of your book.
2. Hold your ruler vertically against the page, parallel to the book's binding, lining up your ruler with the mark you just made.
3. Gently pull the page toward you, ripping until it's completely removed from the book.

Altered Alert

Don't give in to the temptation to simply rip out pages from your book carelessly. Removing pages too close to the binding can damage it, causing your entire book to fall apart.

Creating Support

The other step to preparing your book is to create support for your artwork. If you selected a standard book such as a novel or textbook to alter, the pages will be too thin to support your artwork on their own. Adding paint or embellishments will cause the pages to curl or tear. To avoid this, you want to create a stronger foundation for the art in your book by gluing two consecutive pages together. The combined weight of the two pages, plus the adhesive, will be enough to support most basic techniques.

Altered Alert

Begin by supporting the pages you plan to alter first. That way, if you make a mistake, you can easily rip out the page, glue two more together, and start again. Eventually, you'll want to be sure you add support to all the pages you plan to alter.

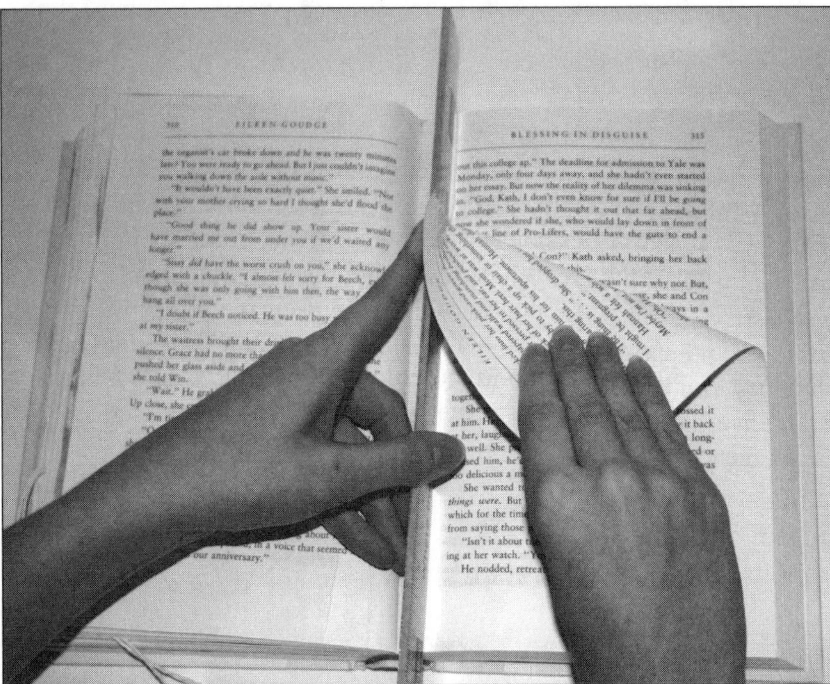

Keep even pressure on the ruler as you tear out your page to provide a crisp, even tear.

Follow these easy steps to glue your pages together:

1. Using a glue stick, apply adhesive to the entire surface of one book page. Be sure to pay special attention to the corners and edges of the page.
2. Smooth the second page out over the adhesive so the two pages are stuck together.
3. Using a brayer, roll evenly over the top page to smooth out the glue and any air bubbles.

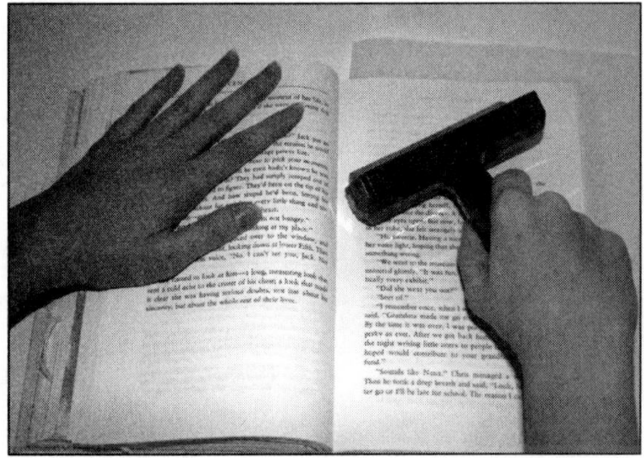

Using a brayer helps smooth out your pages and removes any trapped air bubbles from the adhering process.

If you're having trouble with your glue stick, you might want to use *gel medium* as an alternate adhesive. It's more expensive than a standard glue stick, but it has many qualities that make it an ideal choice for most of the altered art projects in this book. Use it as an adhesive any time you're working with paper, or as a protective sealant for your pages.

Transforming Talk

Gel medium is a liquid gel that acts an adhesive for altered art and collage, drying to a smooth finish. It's available in matte or glossy finish, and can also be used to create a protective coating on top of your artwork, sealing out air and dust. Finally, it can be mixed with acrylic paint to extend drying time and add dimension to the dried paint.

Congratulations! You're now armed with a perfectly prepared book, along with the knowledge and desire to add your own artwork. No matter whether you choose to create a series of unrelated pages or you're working on a themed project, you are now ready to enter the world of altered art with confidence.

The Least You Need to Know

- Altered art is the craft of taking a secondhand item and artistically changing it to create a new, artistic purpose.
- Creating altered art consists of working with two basic components: the item you want to alter and your own artsy additions.
- Self-expression, memory preservation, connecting with others, and decorating your home are four primary reasons to create altered art.
- Creating a sampler can be a great way to get started as an altered book artist.
- Before adding artwork to your book pages, be sure to thin out your book and create support for your artwork.

In This Chapter

- Creating backgrounds for your altered book pages
- Using paint, ink, and paper to create artistic looks
- Making a woven background page

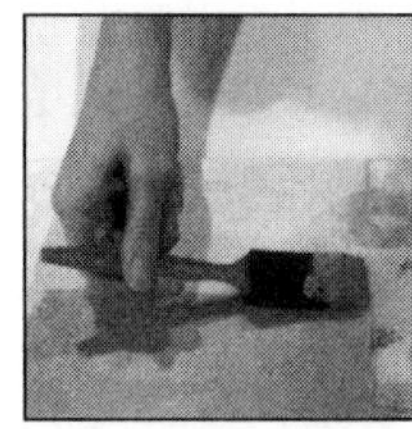

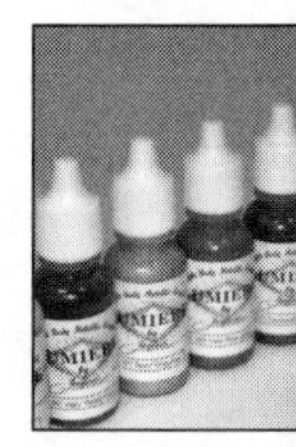

Chapter 2

Basic Backgrounds

You've learned about altered art, and you've prepped your first book for creation. What's next? It's time to get creating! You've probably garnered a few ideas, and you might have even set aside a few special photographs or mementos you'd like to include as part of your first altered book. It's almost time to add them. But first, it's time to learn how to create the perfect foundation for your project—by discovering some easy and fun background techniques.

Isn't the *Book* the Background?

Part of the fun of working in altered books is that the text and images in the book provide a ready-made background for your art. This is indeed a good thing, but sometimes it poses a problem. Perhaps the text on the page you want to work on is too dark, and you're worried it will overpower your art. Or maybe you only want to use a certain part of the text, and you'd like to cover up the rest. Or maybe you want to add some fabulous color and texture to your artwork.

No matter what you plan to include in your book, and regardless of the theme you're thinking of, it's a great idea to begin each altered book by giving it a solid background treatment. The products and techniques in this chapter help you create backgrounds that can serve as the foundation for almost any project.

Brush It On: Paint and More

Using paint and similar mediums on your altered book pages is easy to learn and quick to do. You can easily add color, as well as a bit of texture, with a quick swipe of the brush. And because you control the paintbrush, you decide exactly how much color you want and exactly where you want it—making it the ideal choice for one of your first pages.

Gesso

Using *gesso* on book pages is a common first step for many altered artists. Similar to acrylic paint in many ways, gesso comes in a jar, is liquid in form, and can be applied to your painting surface using a brush. Gesso is thinner than paint but dries hard. In addition, gesso is formulated for strong paint adhesion. Some surfaces, particularly glossier ones, don't hold paint well, causing the paint to flake off over time. Using gesso as a base coat prevents this.

Transforming Talk

Gesso is a primer commonly used to prepare painting surfaces for decoration. It's generally white or black in color and can be applied like paint.

To apply gesso to your pages, simply use a foam paint brush. I like to use the disposable ones you can purchase in bulk from most craft and hobby stores.

Apply the gesso over the entire page surface, working from the top of the page toward the bottom. Be sure to apply the gesso all the way to the edge of each page you're working on. A single, thin coat of gesso is enough to prepare your page and usually allows some text to remain visible on the page. If you want to completely obscure the text of the book, opt for thicker coverage.

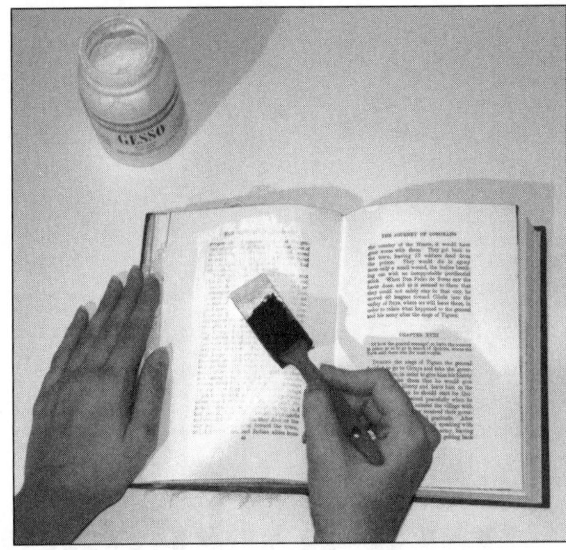

Work quickly when applying gesso, as it dries rapidly.

Your pages might begin to curl as the gesso dries. To prevent this, be sure to have at least two or three pages glued together for added strength. If your pages still curl, don't worry. After the gesso dries, close your book. Gather the book's pages together with a binder clip or two and allow the closed book to set overnight. If your book is particularly thick, gather about half the pages, making sure to sandwich the curled pages in the middle. This should flatten any curls that might have formed.

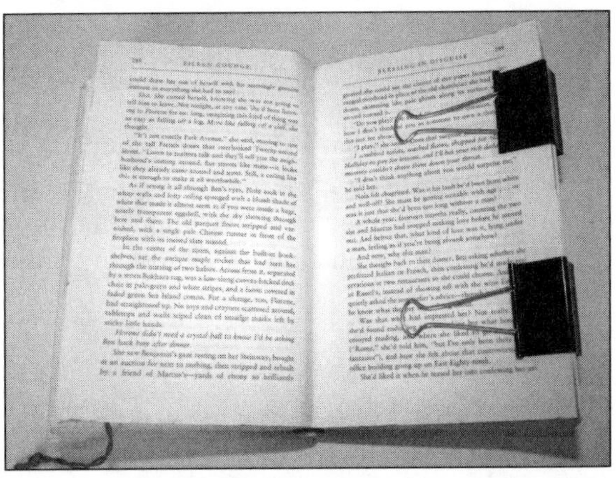

If your pages curl after applying gesso, simply clamp the pages together and close the book. Set overnight, the pages should flatten out.

Altered Alert

When applying gesso to the edges of the paper, it can sometimes be difficult to keep the gesso from getting onto other pages of the book. If you're having trouble, trying placing a sheet of wax paper slightly larger than your book page behind the page you're working on. This covers and protects the book's additional pages.

Gesso comes in both white and black, and both are fun to use to create unique effects in your altered books. White gesso works great as a foundation because it creates an entirely white base for your pages, allowing to you decorate and embellish on a clean slate. Black gesso is creating for creating more dramatic effects and works excellent as a base for metallic paint and inks.

Paint

Paint, widely available in hundreds of colors, is another great product for altered book artists. Gesso can generally only be found in specialty art and craft stores, but you can find paint in many more places, including your local Wal-Mart or other mass merchant store.

All paints are not created equal. There are many different options available to altered artists. Acrylic paints are a great choice for beginning artists. They are highly affordable—many brands start as low as 99¢ for a 2-ounce bottle. At this price, you probably can afford to stock up. I also enjoy using paints formulated for fabric and other surfaces. Fabric paint remains soft after drying, creating a beautiful effect.

I enjoy using Lumiere paints, manufactured by Jacquard. They come in 24 beautiful colors and dry to a beautiful finish.

To apply paint to your pages, you can use a variety of techniques. My favorite method is the tried-and-true disposable foam brush.

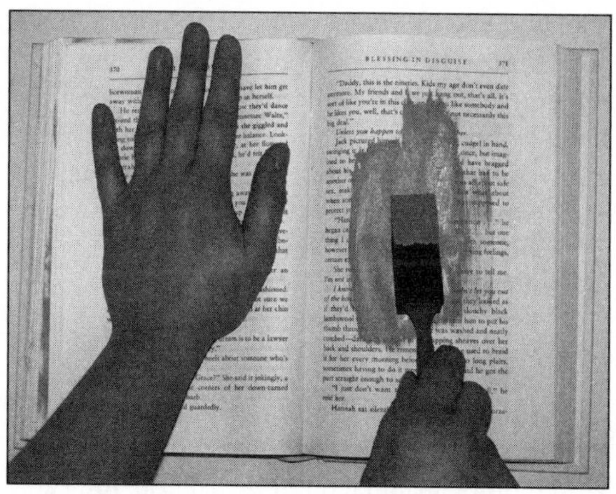

Paint the entire page, edge to edge, or just a select area. The choice is yours!

Feel free to experiment with paint on your pages. You can apply paint to the entire page, or try one of these fun techniques to jazz it up a bit:

- Create a border for the painted page from a contrasting paint color.
- Apply paint with a standard artist's brush or watercolor brush.

- Apply paint to bubble wrap or another textured surface and press onto your page.
- Paint each page in a different color or combination of colors.
- Paint around a text block or image on your page, leaving that area untouched.
- Paint over only a certain element or portion of your book page.
- Mix one or more paint colors to create your own unique shade.

No matter how you choose to use paint, you'll be glad you did. The color options are endless, and so are the looks you can achieve when working with paint in your altered books.

Watercolors

You might think watercolor paint would be a poor choice for altered books, but that just isn't so. You do have to be aware of a few factors when working with watercolor paint, primarily due to the incredibly fluid nature of the paint, but once you've got the basics covered, you can use watercolor paint in your altered books with ease and confidence.

Watercolor paints come in many forms, from liquid watercolors to the art paint sets you probably remember painting with as a child. My favorite watercolor paints to work with are Koi Watercolors, manufactured by Sakura. You can purchase Koi Watercolors in a small box set, which contains 12 cake watercolors, a brush, and a sponge. It all weighs less than 4 ounces—great for artists on the go. You can also get Koi Watercolors in tube form.

Many brush choices are available for watercolor artists, in a range of quality and price. Feel free to use whatever brush suits you best, but be sure to choose one designed specifically for watercolor painting, as it will ensure the best coverage and application. One of my favorite products, again from the Koi Watercolor line, is the WaterBrush. This unique brush contains a water reservoir in the barrel. Simply fill it with water and begin painting. You need only light pressure to release the water to the brush tip, and you can paint as usual. Using a WaterBrush eliminates the need for a cup of water near your workspace, which can be a disaster waiting to happen. WaterBrushes are available in three different sizes. Koi Watercolors and WaterBrushes can be purchased at your local art supply store, or direct from Sakura. Turn to Appendix D for more information.

To use watercolors in your altered books, you'll first need to cover the pages you want to work on with a strong coat of white gesso. Let this dry completely, and your book pages will be ready for painting.

Altered Alert

Don't skip the white gesso! Without it, your pages will be too weak to support the watercolor, resulting in buckled and torn pages in your book.

Once you've mastered the basics, try a fun technique or two to keep things interesting. Watercolor paint doesn't dry as quickly as acrylic, so you have a bit more freedom to experiment.

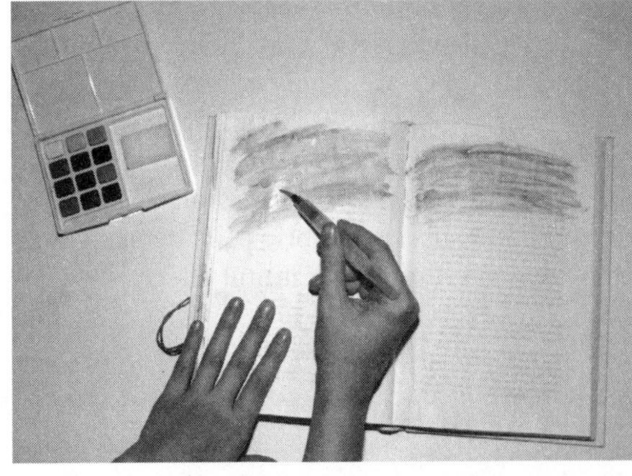

Experiment with your paint stroke size and speed. Different techniques yield lots of exciting results.

After you've applied paint to your page, trying adding a texture effect by crinkling a piece of plastic wrap over the wet paint. Lift it up and notice how the paint holds the crinkled texture. Let dry for a different look. For even more fun, sprinkle salt over the wet paint and watch how a resist effect is created!

Adding watercolor paints to your altered books can provide a soft, light mood and feel to your pages. While acrylic paints are thick and heavy, watercolor enables you to explore a completely different look on the page.

Ink It Up

Another great way to add color and texture to your page backgrounds is to use ink. Let's look at a couple ways you can ink up your pages.

Inkpads

You may have used inkpads before, likely with rubber stamps. That's certainly a fantastic way to use inkpads, but it's definitely not the only way. Inkpads can also be used directly on paper, and this is a great way to achieve amazing background color for your altered book pages.

Inkpads come in hundreds of colors and styles. For this particular technique, I recommend using a pigment inkpad in a strong color. (To learn more about inkpad types, or for help selecting an inkpad, turn to Chapter 6.)

Open the inkpad and turn it upside down over your altered book page so the ink surface faces the page. Using a firm amount of pressure, sweep the inkpad across the page's surface, spreading color across the page as dark or light as you like.

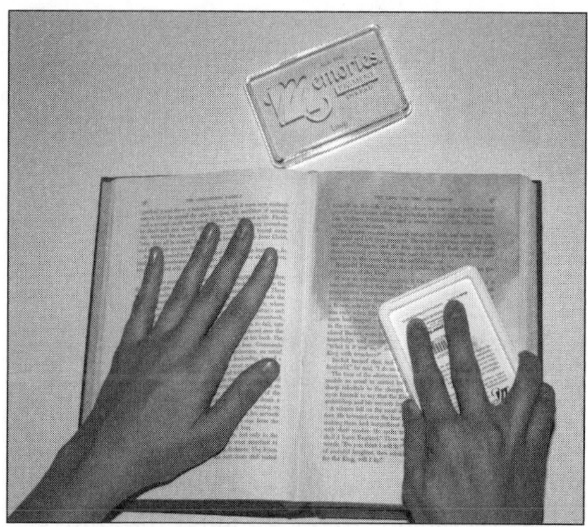

Inking from the top of the page to the bottom helps you avoid messy fingers!

The ink will naturally be thicker in some areas than others, but that's a good thing! This adds the illusion of texture to your page and can be quite attractive. Working to apply the ink darker or lighter at the edges of your pages can create a nice border effect, too.

Bottled Ink

Ink doesn't just come in pads—it can also be found in bottles of all kinds! Bottled inks have the potential to be messy, but the results are completely worth it. My favorite bottled ink is Fiber Scraps's Walnut Ink.

Walnut Ink by Fiber Scraps comes in a variety of bright colors, in addition to traditional brown.

Transforming Talk

Walnut ink, traditionally made from walnuts, is known for its thickness and deep color. Many manufacturers now mass-produce it synthetically as well as naturally.

Most walnut ink manufacturers package the ink in small bottles containing an eyedropper or spray nozzle to apply the ink. As you might imagine, this gets messy quite quickly! Fiber Scraps packages its walnut ink with a unique dauber on the tip. To use it, simply turn the bottle over and, using a light amount of pressure, glide the bottle tip across the surface of your page. Use wide, even strokes, and your entire page will be covered in no time.

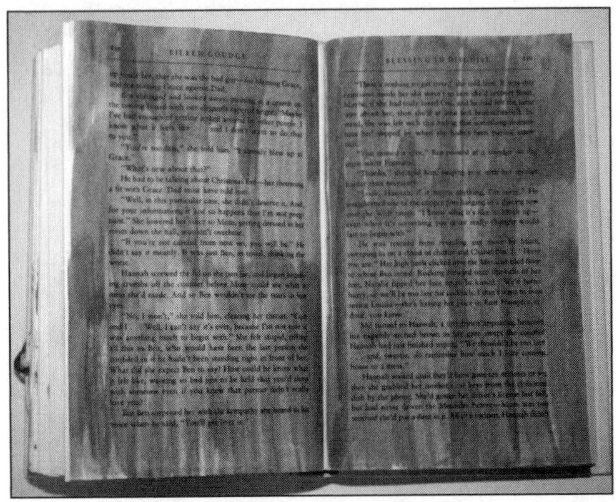

I created this background easily with just a few strokes of the bottle.

With your background ready to go, you are ready for even more possibilities. Notice in the next photo how the background becomes even more striking when images, text, and embellishments are added.

Picture This

Feeling adventurous? Try creating your own walnut ink! For complete instructions, visit en.wikipedia.org/wiki/Walnut_ink.

Paper Backgrounds

If you're coming to altered art with scrapbooking experience, you've probably already thought of this: using decorative and patterned papers to create backgrounds. From stripes and plaids to paisley and florals, you're sure to find just the paper you're looking for. Most patterned papers come in 12×12-inch squares, but you can also find select patterns available in $8^1/_2$×11 inches. To purchase papers, visit your local scrapbooking or craft store. If you can't find what you're looking for nearby, try an online store such as www.scrapbook.com.

Picture This

To effectively use patterned papers in your altered books, you'll need a paper trimmer. You can usually find inexpensive trimmers where patterned paper is sold.

There are several ways you can use patterned papers to create backgrounds in your altered books. One of the easiest methods is to simply use the paper to cover the entire book page:

1. Use a ruler to measure the dimensions of your book page.
2. Trim a sheet of patterned paper to this size, or slightly smaller if you'd like to leave a border.

This inked page uses a variety of techniques and additions you'll learn in future chapters.

3. Adhere the paper into your book using glue stick or a scrapbooking adhesive of your choice.

You can cover both pages completely or leave one blank. Or try one of these fun ideas:

- Adhere various-size blocks of paper to your page, leaving certain parts of the text exposed.
- Use a frame cut from a sheet of patterned paper to highlight an element of your page.
- Use cut paper triangles as border corners for your page.
- Use multiple patterned papers to collage a customized background.
- Cut a mat from patterned paper to use with a photograph or other decorative element.

This fun striped paper sets the stage for a whimsical look.

Woven Paper Background

One of my favorite ways to use patterned papers in altered books is to weave it through the book's pages. This sounds difficult, but it's really quite easy with the right tools and some simple instruction.

To create a woven background, you'll need these supplies:

- Weaving template (WeaverZ by Fiber Scraps)
- Patterned paper of your choice
- Paper trimmer
- Pencil with eraser
- Craft knife with fresh blade
- Cutting mat
- Masking tape or other removable adhesive

Now just follow these easy steps to create your woven paper background:

1. Position the weaving template over your book page where you'd like to create the weaving. Use masking tape to secure it in place.
2. With a pencil, trace through the slits in the template, marking where you'll need to cut.

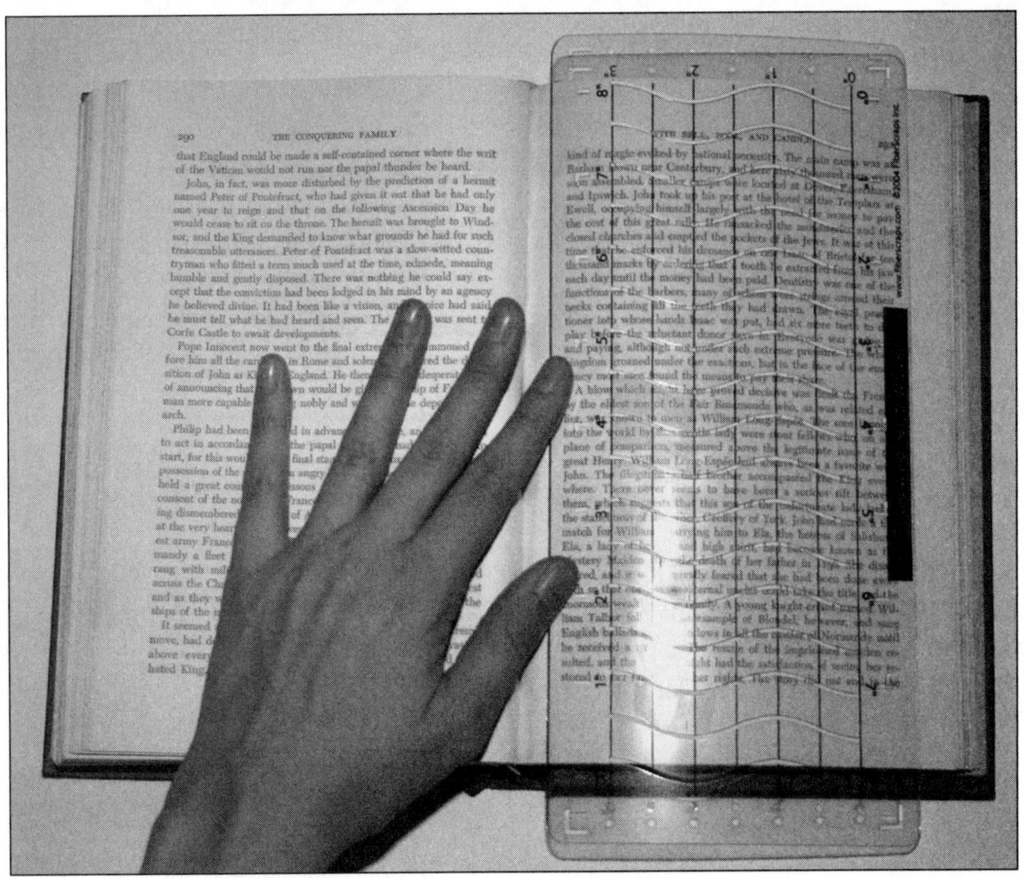

Notice how the template is lined up directly on top of the text.

3. Remove the template from the paper, and place a cutting mat under the page.
4. Use a craft knife to cut along the traced lines, creating slits in your paper.
5. Cut your patterned paper into strips of whatever width you'd like. Narrower strips will create a more intricate weave.

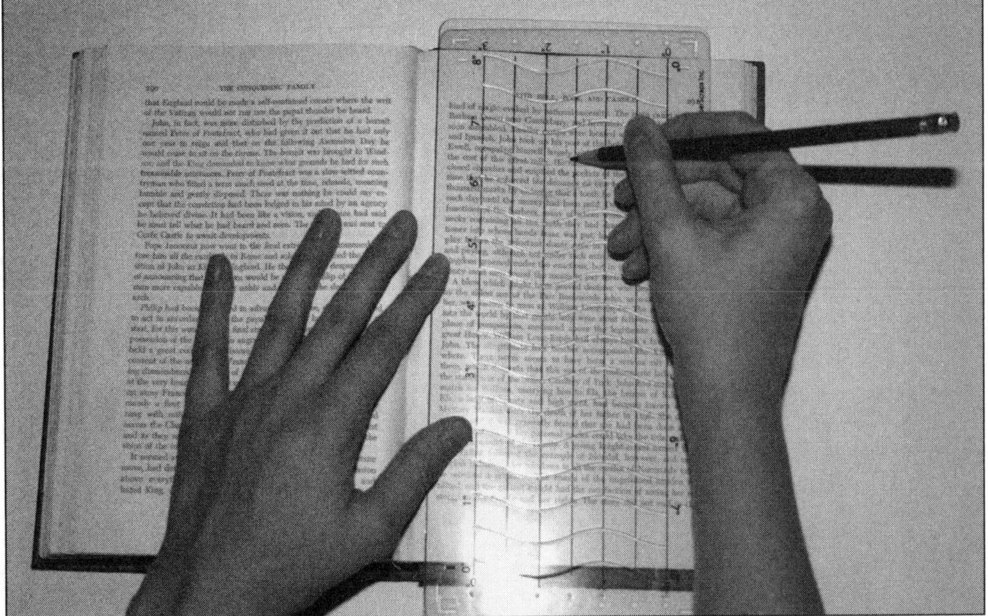

Cut slowly and carefully to avoid tearing your paper.

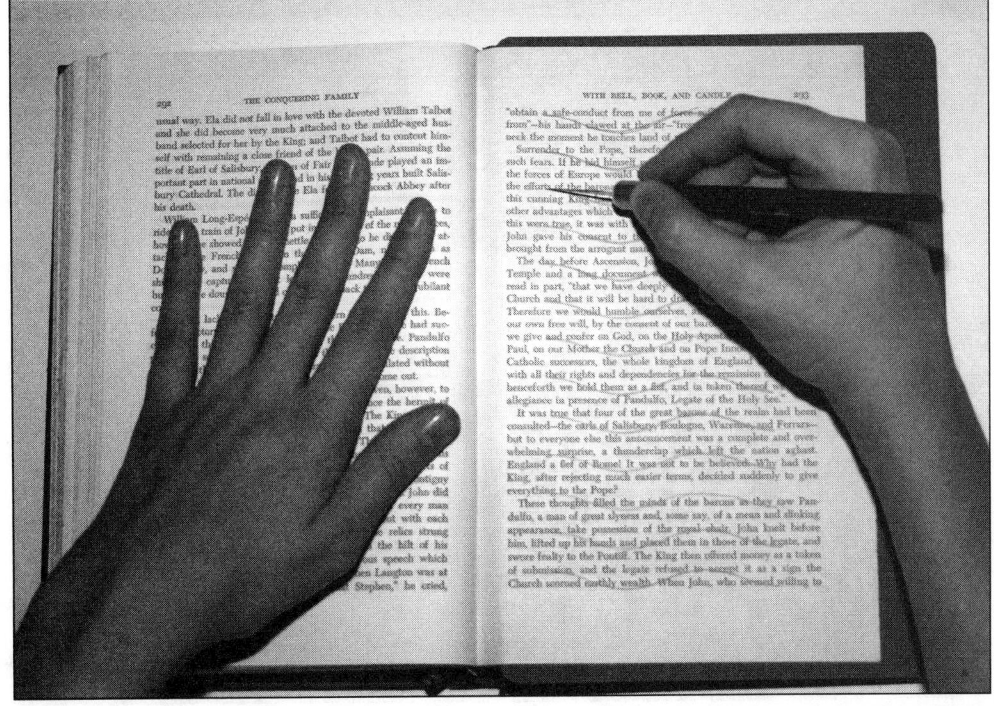

Be sure to trace through each slit of the template all the way from beginning to end.

6. Weave the strips through the openings in the paper, changing your starting position with each strip so the design alternates through the weave.
7. Repeat until paper strips have been woven through the entire cut area.
8. Trim the top and bottom edges, and this background is now complete and ready to be embellished.

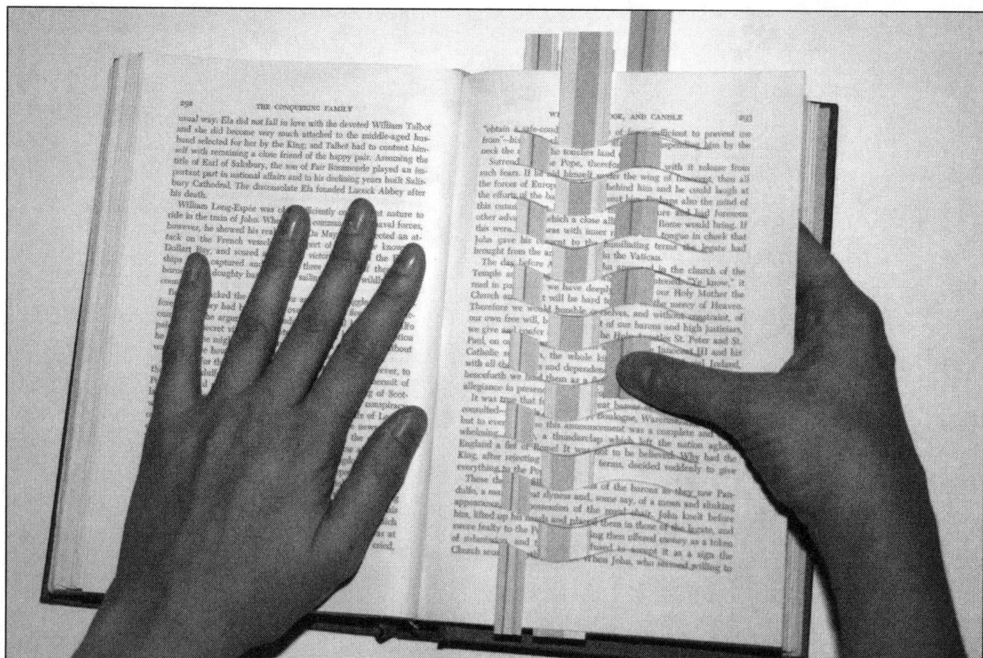

Be sure to line up each strip with the one before it, assuring a straight weave with no gaps.

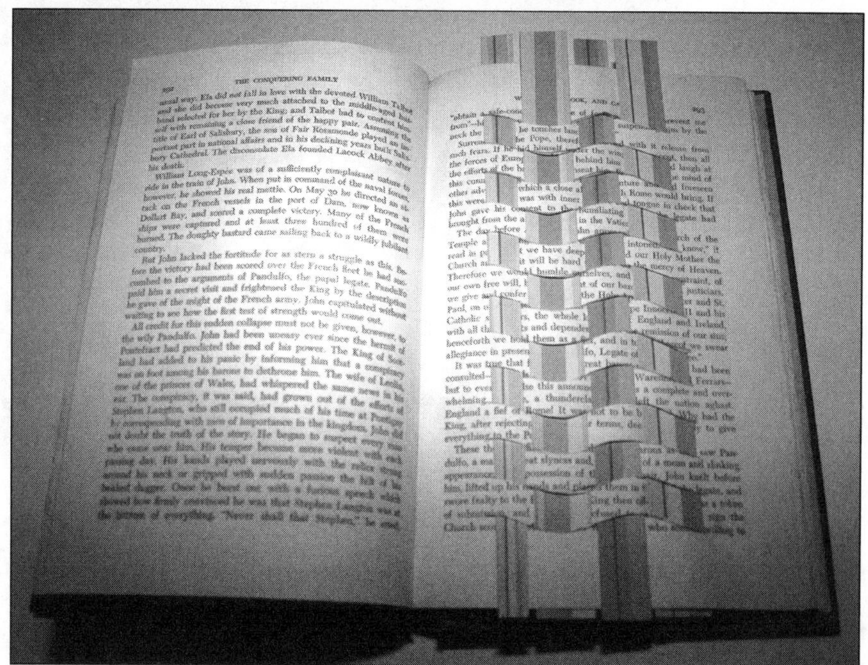

This design uses four wide strips of patterned paper.

> **Picture This**
>
> Want your weaving to be wider than the template? After you remove the template from the paper, place it again so your traced lines match up to the edge of the template. Repeat steps 1 through 3 so you have a traced design twice as wide as the original and then complete the process as shown.

Woven backgrounds add a unique flair to your altered book pages. Try combining a woven design with a solid patterned paper background or other background technique to create a beautiful effect.

Using patterned papers results in fun and whimsical pages, and brings a stylistic flair to your altered book.

The Least You Need to Know

- Background techniques provide the foundation for your altered book art.
- Use gesso to create a solid background or a white painting surface for watercolors.
- Paint provides a strong and fabulous look on your altered book pages.
- Ink, both bottled and in pads, creates a soft, textured look for your pages.
- Patterned paper makes a fantastic background when used on altered book pages. Create a weaving with patterned paper to add visual interest.

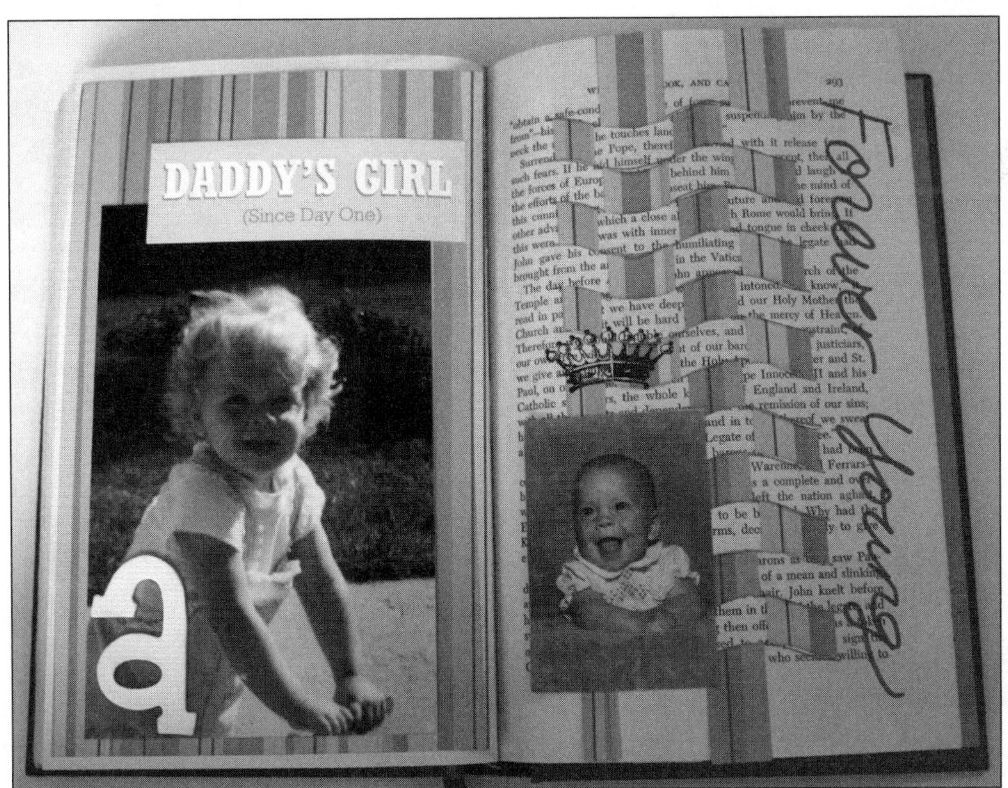

Baby photographs complement these papers perfectly. Turn to Chapters 4 and 12 for more fun photo ideas!

In This Chapter

- Securing your book's binding
- Covering altered books with fabric and decorative paper
- Decorating journals and notebooks

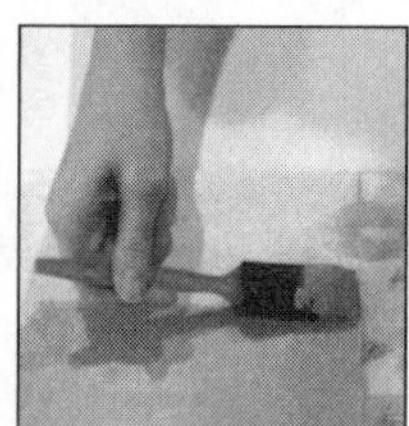

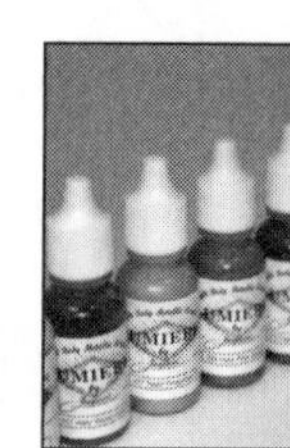

Chapter 3

Covering Your Book

You've chosen a book to alter, learned the basics, and even made a few background pages. Now it's time to discover how to cover and embellish the outside of your altered book. Many altered artists choose to cover their books after they've decorated all the pages inside. This allows the artist to create a cover that reflects the interior of his or her altered book. I generally choose to cover my books when I'm about halfway through the inside pages. By this time, I usually have a general idea of how I'd like my book's cover to appear. Plus, I enjoy working in my books quite a bit more when the outside has been covered. Somehow, it makes the process seem a bit more complete. When you choose to cover your book is entirely up to you.

Securing Your Binding

Before you can creatively cover your book, be sure your book's binding is secure. You likely chose a book with a strong binding when you first began your altered art journey, but there's a chance it's come loose by now. Or perhaps your book has somehow been damaged since you first began working in it.

If your book's binding has become loose, you'll want to secure it with *bookbinding tape* before you move on. You can find bookbinding tape in some fine art stores or online. In the last couple of years, a few major scrapbooking manufacturers (such as Making Memories and 7gypsies) have introduced bookbinding tape in decorative colors and patterns. Local scrapbooking stores can be a great source for this tape as well.

Transforming Talk

Bookbinding tape is a self-adhesive cloth tape printers and bookbinders use to hold the covers and pages of a book together.

To use bookbinding tape to secure your binding, follow these steps:

1. Be sure your book's covers are positioned as you want them. If they have completely detached from the spine, use a large binder clip or clamp to hold them in place while you work.
2. Adhere a length of bookbinding tape vertically across the spine and front cover, attaching the two parts of the book together.
3. Repeat the process with the back cover.

Your covers should now be taped to your book's spine. This ensures that your book is strengthened and the binding will last a lifetime.

Altered Alert

Bookbinding tape is not forgiving! Work slowly and carefully to avoid mistakes. Once you've adhered it to your book, it's not removable.

Creative Book Covers

When you're certain your book's binding is secure, it's time to have some fun. You can cover your book with fabric or decorative paper. Regardless of which you choose, the end result will be a beautifully covered book you'll cherish for years to come.

Decorative Paper Book Cover

Covering your book with decorative patterned paper is simple and fun. You'll need these supplies:

- Hardcover book for alteration
- Glue stick or other adhesive of your choice
- Scissors
- 2 to 4 sheets of 12×12-inch patterned paper (depending on the size of your book)
- Bookbinding tape

To cover my book, I chose to work with coordinating papers manufactured by Fiber Scraps along with purple bookbinding tape from Making Memories. When you have your supplies, follow these steps to cover your book:

1. Cut a sheet of patterned paper slightly larger than the front cover of your book. A margin of about 1 or 2 inches is perfect.
2. Using the glue stick, adhere the patterned paper to your book's cover, in line with the spine edge with the larger sides extending past the top, side, and bottom edges. Let this dry.
3. Open your book. Trim the paper's corners from each outside edge, then fold the paper to the inside of your book, and adhere to the inside cover. Let this dry.

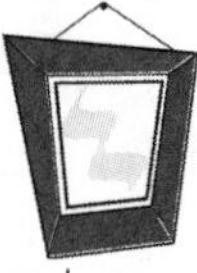

Picture This

Remember that you don't *have* to cover your book at all! If you selected a book with a meaningful title or beautiful artwork, you're already set to go.

Lay the paper on top of the book and make sure that the edges hang over the sides of the book.

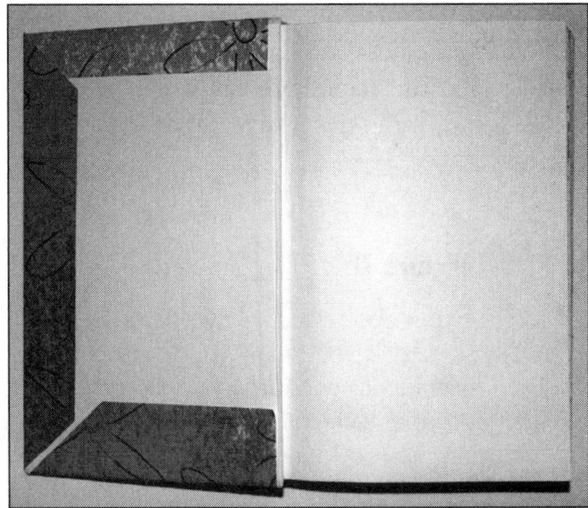

Glue each edge to the inside of your book securely.

4. Cut a coordinating sheet of patterned paper to fit inside your book's cover. (This covers the edges of the paper you just glued down.) This should be roughly $^{1}/_{4}$ inch smaller all around than the inside cover of your book. Adhere this to the cover, and let it dry.

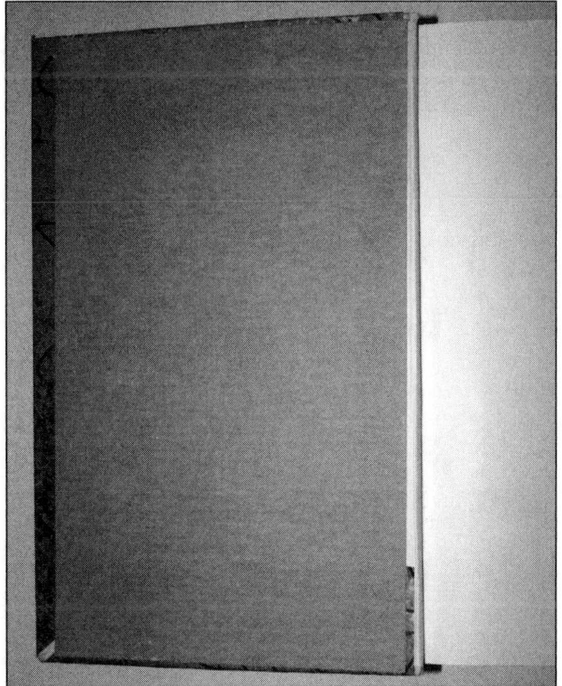

This sheet covers the messy edges left behind from covering the outside of your book.

5. Repeat steps 1 through 4 for the back cover of your book.
6. Use a colored bookbinding tape to cover the entire spine. Cover the two spine edges first, connecting the covers. If you have a thick book, you might need to add an extra piece of tape down the middle of the spine so the spine is completely covered.

At this point, all that remains is covering the spine.

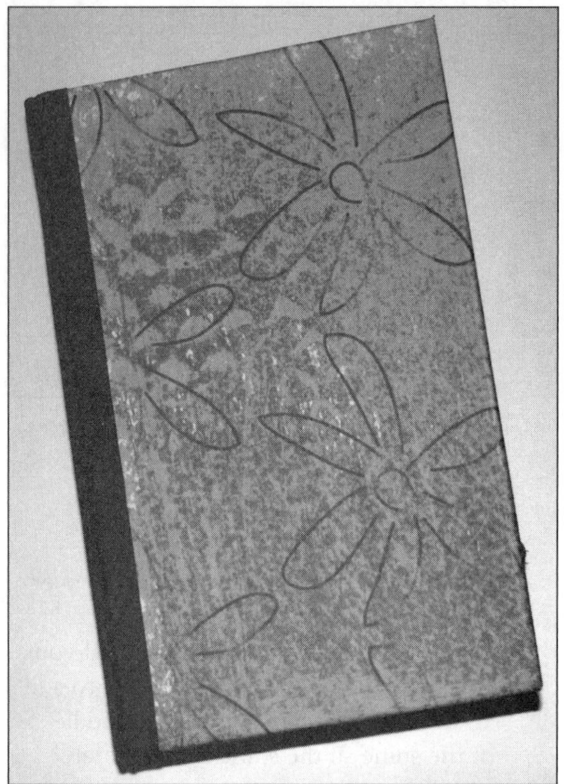

Your cover is now complete and ready to be embellished.

If you want, take a moment to decorate your book's front or inside covers. In my altered books, I enjoy stamping the inside front cover and signing my book. (If you need help with rubber stamping, turn to Chapter 6.)

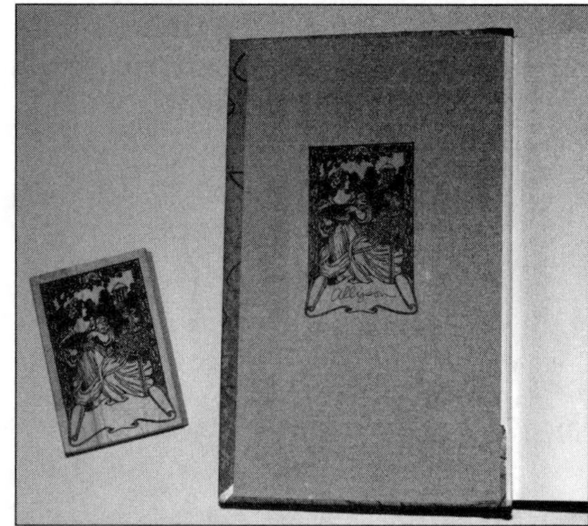

This stamp from 100 Proof Press provided the perfect touch for my book's inside cover.

Fabric-Covered Book

Fabric is a fun and beautiful way to cover your altered books. Note that this technique works best with books that have open spines. To see if your book has an open spine, simply open it. If there's a space between the book's spine and the glued pages, this technique will work for your book. If not, using decorative paper is a better option.

Picture This

If your book doesn't have an open spine and you really want to cover it with fabric, consider trying the patterned paper technique with fabric paper—specially treated fabric that works and acts just like paper with the texture of fabric. Michael Miller Memories (www.michaelmillermemories.com) manufactures a wide variety of fabric paper.

When you have a book you'd like to alter, gather these additional supplies:

- ½ yard of a favorite fabric (Michael Miller Memories)
- Two coordinating pieces of fabric paper (Michael Miller Memories)
- Altered Book rubber stamp (Catslife Press)
- Fabri-Tac liquid adhesive (Beacon Adhesives)
- Black pigment inkpad
- Scissors
- 1 yard decorative ribbon (Strano Designs)
- Large floral embellishment (Michael Miller Memories)

Altered Alert

All adhesives are not created equal. If you can't find Fabri-Tac, be sure you use an adhesive formulated for fabric. Otherwise, the glue won't hold and your project will fall apart.

With everything ready, follow these simple steps:

1. Cut a piece of fabric about twice as wide as your book, leaving a 1- to 2-inch border around the edge.

2. Wrap the fabric around your book. Adhere it to the front and back covers with Fabri-Tac. Do *not* use any glue on the spine.
3. Right at the spine of the book, use scissors to make a cut in the fabric from the edge of the fabric to the book at each spine edge, leaving a small fabric tab at each end of the spine.

4. Use your fingers to press the extra fabric up into the book's spine. Use Fabri-Tac to ensure it stays in place.

5. Open the book to the front cover. Wrap the edges of the fabric to the inside front cover, and adhere with Fabri-Tac. Trim the corners if necessary to eliminate any bulk.

6. Cut a piece of fabric paper to fit your book's inside cover, and adhere.
7. Stamp image on to a coordinating piece of fabric paper. Trim to size, and adhere this to the inside front cover.

8. Open your book so the spine is open. Thread decorative ribbon through the opening down the spine (where you tucked in the cover fabric tab earlier).

Picture This

Having trouble threading the ribbon through the spine? Use the blunt end of a pencil or capped pen to help poke it all the way through.

9. Tie the ribbon into bow. Secure ribbon anywhere along the spine with Fabri-Tac, if desired.
10. Adhere a flower to your book's cover with Fabri-Tac.

This cover is now complete and makes a beautiful showcase for your altered artwork.

Congratulations! You now have a fantastic book that's ready for your artwork or display.

Creative Journals and Notebook Covers

So far, we've explored two primary ways to cover hardbound books—with decorative paper and with fabric. Perhaps, though, the book you want to cover isn't an ordinary book. Maybe you're looking to add extra pizzazz to a notebook or journal.

Covering and decorating spiral notebooks and composition books can be a fun and exciting way to explore your creativity. Plus, just like the books we've been working with so far, they make an excellent container for your pages of altered art.

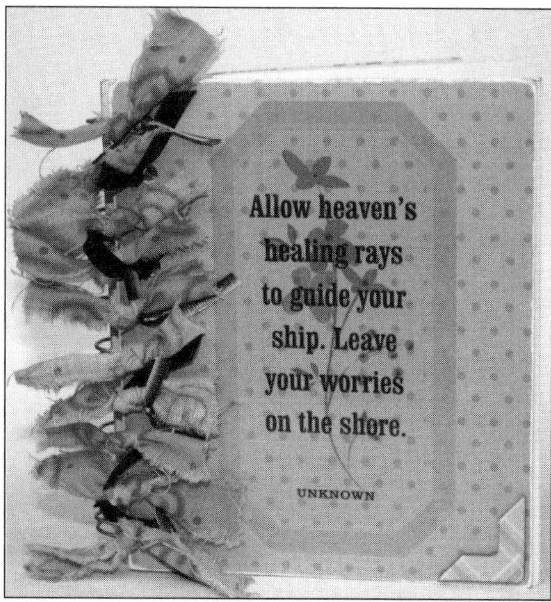

This beautiful journal makes an excellent gift.

(Book by Carolyn A. Lontin)

UNALTERABLE FACT

Decorative blank books are excellent gifts for family and friends. You can fill them up yourself with altered artwork, photographs, quotes, or just about anything else—or leave them blank for the recipient to alter.

To create this gorgeous covered journal, you need the following:

- Spiral-bound blank or lined journal
- Patterned paper, transparent quote sticker, and chipboard photo corner (Chatterbox)
- Assorted fabric strips and ribbons
- Glue stick or other adhesive of your choice

Then, just stick to these easy steps:

1. Gently pull apart the spiral binding, remove it from the book, and set it aside. Do not discard it.
2. Cut patterned paper to fit the front cover of your journal. Your paper should be the exact same size as the book's cover. Adhere the paper to the cover.
3. Adhere the quote sticker to the center of your journal's cover.
4. Adhere the photo corner to the bottom right corner of your journal.
5. Use a small object to poke through the paper into the holes of the spiral binding. Because holes are already present in the book's cover, you just need to poke through them enough for the spiral to pass through them again. They won't be exact, but once you place the spiral through the holes again, it won't matter.

6. Carefully rethread the journal's spiral binding into the journal cover and pages. If necessary, use pliers to ensure a tight binding.
7. Tie ribbon and fabric strips to the spiral coils.

You now have an amazing journal ready for your own thoughts and feelings, or to give to a special friend or relative.

The possibilities for decorative journal covers are endless. Consider trying one of these fun ideas:

- Make a journal celebrating your favorite game, and use it to keep scores and ratings in.
- Decorate a journal for your favorite holiday or another upcoming event, and use it to keep track of all your planning and preparations.

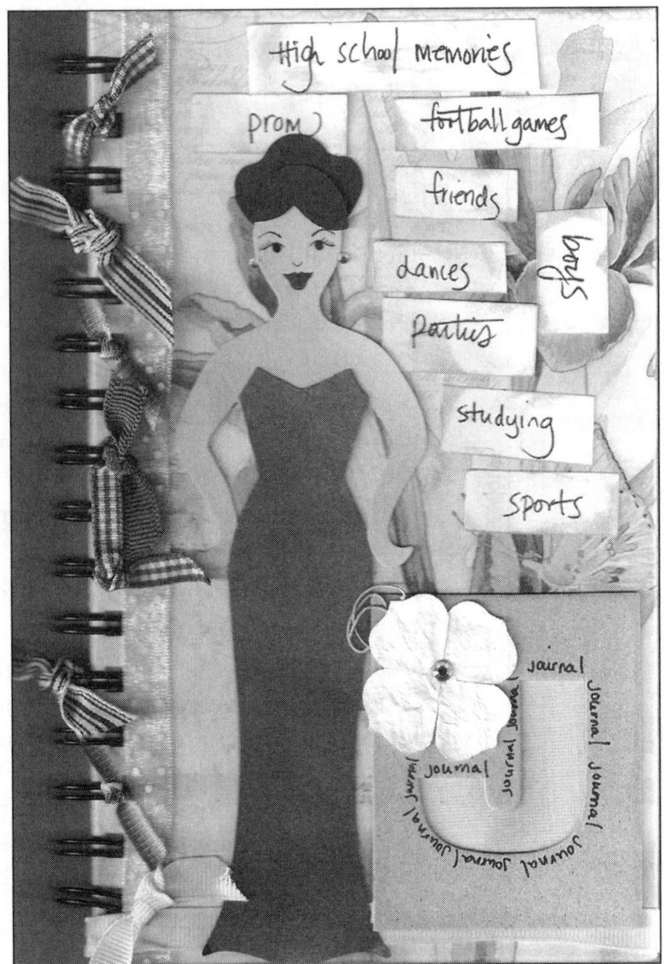

This journal is ready for all sorts of prom and other high school memories.

(Journal by Pam Callaghan)

- Use a favorite photo on a journal cover.
- Try one of the altered art techniques shown throughout this book as a cover technique.
- Add a large monogram letter to the front of your journal or notebook.

No matter how you choose to decorate the covers of your journals and books, you'll be glad you did. The results are fun, beautiful, and ready to be treasured.

The Least You Need to Know

- Be sure your binding is secure before decorating or covering your book. If it's not, use bookbinding tape to repair the book.
- Hardbound books can be easily and beautifully covered using patterned paper and fabric.
- Covering spiral notebooks, composition books, and journals is fun and easy. These books are excellent for altered art, or simply to be left blank and given as gifts.

In This Part

OK, OK. WE'LL GO TO FRANCE NEXT SUMMER. JUST DON'T PASTE A BERET ON ME.

Part 2

Creative Imagery

Images are a key element in any altered project. In Part 2, you encounter four key sources of imagery to use in your altered books. First, we take a detailed look at the most basic image form—the photograph. Next, we discover how to use your memorabilia—as well as antique memorabilia reproductions—to create totally unique looks. You'll learn how to become an expert rubber stamper and even discover the art of drawing in your books—regardless of your artistic experience. Finally, I'll teach you the basics of image transfer—the art of printing an image directly onto your project using special techniques and products.

After reading through Part 2, you'll be certain to have the knowledge and skills you need to find the perfect image for any project.

In This Chapter

- Using photographs in your altered books
- Vintage photography tips and tricks
- Creating an altered book with historical photographs

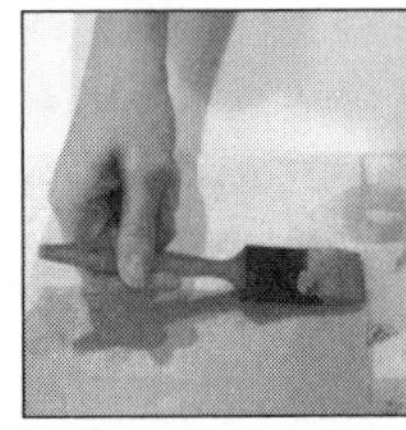

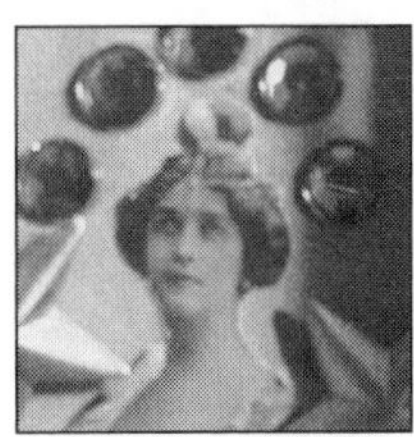
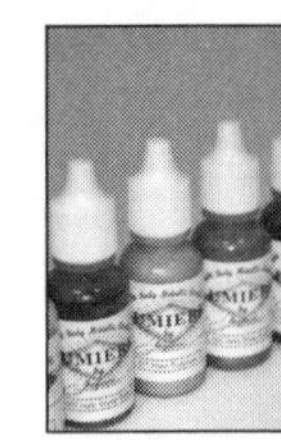

Chapter 4

Snapshots: Working with Photography

A photograph is the most basic way to preserve a memory, and it's the most basic form of imagery available to you as an altered book artist. Both modern photographs and vintage historical photos have a place in your altered books and can enable you to create fantastic and fun works of altered art.

Modern Photography

Altered books make a great home for some of your modern snapshots—particularly those that might not otherwise find a place to be used. For example, let's say you've recently taken a vacation. You framed your favorite photo and used most of the rest in a special scrapbook project. Only a few photos remain. You still enjoy these photos, but you don't really have a use for them. Enter the altered book.

Altered books allow you to pair nearly unlimited artistic options with your photograph. You can work freely, focusing on the memory at hand and the art you want to create, without having to worry about the "rules" of scrapbooking and photo storage.

Altered Alert

For the most part, altered books are not photo-safe. When using photographs in your altered books, use a copy, or plan to use a photograph with the understanding that it may age over time.

When using photographs in your altered books, look for products and use techniques that match the mood of your photo. For example, consider matching a beach vacation photo with tropical blue paint, a palm tree rubber stamp, and small seashells. The result will be a page you'll love to share and display.

These fun and whimsical altered book pages reflect the mood of the photograph.

Altering Your Photographs

Part of the fun of working with photos in altered books is that altering isn't limited to what you can do to or glue on the page. Why not take it a step further and alter the photographs, too?

Most computers come equipped with a photo-editing program with which you can make adjustments or additions to your photo. You can print the new version either at home with a photo printer or save the file to a disc and take it to your local photo development center.

The most basic way to alter a photograph is to change its color. Try converting a color photograph to black and white. For a nostalgic feel, opt for sepia tone.

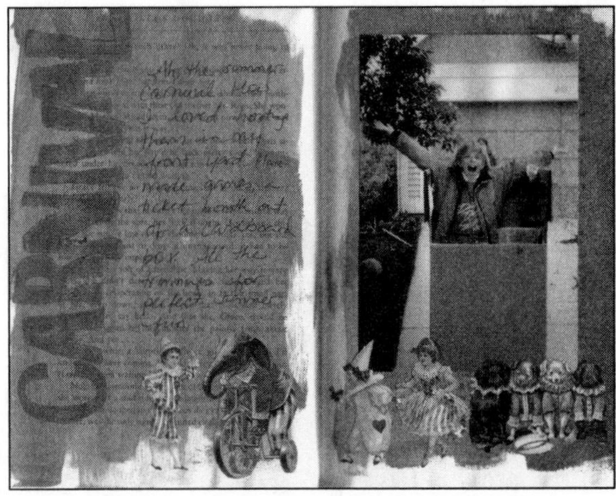

These pages use a photograph I changed to sepia tone, which adds to the vintage circus theme of the spread.

Depending on the photo-editing program you're using, you might be able to try some of these other effects:

- Changing the surface texture of the photo (I love adding a canvas texture!)
- Adding decorative borders and frames
- Creating a collage of two or more photographs
- Converting a photograph to all one color, such as blue or pink

These are just a few possibilities. Consult your program's manual or online help center for the full menu of choices available to you. Try searching for "artistic effects" and see what you get.

If you don't have any kind of photo-editing program, don't skip this section! Keep reading, and try using an online photo developer. Typically, online developers offer several options, including color manipulation, creative borders, and more. Most offer easy-to-use sites where you can upload your photographs and order prints in minutes. Here are some of my favorite online photo developers:

- www.scrapbookpictures.com
- www.shutterfly.com
- www.snapfish.com

Plus, these sites often offer several free prints in exchange for signing up for their services. Try a few different developers, and see which one you like best!

Vintage Photography

Working with antique photographs is one of my favorite altered art techniques. I love the timeless look and feel of old photos, and I often find myself wondering about the people in them—what they were like, what they were thinking about. Creating altered book pages with antique photographs allows you to explore these ideas or simply celebrate your own ancestors.

One of the primary challenges of working with old photographs is finding them! You likely have piles and piles of current snapshots, but your stock of older photos is probably much more limited—and probably much more precious. While I do have quite a few antique photographs featuring my relatives, I choose to create most of my altered art with photographs I've found elsewhere. Something about cutting up an old photograph of my great-grandmother just doesn't feel right.

> **Picture This**
>
> If you'd like to work with antique photographs from your own family but don't want to use the original photo, make a copy. Your local photo store can usually produce a copy that looks as good as the original (sometimes better!). This way, you can work with the photos you love without having to worry about destroying a family heirloom.

One of the best places to find vintage photographs is your local antique store or flea market. Often you'll find quite a selection—and cheap, too! Many are priced from $1 to $3 per photo. Look for photographs that interest you and catch your eye. Purchase several so you have plenty to choose from when you sit down to create your artwork.

If you can't find a local resource for antique photos, try an online auction site such as eBay (www.ebay.com). eBay usually has hundreds—if not thousands—of antique photographs available for purchase at any given time. Look for large lots of several photographs. This keeps your shipping costs down, and ensures that you can get a good variety of photos to start with.

These photographs were a fun eBay find and only cost me a couple of dollars.

UNALTERABLE FACT

Need a lot of photos and can't find what you need? Visit www.amandacallahan.com to purchase a CD full of photos you can use on your projects.

Getting to Know Your Photos

Take a minute to think about the photos you're going to work with. If they're from your own family, you probably have a good handle on the details. But what if they aren't? It can be so much fun to create your own fictional history using the photographs you plan to include in your artwork.

You'll likely find that antique photographs take on a life of their own. Even though you might not know anything about the people in the photographs you're working with, try inventing little details about their lives. These details can guide your art and help you as you make choices regarding color selection, additional products to use, and more.

If coming up with these little details is difficult, try this exercise to jump-start your creativity: choose an antique photograph from your pile and place it in front of you. Work with any photo you like, but you might find it easiest to work with a photo of someone of your own gender and appears to be about your age. As you look at the photograph, notice these details:

- Facial expression—is the subject smiling? Does he or she look angry? Bored?
- Position—is the subject sitting? Standing? Dancing?
- Dress—are the subject's clothes fun or practical? Fancy or simple?

Taking these factors into consideration, think about the following questions. Answer them with the first idea that pops in your head, and invent your own answers—there is no "right" or "wrong." Remember that there's usually no real way to find out the truth about these photographs—so go ahead and be creative!

- What was the subject thinking about? Is she in love? Is he bored? Is he worried about money or his career? Is she thinking about how uncomfortable her clothes are?
- Where is the photo being taken? Was she on vacation? At home?
- Is the subject married or single?
- Has the subject been through school of any kind?
- Where does the subject live? In a rural area? In the city?

Inventing the answers to these questions can help guide your artwork. When I was creating the altered book spread you're going to work through in the next section (go ahead and take a sneak peek now if you want), I started with the photo of the young woman. I noticed her smile and style of dress and imagined that she found herself quite trendy for the time. But I also thought she had a bit of a twinkle in her eye and decided she must be in love. So I then looked for a photo of a young man and decided to choose someone who appeared to be her opposite—a serious man with a somewhat sour expression. Putting the two photographs together allowed me to create a fun piece of art. The elegance of her photo contrasted with the simplicity of his, and it all was enhanced by the design of the pages.

Picture This

Still having trouble with details? Model your photograph subject after a favorite friend, family member, even literary character!

It all starts with one photograph. By taking just a few moments to really analyze that photo, you'll find that design decisions come much more easily. Choosing additional photos, your color scheme, and even complementary products all seem to come together more smoothly. The more you get to know your subject, you'll discover that designing a page to suit him or her becomes easier and easier.

Ancestors Altered Book Spread

Creating an altered book spread using vintage photographs can be so much fun. You get to imagine what each individual was thinking about, what he or she loved, the choices that person made, and more. The photographs are the starting point, and you get to create the details.

Because this likely will be your first complete altered book page, I'll walk you through the process. Follow these easy steps and you'll have a beautiful page of your own.

Gathering the Goods

Start by rounding up a few supplies:

- Book with pages to alter
- Acrylic paint (any color) and foam brush(es)
- Scissors or a craft knife and cutting mat
- 2 vintage photographs, 1 each of a man and a woman
- Old place card and travel tag, or other vintage papers of your choice
- Decorative trim (I used Victorian Scrapworks.)
- Black pen

Altering Your Book

When you have your supplies gathered at your workspace, you're ready to get altering!

1. Begin by painting your background pages, using a method from Chapter 2. I chose light purple. Let the paint dry.

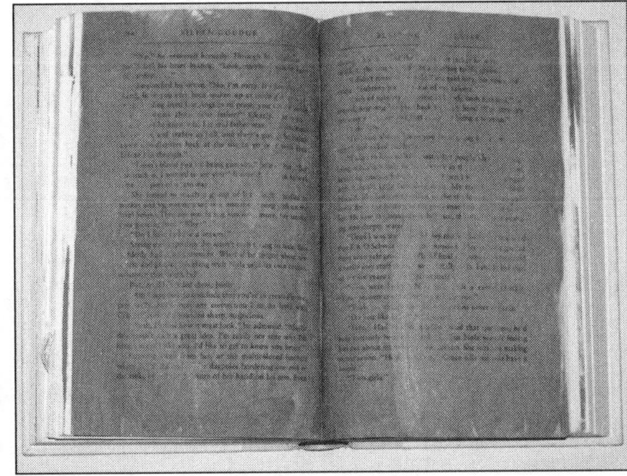

Be sure to use a light, even coat of paint across the entire page background.

2. Cut out around the photographs you've chosen. Most antique photos have large borders or frames. These aren't necessary for altered artwork, so feel free to cut them off using scissors or a craft knife.
3. Adhere the photos to your pages.

Altered Alert

Be sure to use an adhesive formulated for photographs when adhering photos in your altered book. This helps prevent deterioration over time.

4. Add vintage papers. (See Chapter 5 for more about working with these items.)

I love these photographs. The woman looks so stylish, and the man is so serious—I like to think they were in love despite these differences.

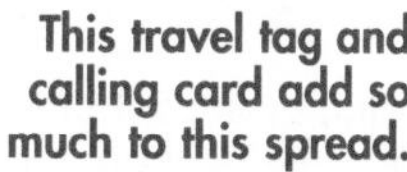

This travel tag and calling card add so much to this spread.

Feel free to alter your handwriting as you add your title. I wrote in a script to add to the antique feel of the pages.

5. Add a title or text using a black pen or another art pen of your choice. (See Chapter 7 to learn more about art pens and markers.) I chose to use "Still she yearns for him" as the title.
6. Now take a look at your pages. Does anything feel missing? I thought so, too. Adhere a final strip of decorative trim on the right page, and your book pages are complete.

See how much fun it can be to work with old photographs? Now you're ready to create an altered book spread of your own design!

The Least You Need to Know

- Snapshots and modern photographs can be fun additions to your altered book pages.
- Creating altered book pages with antique photographs is easy—and a great way to preserve family memories.
- Taking a moment to analyze your antique photos and invent details about the subject's life can lead to easier design choices and well-balanced art.

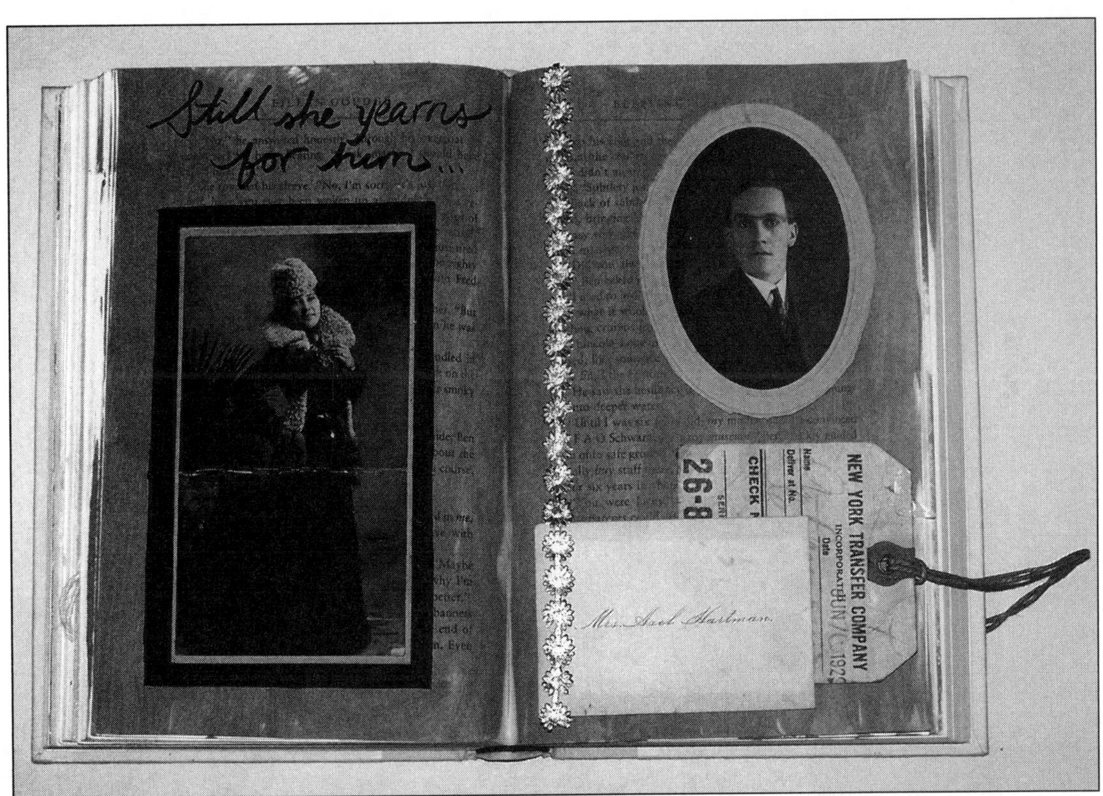

The floral trim adds just the right finishing touch to the spread.

In This Chapter

- Using memorabilia in your altered books
- Locating historical memorabilia and ephemera
- Creating a beautiful and unique dream journal altered book

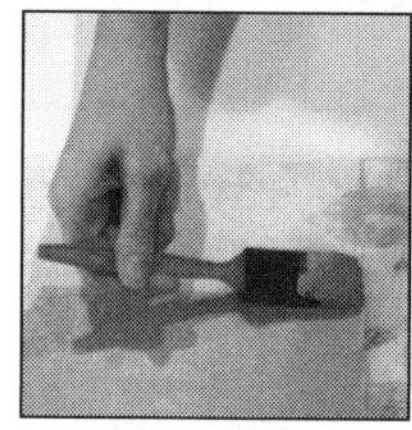

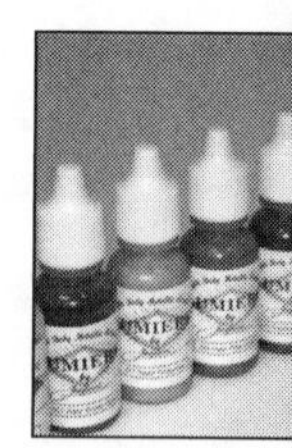

Chapter 5

Ephemera and More

As you've learned in previous chapters, using photography on your altered book pages can add a special touch. But what happens when you can't find the photograph you're looking for? Or when you have a fantastical subject in mind you just can't capture in a photograph? The perfect image for your altered art creation just might be lying in the world of ephemera.

Historical Ephemera

One of the most unique ways to add a touch of history and whimsy to your pages is to use *ephemera*. For example, you could enhance an altered book page featuring a photograph of a Ferris wheel by adding an old ticket stub or fairground map.

Transforming Talk

Ephemera are printed materials with little or no lasting value. Examples include memorabilia, junk mail, receipts, and maps. Junk mail? Sure. Just as you might include current memorabilia, ticket stubs, etc., in a scrapbook, these items from the past can add a historical and artistic touch to your creations.

Try looking for these types of ephemera, all of which can add interest to your altered pages and projects:

- Old postcards
- Can labels
- Ticket stubs
- Street maps
- Food stamps and coupons
- Magazine advertisements
- Place cards
- Wedding announcements and invitations
- Newspaper clippings
- Greeting cards

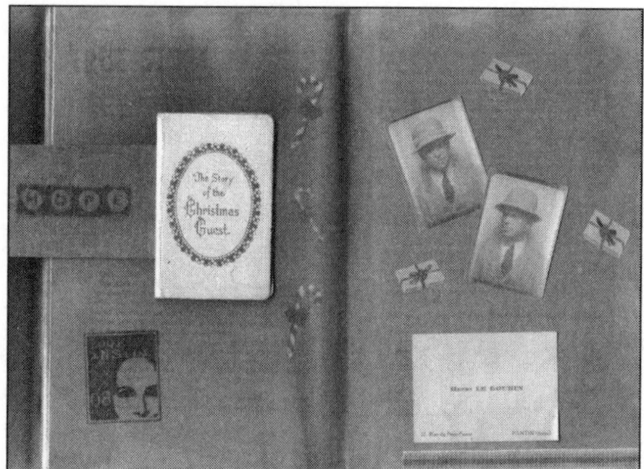

The small booklet and calling card complement the photographs and stamped images on these pages.

(Pages by Kate Schaefer)

By adding historical elements to your pages, you can create a timeless, vintage look that has lasting appeal.

Finding Ephemera

If you're lucky, you might have a relative who saved ephemera and other interesting items in a scrapbook that's yours for the taking. If not—as is most often the case—you'll have to look elsewhere to locate some ephemera to use in your work.

As we learned in Chapter 1, one of the earliest forms of the altered book was the practice of keeping ephemera and photographs in oversized books and scrapbooks. These kinds of albums can often be found at flea markets and antique stores. Occasionally, a trip to an estate sale or even your neighborhood garage sale can yield such a find.

If all else fails, try searching for ephemera on an online auction site, such as eBay. Simply type *ephemera* into the search box, or try mixing and matching some of these keywords to ensure a better search result:

altered	old	vintage
antique	photograph	
map	ticket	

When you've found the ephemera you'd like to use, you're all set to get creating!

Picture This

Altered book art is a growing craft, so lots of ephemera and old scrapbooks are in high demand. You don't want to have to pay for items you don't plan to use. When purchasing ephemera online, use a specific search so you don't end up with too many results or too many extra items.

Collage Sheets

Still can't find what you're looking for? (Or simply can't afford it?) Enter the *collage sheet*. Collage sheets are designed for altered artists, scrapbookers, and collage artists who want a wide variety of images at their fingertips, without having to spend time and money hunting for original images.

Transforming Talk

A **collage sheet** is an $8\frac{1}{2}\times11$-inch page featuring several small-scale reproductions of vintage art and ephemera.

You can purchase collage sheets at many different online stores. These are a few of my favorites:

- www.alteredpages.com
- www.artchixstudio.com
- www.scrapsmart.com
- www.tuscanrose.com

When shopping for collage sheets, pay attention to different pricing and printing options. Many stores allow you to choose the material your images are printed on from a variety of media, including plain cardstock, transparency, fabric paper, and more. These options enable you to further customize the images you'd like to use so they best meet the needs of your specific project.

Think outside the box when working with collage sheets, altering the images to your heart's content. If you're stumped for ideas, try one of these ways to use collage sheet images in your artwork:

- Use fine-tipped scissors to cut a silhouette of the image you're working with.
- Layer two images on top of one another. This works best with images printed on transparency and vellum.
- Cut an image into multiple sections and then adhere the pieces to your page in a new way.
- Combine parts of several images into a new image.

Altered Alert

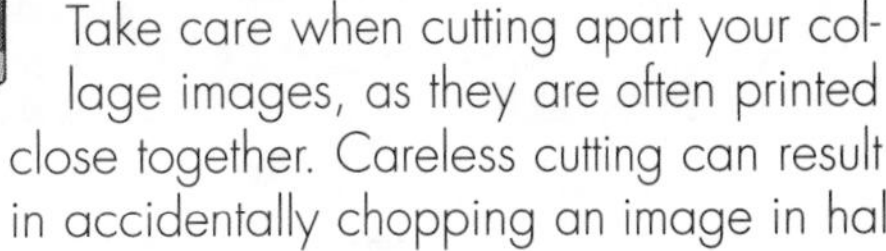

Take care when cutting apart your collage images, as they are often printed close together. Careless cutting can result in accidentally chopping an image in half!

However you use them, collage sheets are sure to provide a fantastic touch to your altered book pages and projects.

Victorian Scrap Art

Another great source of vintage imagery for the crafter exists in *Victorian scraps*. Popular during the late 1800s and early 1900s, Victorian scraps were commonly used as accents in scrapbooks and on calling cards but were most often used on greeting cards. You're probably most familiar with these images as the focal point of handmade Victorian valentines—a look that's still commonly imitated today.

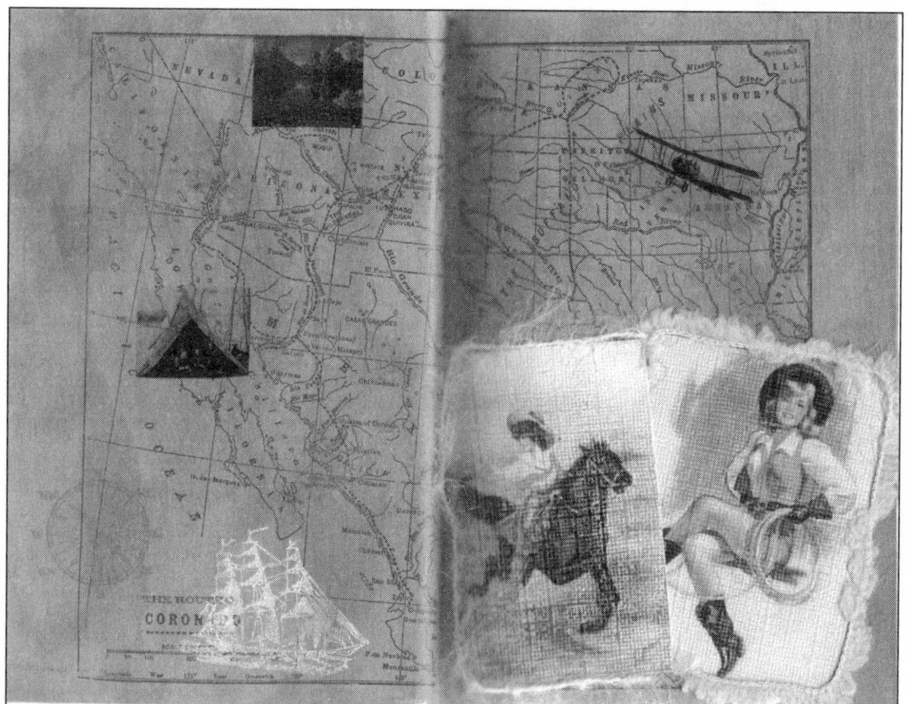

These vintage cowgirls, from a collage sheet by Altered Pages, add the perfect touch to these pages.

(Pages by Kate Schaefer)

Cutting apart the image of the dancers and arranging them in a downward sequence enhances the feel of movement on these pages.

(Pages by Kate Schaefer)

Transforming Talk

A **Victorian scrap** is a die-cut, embossed, lithograph image from the Victorian era, often featuring playful images of children or animals, and usually brightly colored. Original Victorian scraps as well as reproductions are widely used in altered art.

You can find many Victorian scrap images on collage sheets from various publishers, but you can also still find real Victorian scraps with deep color and embossed texture. Try looking at your local papercraft or stationery store, or visit www.victorianscrapworks.com.

Victorian scraps are perfect for adding a touch of texture and whimsy to your next project.

Picture This

For an interesting look at Victorian scraps and their historical uses, visit www.scrapalbum.com.

Altered Dream Journal

Collage sheet images are the focus of this beautiful small dream journal. Create this altered book to keep as a journal for yourself or to give as a gift.

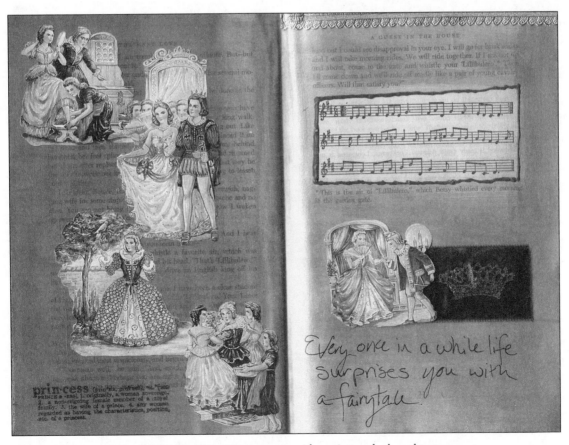

These fairytale Victorian scraps provide a vintage look and texture to the book's pages.

(Pages by Kate Schaefer)

This dream journal is perfect for your bedside table.

Getting Started

To begin your project, gather the following supplies:

- Small to medium-size hardcover book for altering
- Tropical print fabric paper (Michael Miller Memories)
- 1 or 2 yards coordinating ribbon (Strano Designs)
- Fantasy collage sheets featuring fairies and mermaids (Altered Pages)
- Butterfly stickers (Violette Stickers)
- Antique white acrylic paint
- Purple and blue ink pads (Stewart Superior)
- Assorted rubber stamps (Catslife Press)
- Fabric Adhesive (Fabri-Tac by Beacon Adhesives)

When you have all your supplies, prepare your book as described in Chapter 1. When your book is thinned out and you've added support, you're ready to go.

Creating Your Journal Pages

Follow these easy steps to create your very own dream journal:

1. Apply a thin layer of acrylic paint to each page.

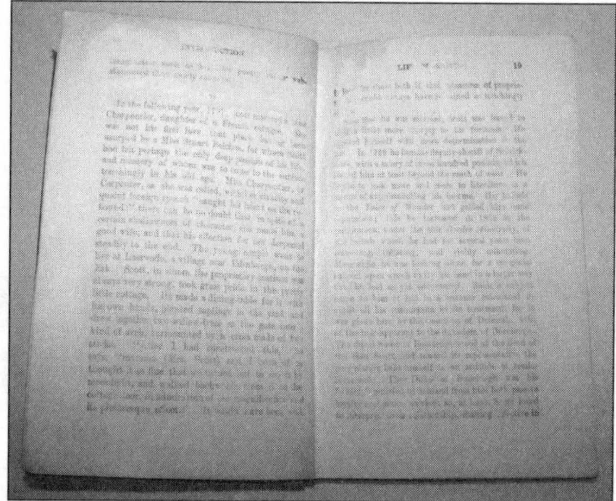

Use just enough paint so the text barely peeks through.

2. Add a collage sheet image to the left-hand page.

Images printed on vellum, such as this one, look particularly beautiful in this project.

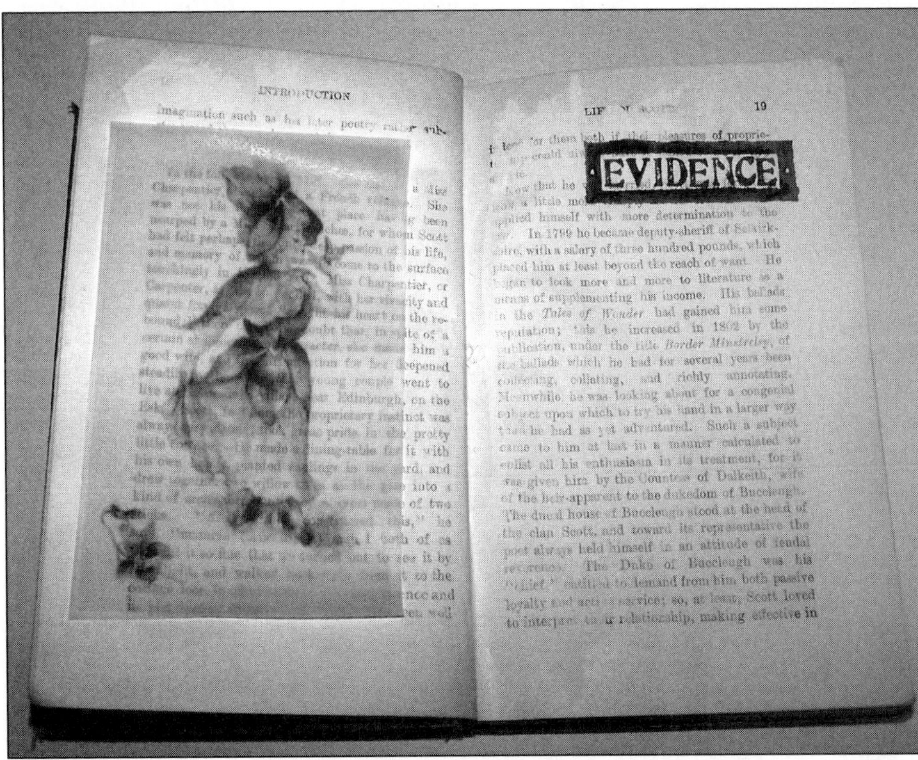

This page is now complete.

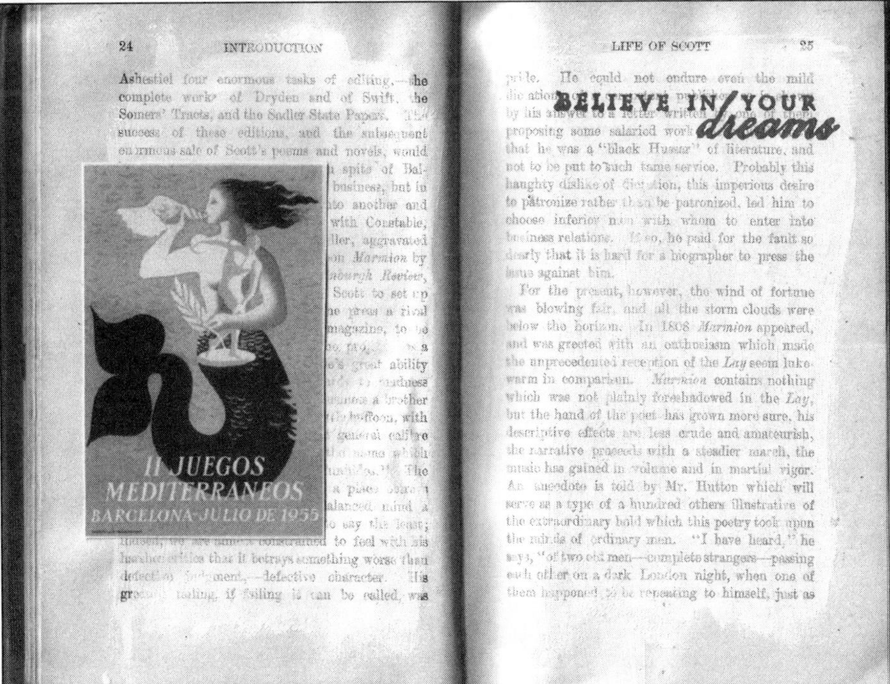

These pages follow the same basic layout as the other interior pages.

3. Add a rubber stamped image to the top corner of the right-hand page. (If you need help rubber stamping, turn to Chapter 6.)
4. Leave most of the right-hand page blank so the journal's owner can add his or her own thoughts and writing.
5. Repeat this process for the rest of the pages in your book. You can alter as many (or as few) spreads as you want, allowing the journal's owner to complete the book on his or her own.

Your inside pages are now complete. Be sure to vary your collage image and rubber stamp choices as you work throughout the book to add visual interest.

You might want to alter your book's inside front and back covers as well. I chose to alter the front inside cover of my book by following these basic steps:

1. Apply a thick coat of acrylic paint to the inside cover.
2. Add the "dream journal" stamped image.
3. Add a butterfly sticker.
4. Adhere the collage image to the right-hand page.

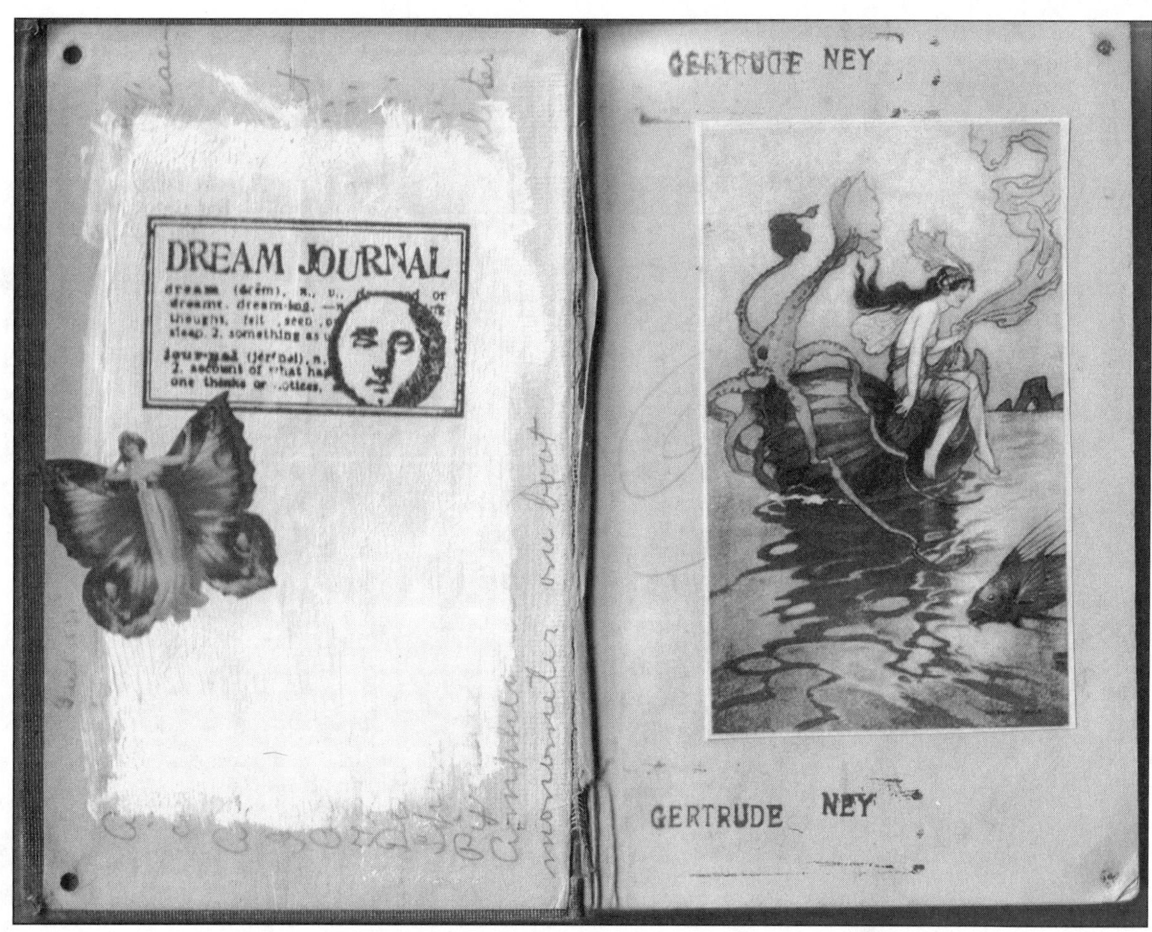

If you're giving the journal as a gift, leave room on the left-hand page for the journal's owner to sign his or her name.

Adding the Final Touches

Finish off your dream journal by covering the book and adding a closure:

1. Using the method described in Chapter 3, cover the outside of your book using fabric paper. Be sure to smooth out any wrinkles and check that your book opens and closes easily.
2. Adhere a length of ribbon along the top and bottom edge of the book's cover using fabric adhesive. Leave several inches of ribbon hanging from each end.

Your covered book can be tied closed for added durability and privacy.

Tie your book shut and you have a completed altered book dream journal!

Picture This

Not all dreams occur while you're sleeping! Consider using this book to record your goals and wishes for the future.

Regardless of how you choose to use your dream journal, you now have a beautiful and fun book that will become a lasting keepsake.

The Least You Need to Know

- Ephemera make a fantastic addition to your pages, especially when you want to create a vintage or aged look.
- Collage sheets are an excellent source of imagery without the added cost of using original artwork.
- Victorian scraps are still available today and can add fabulous color and texture to your book pages.
- Creating a dream journal is a fun and easy altered book project that makes a great gift.

In This Chapter

- Stamping with mounted, unmounted, and unmounted acrylic stamps
- Discovering inks and colorants
- Learning the craft of heat embossing
- Recovering from your stamping mistakes

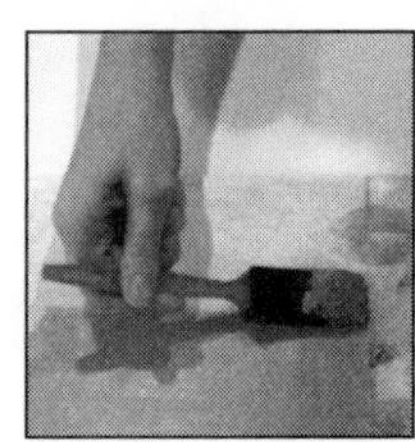

Chapter 6

Rubber Stamping

Rubber stamping is one of the most popular hobbies in the United States today. Many artists enjoy stamping because it enables them the freedom to experiment and play with different colors and designs as part of their artwork. Plus, stamps have a virtually indefinite life span. When properly cared for, they can last for thousands of uses, allowing you to create as many altered art and other craft projects as you'd like, all from the same stamp.

The advantages of stamping are clear. So let's take a look at the different types of stamps available to today's crafter.

Understanding Stamps

Stamps come in all sorts of styles—and not just when it comes to images. The earliest craft stamps were almost always made of a piece of rubber mounted on a wood block, but today, stamps come in mounted and unmounted forms, made of both rubber and acrylic. When it comes to stamps, innumerable options await the altered artist.

Wood-Mounted Rubber Stamps

Wood-mounted rubber stamps are the most common type of stamps, and probably what first pops into your mind when you think of the art of stamping.

These wood-mounted stamps from 100 Proof Press and Catslife Press are just a handful of my personal favorites.

Wood-mounted stamps are also the easiest to use. Here's a quick example of how to use a wood-mounted stamp:

1. Use an inkpad to cover the rubber surface of the stamp, making sure the entire design is covered in ink.
2. Press the stamp firmly on the paper or other surface you want to decorate. Do not rock or move the stamp.
3. Carefully lift the stamp up from the paper.

This image is stunning when stamped in all black ink.

(Stamp by Enchanted Ink)

Wood-mounted stamps are an excellent choice for the beginning crafter. They require no assembly or special accessories to use. Because the stamp image is printed directly on the block, there's little chance for error.

Unmounted Rubber Stamps

Unmounted rubber stamps are also popular with altered artists. These stamps come as cut-out single images of rubber or as a series or group of images on one larger sheet of rubber. This makes them significantly cheaper than traditional wood-mounted rubber stamps.

Because unmounted stamps don't come with a cushion or wood block, using them isn't quite as easy as using wood-mounted stamps and requires a bit of preparation—namely mounting them. You can mount unmounted rubber stamps many different ways. I prefer to use a temporary mounting system, known as EZ Mount, manufactured by Sunday International (www.sundayint.com). The EZ Mount system uses sheets of gray foam cushion; one side permanently sticks to your stamp image, and the other temporarily clings to a clear acrylic stamping block. This enables you to attach your stamp to a clear block when you're ready to use it and then remove it when you're finished stamping.

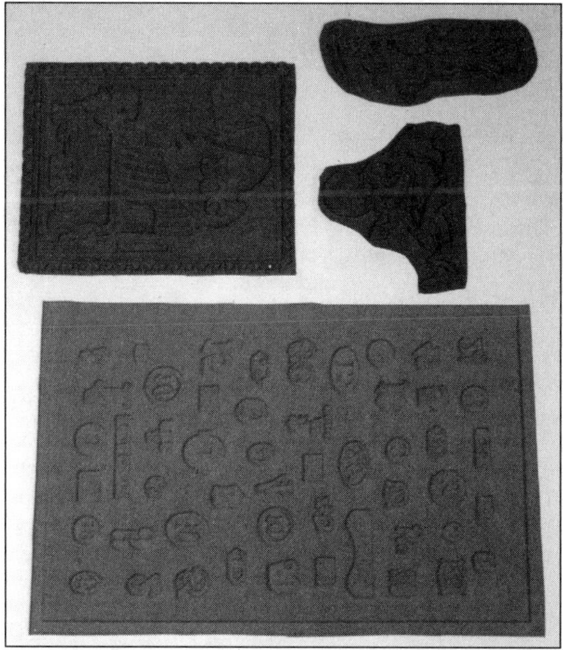

Here are some examples of unmounted stamps. These are from Enchanted Ink and 100 Proof Press.

UNALTERABLE FACT

Many mounting systems are available for unmounted rubber stamps. If EZ Mount doesn't strike your fancy, try another, such as HALOS (www.halosrubberstamps.com), which uses Velcro technology to mount and unmount stamps.

To mount your stamps, you'll need the following:

- Images to be mounted
- Sheet of gray EZ Mount foam
- Sharp pair of scissors

Then, simply follow these steps:

1. Peel away the protective covering on the sticky side of the EZ Mount foam, and stick your rubber images to the foam.
2. Peel away the paper backing from the static-cling side of the EZ Mount foam.
3. Cut out each image, trimming away any excess foam from the rubber's edge.

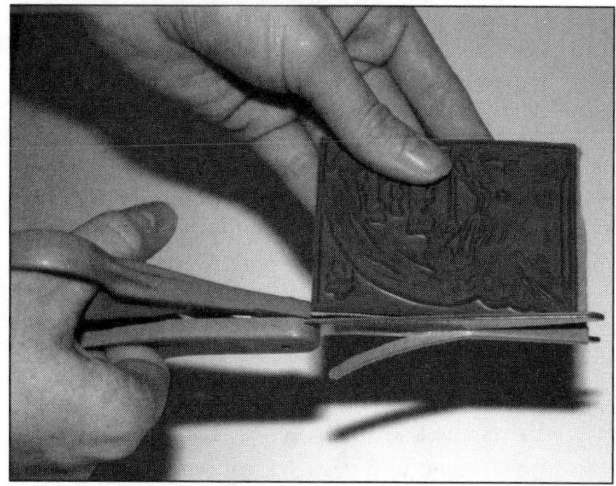

Don't be afraid to cut away any excess rubber as well—all you need for a good impression is the actual stamp image.

Picture This

Mount several stamps at once so you can maximize space when using the EZ Mount foam. I like to wait until I have a bunch of different stamps that need to be mounted and then cover the entire sheet with stamps at one time.

Now that your stamps are mounted, they are ready to use. This process couldn't be simpler. All you need is your favorite stamp, an acrylic block, and an inkpad in a color of your choice.

1. Press the stamp image onto the acrylic block. The cling side of the EZ Mount foam allows the stamp to stick to the block, holding it in place while you work.

2. Use an inkpad to cover the entire image surface with ink.

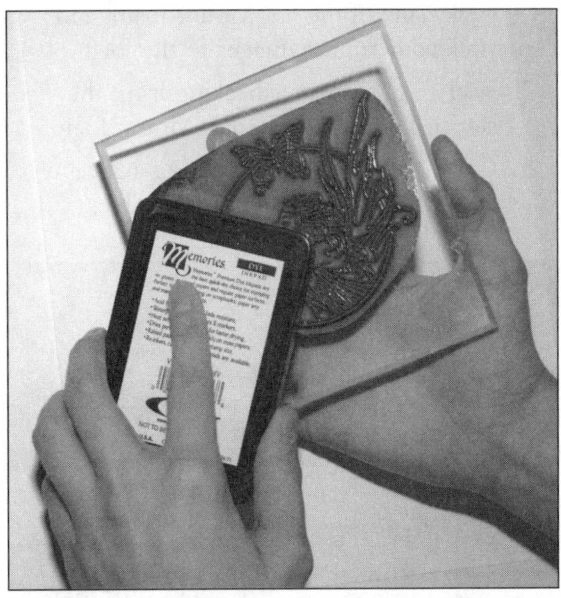

3. Press the stamp firmly on the paper or book page you're working on.

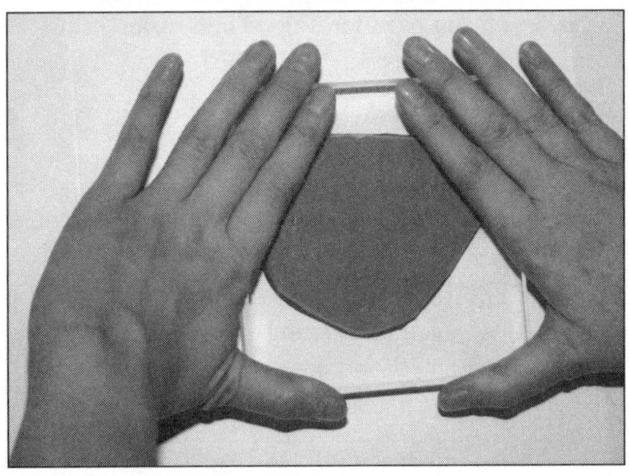

4. Carefully lift stamp straight up off the paper to reveal your stamped image!

Once you discover the fun and ease of working with unmounted stamps, you'll want to use them more and more.

Unmounted Acrylic Rubber Stamps

Unmounted acrylic stamps have become increasingly popular in the last few years. These work just like unmounted rubber stamps, except there's no extra mounting work required. Plus, the stamp itself is clear, so when you're working with unmounted acrylic stamps on a clear block, you can see directly through the stamp, letting you know exactly where your image will end up—a real bonus in the eyes of most crafters.

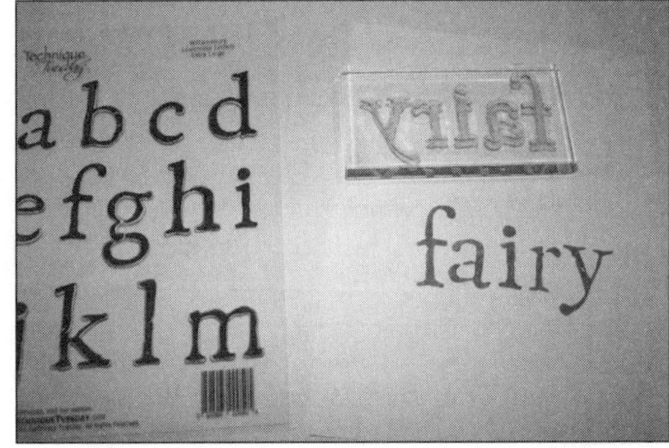

Notice how you can see directly through the letters on the acrylic block. This way, you'll get perfect placement and coverage every time you stamp.

Unmounted acrylic stamps generally come packaged stuck to a transparent Mylar film, often the with the stamp image printed directly on the film. This enables you to see the stamp image clearly and also offers you a place to return the stamp when you're finished stamping.

Picture This

Here's another bonus of acrylic stamps: many companies, such as Technique Tuesday (www.techniquetuesday.com), package their stamps on full-size $8\frac{1}{2} \times 11$ sheets, which you can easily insert into in a 3-ring binder for easy storage and transport.

Inks and Colorants

One of the most important factors to consider when stamping is the type and color of ink you'd like to use on your project. Many different types of ink pads are on the market today—so many, in fact, that the choices can be extremely overwhelming to the new crafter.

In the following sections, I cover a couple types of inking options. I recommend experimenting with different brands and types of inks and colorants to discover what you like best.

Inkpads

The most common way to add color to your stamped images is to use an inkpad. You simply use the pad to cover the surface of the stamp with ink, press the image onto your paper, and you're all set. It's simple, fast, and fun.

My favorite inkpads are Memories pads manufactured by Stewart Superior (www.stewartsuperior.com). They deliver consistent, even coverage and are quite affordable compared with some other brands. Memories inkpads come in a variety of styles, including these:

- *Dye.* These inkpads are quick-drying and easy to use. They deliver a strong, solid impression—making them an excellent choice for altered artists wanting instant results.
- *Pigment.* Pigment inkpads contain a thicker ink that might require a little more drying time. They are permanent and waterproof—perfect for scrapbookers as well as altered artists. Pigment inks deliver strong, rich color, often even on darker surfaces.
- *Chalk.* Chalk inkpads are excellent for pastel and dreamlike effects. They create soft, beautiful colors on dark backgrounds. Chalk inks also work well on vellum and other coated surfaces.
- *Metallic.* These are one of my new favorites! Metallic inkpads create dramatic, shimmering effects on almost any surface.

This altered book page was created using black metallic ink on the stamp in the center of the window. The background is gold metallic paint, making the entire piece a glimmering work of art.

(Stamp by Enchanted Ink)

All these ink pads come in a rainbow of colors. Experiment with some or all of these on your next projects.

Colored Pencils and Pens

One of the greatest ways to add color to a favorite stamped image is to use an outline stamp and color it in using your favorite colored pencils or pens.

Colored pencils are fun and easy to use, and most work well in your altered books. My favorite colored pencils are oil-based, because they deliver strong, vibrant color that lasts. In a pinch, you can even raid your child's art supplies for pencils that will deliver colorful results.

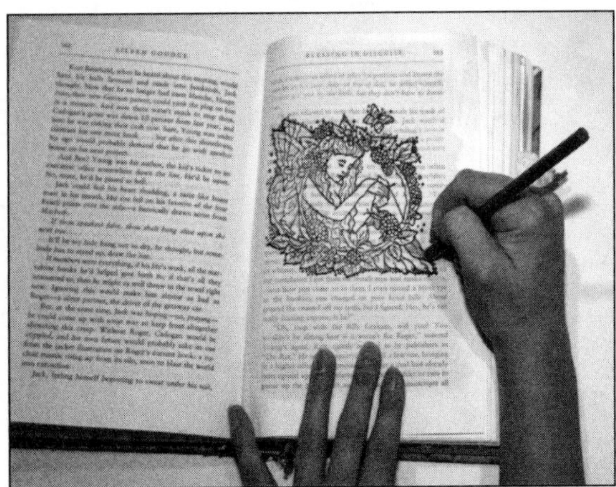

Oil color pencils by Walnut Hollow allow this image to really stand out.

Altered Alert

Work slowly with colored pencils so you don't accidentally smear your project.

Gel pens and other colored pens are also a great choice for working with stamped images. To learn more about working with pens in your altered books, turn to Chapter 7.

The Metallic Effect: Heat Embossing

It doesn't matter how many new stamping techniques I discover, *heat embossing* will always be my favorite. The first time I saw this technique, my jaw hit the floor. It was so easy to do, and the results were so dramatic. Whenever I teach this technique, it always gets the same response.

Transforming Talk

Heat embossing is the act of applying embossing powder to a stamped image and then heating the image. The heat melts the powder, resulting in a raised, fully metallic image.

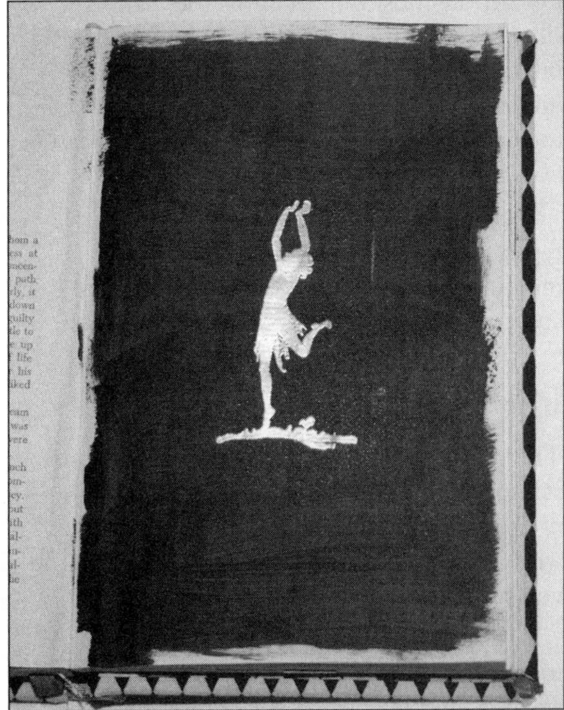

Heat embossed images can deliver fantastic results on any altered page.

Heat-embossed images look amazing on dark backgrounds but work well on any surface. Because embossed images are generally metallic, using them on dark backgrounds really pops the image away from the page.

Embossing Tools

To create a heat embossed image, you'll need a few special tools. These tools can be purchased at almost any craft store, or try searching online:

- *Embossing heat tool.* This handheld tool resembles a hair dryer and is designed to deliver a concentrated amount of heat to your paper surface.

Altered Alert

Many new crafters are tempted to try to use an actual hair dryer in place of the heat tool when embossing. Don't be a victim of this temptation! Hair dryers do not get hot enough and release too much air, creating a significant mess!

- *Embossing inkpad.* This is a specialty inkpad designed just for embossing. The clear ink in the pad remains wet for a long time, which allows the embossing powder to stick to the ink after the image is stamped. In place of an embossing inkpad, you can also use a pigment inkpad, as these take slightly longer to dry and allow the powder enough time to stick.
- *Embossing powder.* This is a fine powder you use to sprinkle over the stamped image and then melt to get the raised embossed image. Look for powders in a rainbow of colors.

When you have these tools on hand, grab a favorite stamp and you're ready to create your first embossed image.

The Heat Embossing Process

Heat embossing is quite simple—and lots of fun to do. Here's how:

1. Cover the surface of the rubber stamp with embossing ink, and press the stamp on the background of your choice.

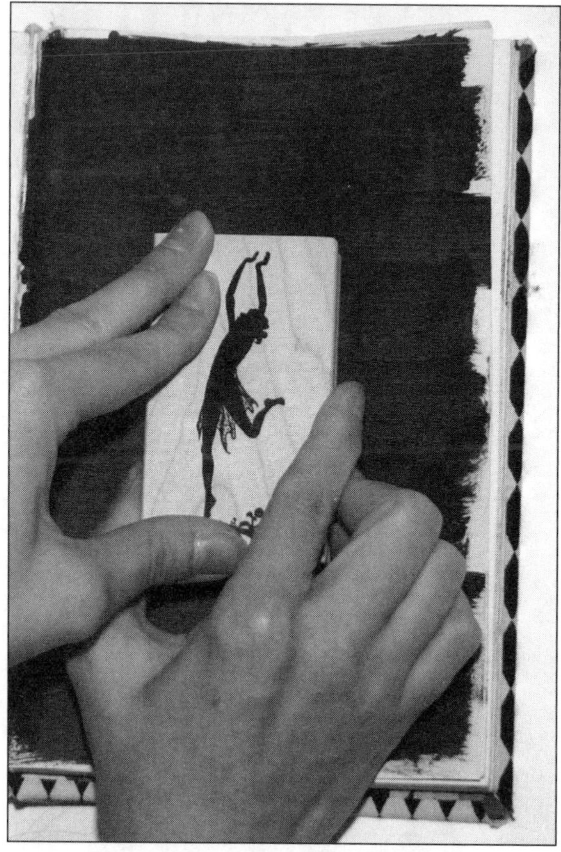

2. Pour embossing powder liberally over the wet stamped image. Note that because the stamped image is clear, you may want to tilt your book so that the ink will catch the light, making it easier to see the exact placement of your stamped image.

3. Immediately tilt your book at an angle, allowing the excess embossing powder to fall away from the page. I like to catch the extra powder on a scrap of paper and return it to the jar for later use.
4. Wipe away any excess powder using a tissue or your fingertip, so only your image is covered with powder. Be sure not to touch the stamped image at this stage.
5. Use the heat tool to heat powdered image. Move the heat gun over the surface of the paper in circles.

Altered Alert

When using the heat tool, avoid hovering over any single area for too long, as this can warp or even burn your paper!

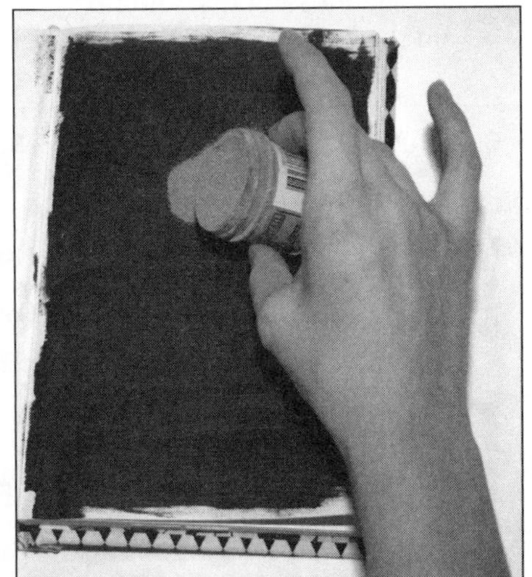

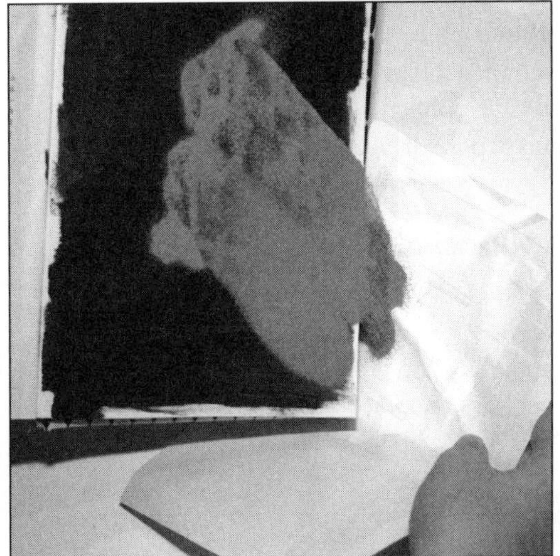

6. Continue to heat until all the powder over your image is fully melted.

You now have a shimmering, raised metallic design! Finish the page any way you like, adding text or other decorations to complete the look you're going for.

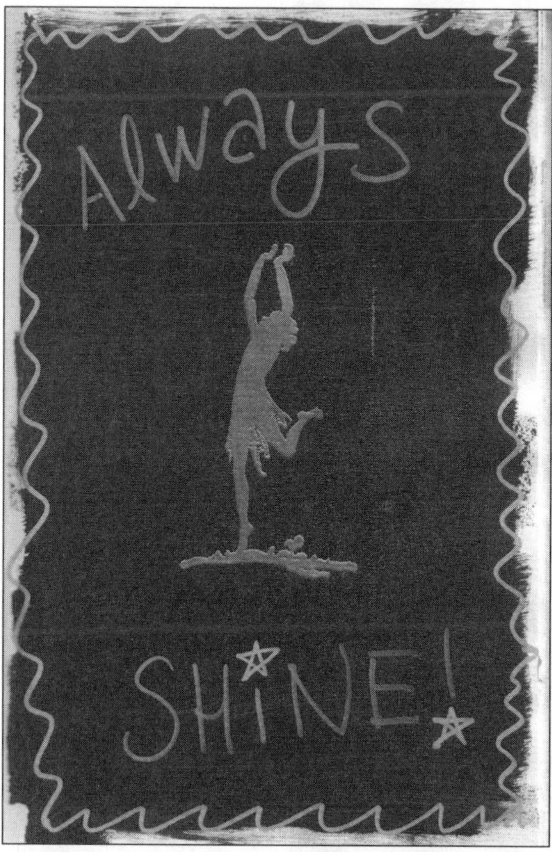

I finished this fantastic page by adding text with a variety of metallic markers from Stewart Superior's Memories line.

Covering Your Mistakes

Let's face it. Stamping isn't always a perfect science. Maybe you've got your entire altered book page complete except for one final stamped image. You ink your stamp, press firmly, and do everything right. But for whatever reason, when you lift up the stamp, you discover that you didn't get a full print. Or part of your image is blurred. Or you stamped the image upside down. Whatever the accident, don't worry. You can creatively fix your error, and no one will ever know the difference.

> **Altered Alert**
>
> Avoid the perfectionist trap! Art is art, and even famous artists make mistakes. Remember that it really is okay if you make an error—trust me, you're the only one who will notice. Some of my best work has come from finding ways to creatively fix "mistakes."

If you were lucky enough to be using unmounted acrylic stamps, the solution is easy: simply line up the stamp again on top of your erred image, and re-stamp. Because the stamps are completely clear, you can get the alignment right-on.

If you weren't using clear stamps, perhaps the easiest way to fix a mistake is to simply cover it:

1. Stamp the image again on a scrap of paper.
2. Cut out or decoratively tear around the stamped image, and adhere it to your artwork on top of the area where you made an error.

Now, not only is your original error hidden, but you've added a second layer to your art, a new dimension. I've often found that when I employ this technique, I enjoy the "fixed" final product better than I would have liked the original.

If you don't want to cover up your design, just find a way to make it work. This is sometimes easier said than done, but use your imagination to get an even more creative piece of artwork. When artist Kate Schaefer was creating this altered book page, she became frustrated as she pulled up her second stamped image and her hand accidentally moved the stamp as she lifted it. The result: the stamped woman's head came out completely blurry.

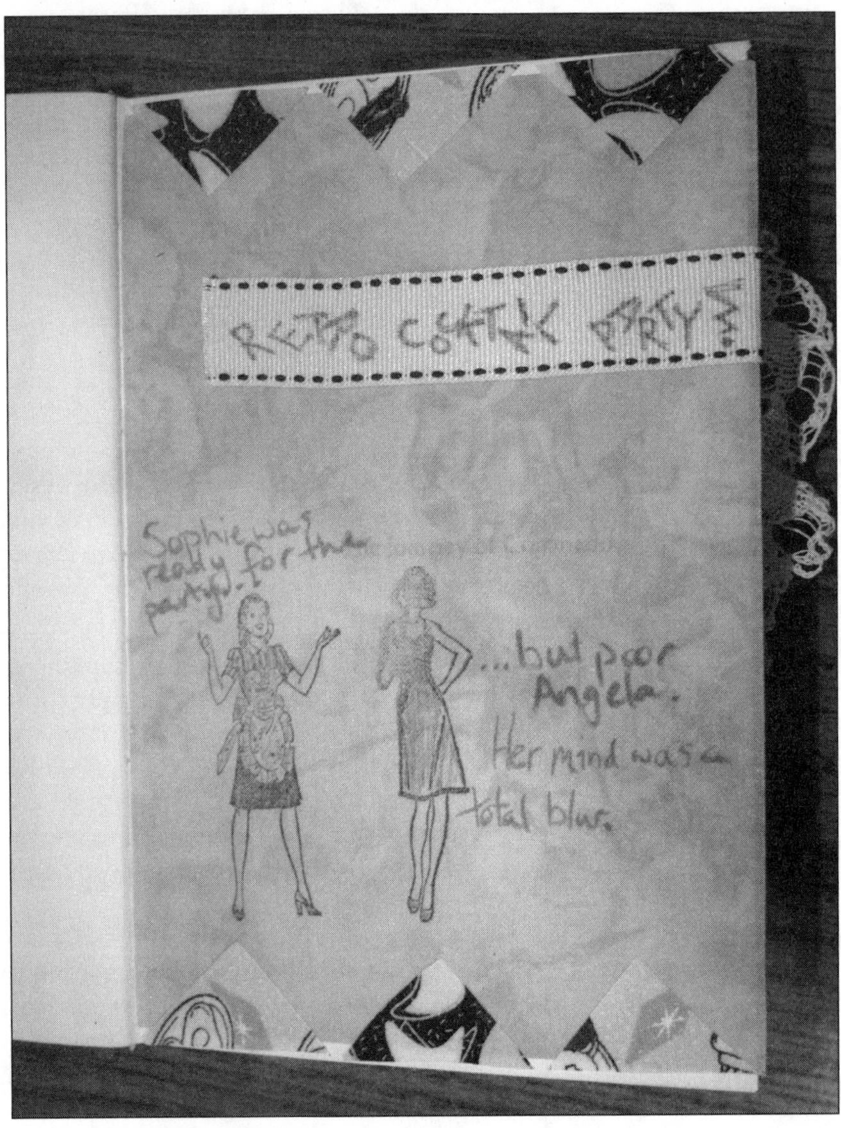

Notice that the top half of the woman on the right is blurred.

(Page by Kate Schaefer)

After examining the piece, Kate decided to simply add two lines of text, one next to each woman:

> *Sophie was ready for the party …*
> *… but poor Angela. Her mind was a total blur.*

Simply by adding these lines of text, Kate turned her "mistake" into a mark of creative genius. People are always asking her how she was able to get only half of the image to blur, imagining it to be a complicated technique. And to think, this fantastic piece of unique art started all because of an "error."

Have fun with your stamping! And if you do happen to make a small mistake, don't worry. Simply cover it up or make it part of your design. The results can be even better than you originally envisioned.

The Least You Need to Know

- Stamps are available in three forms: wood-mounted, unmounted rubber, and unmounted acrylic. All are fun and easy to use with the right set of tools.
- Use a variety of inkpads with your rubber stamps to create beautiful effects.
- Heat embossing creates amazing raised metallic images for your altered artwork.
- Don't be afraid to make a mistake when you're stamping. You can easily correct it by covering it up or incorporating it into your overall design.

In This Chapter

- Using different types of specialty pens in your altered books
- Conquering the fear of drawing and embracing imperfection
- Creating an illustrated altered book spread
- Using masking fluid to create resist designs
- Playing with drawing tools in your altered books

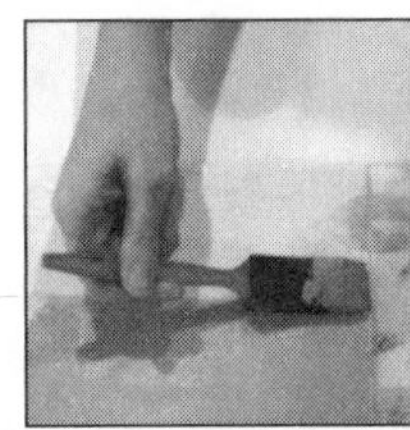

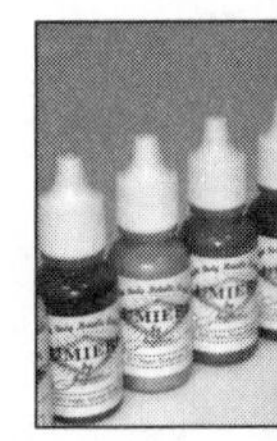

Chapter 7

A Fine Line: Drawing in Your Book

You've learned how to creatively add images to your altered books by using photographs, ephemera, and rubber stamps. Now it's time to pick up the pen and add designs and images of your very own to your altered books.

Drawing and doodling in altered books can seem intimidating at first, especially if you're like me. I grew up believing I "couldn't" draw. I've since discovered that a lack of artistic training doesn't have to stop you from adding your own drawings to your books.

Why Draw?

Right about now, you might be thinking I'm crazy. *What? You want me to draw on my artwork? Are you kidding? That will ruin it!* These are the same thoughts I struggled with when I first sat down to draw in my altered books. I thought that because I have no special art training, and because my drawings are much more doodlelike than artistic in nature, they had no value. This simply isn't so.

When I teach scrapbooking classes, I try to convince my students that they should include journaling and details in their own handwriting, even if they hate it. Why? Because handwriting is a natural part of who you are. By including your handwriting and your hand-drawn designs in your altered books, you have the ability to create a one-of-a-kind piece of artwork. Other artists might purchase the same stamps you select or choose a similar paint color, but no other person can write or draw just like you. And that's something worth celebrating!

The Right Supplies

Like most techniques, drawing in your altered books begins with gathering the necessary supplies. Sure, all you need is a pen. But getting the *right* pen helps ensure you get the results you want.

Many types of drawing and art pens are available, but I recommend starting with a high-quality gel, paint, or writing pen. First and foremost, you'll want to be sure the pen you choose for your book contains *archival ink*. This helps keep your design looking fresh for generations to come.

Transforming Talk

Archival ink is ink that is permanent, waterproof, and lightfast. It's specifically designed to last for hundreds of years, ensuring that your artwork will last.

Many brands of pens are available to choose from. My favorite pens are produced by Sakura. This company offers several lines of pens, all in a variety of colors and tip sizes.

These pens from Sakura represent just a few of the choices available to the altered artist.

Let's take a look at a few of Sakura's best pen types.

Pigma Pens for Drawing and Illustration

The most common pen type available to artists is the fine-line drawing pen. Sakura's Pigma pens are my favorites because they contain archival ink, and they deliver such a strong line. This helps extend the life of the drawing and ensures its permanence.

Pigma pens come in a variety of colors and tip styles, including the following:

- *Pigma Micron*, a fine-point drawing pen available in 15 colors and 6 tip point sizes.
- *Pigma Brush*, a brush-tipped pen that enables the artist to create a variety of looks, available in 8 colors.
- *Pigma Graphic*, a chisel-tipped pen that also comes in a variety of colors and styles. This pen is excellent for calligraphy and other graphic effects and is available in 3 colors and tip styles.

Unalterable Fact

Pigma pens were originally produced as tools for architects and engineers to replace highly expensive and unreliable dye-based drafting pens.

Choose a Pigma pen when you are …

- Working on a light- or medium-colored background and you want a solid, dark contrasting line.
- Creating a project you want to last for generations.
- Looking for a specialty pen tip to create decorative lettering or another special effect.

While Pigma pens are favorites of many altered artists, there are other choices available to you. If you can't locate Pigma pens in your area, feel free to substitute another brand. As long as you look for a pen that features archival ink, you should be all set.

Gel Pens

Gel pens are pretty popular lately because their ink shows up on light or dark paper—ideal for altered artists who want to work with a darker background.

Gel pens come in hundreds of colors and sizes. Be on the lookout for specialty gel pens. A few of my favorites from Sakura's Gelly Roll line include the following:

- Gelly Roll Moonlight pens, which come in 10 fun, bright colors that glow under black light!
- Gelly Roll Stardust pens, available in 12 glittery colors. Try the medium point pen for a good, solid line.
- Gelly Roll Silver Shadow pens, which write in silver and create a colored border automatically as you write. These pens are available in 5 outline colors.

As you can see, you have tons of choices right at your fingertips.

Picture This

Need help keeping track of your pen colors? Visit www.gellyroll.com/products/pens/colorchart4.html for an easy-to-use color chart!

Choose a Gelly Roll pen when you are …

- Looking to add sparkle and shine to a project.
- Creating a drawn or doodled design with many layers of color.
- Working on a dark background.
- Wanting to create a metallic look.

Gel pens are perfect for adding sparkle and shine to any project. Their shimmering colors add a real "wow" factor to your writing and drawing, making them a perfect choice for your next work of art.

Specialty Pens

Still haven't found what you're looking for? Sakura also offers many specialty pens are available to the altered artist to create just the right look. Try some of these specialty pens on your next project:

- *Permapaque pens*, fine-point paint pens that deliver a bold and completely opaque line on almost any surface. They work just like traditional paint pens but without the mess, odor, and shaking.
- *Glaze 3D Transparent Ink pens* enable you to create an embossed, 3D textured line of shimmery, semi-transparent ink.
- *Soufflé pens* create a 3D, embossed, opaque line in a variety of pastel colors.

All these pens offer great possibilities to the altered artist. Try a specialty pen when you are …

- Hoping to create a 3D effect.
- Wanting the ease of paint in pen form.
- Looking for a truly opaque line on a dark surface.
- Wishing to add just a hint of texture to an otherwise flat project.

The hand-drawn flowers on this altered book page were first created with Gelly Roll Stardust pens and then outlined with Permapaques for extra pizzazz.

Getting Past the Fear of Drawing

It's time to grab that perfect pen and make your mark. Unless you were blessed with a talent for drawing, this is where things can start to feel a bit intimidating. The key is to go with the flow and allow yourself to draw and create without judging the final product.

Have you ever watched young children draw? They simply create for fun, making picture after picture of whatever happens to be in their mind at any given moment. The creation is about the process, not the end result. It is about the joy of creating, not the fear of judgment. Challenge yourself to get back to that place and simply allow yourself to create freely—and just for fun—in your altered books. Just play.

Picture This

Remember, no one else has to see your drawings or your final altered object unless you choose to share it. Work like only you will see this work. Let yourself go and draw!

Ready to get started? Follow these steps:

1. Create a background on your page using a technique from Chapter 2.
2. Add paint or decorative detailing if you like.
3. Pick up a pen. I highly recommend starting out with a Pigma pen. They are guaranteed to work perfectly almost every time and produce a strong line for you to work with.
4. Get drawing!

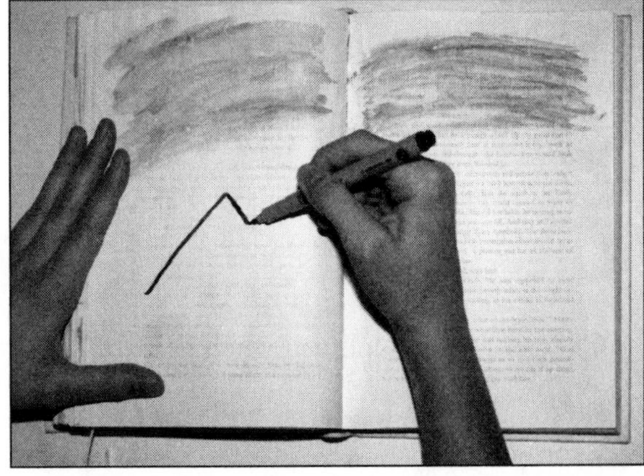

Allow yourself to relax and draw whatever comes to mind.

5. Look at your design. Is it missing something? Keep drawing. Don't judge yourself!
6. Complete your design. Add more paint or accents if you want.

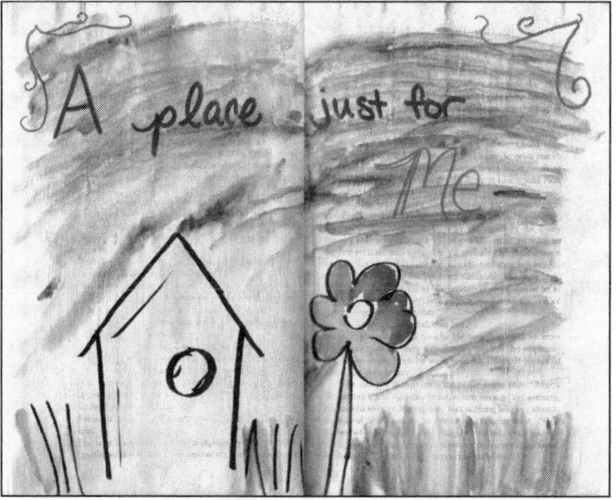

These pages were my first attempt at drawing in my altered books. Very childlike, I know, but they're still fun!

Take the time to create a drawing or two in your altered books, and allow yourself to explore whatever you want. Do whatever feels right to you. Remember, this book is just for you.

Picture This

Your designs don't have to consist entirely of drawing. Try adding a just a few hand-drawn touches to an altered book page you've already created. Flowers, swirls, and borders are easy designs to create and can be added quite easily to another design.

Fairytale Altered Book Spread

Creating an altered book page with hand-drawn accents and elements is easier than you might think! Follow these easy steps to create this fun 2-page spread for your altered book.

Rounding Up the Goods

Start by gathering the supplies you'll need:

- Book to alter of your choosing
- Acrylic paints in metallic blue and green
- Foam brush
- Paint texture comb, if desired
- Queen stamp (Catslife Press)
- Girl Dress Die Cut Shape (Poppets designed by Claudine Hellmuth, manufactured by Lazar StudioWERX)
- White Opaque Inkpad (Memories Chalk by Stewart Superior)
- Gel pens in a variety of colors (Gelly Roll by Sakura)

With your supplies in hand, it's time to get to work!

Preparing Your Pages

Begin by giving your pages a simple background:

1. Cover the entire page surface in blue paint. (If you'd like, leave a small passage of text exposed, as shown in the following photos.) Let the paint dry.

This fun altered book spread is easy to create and provides a whimsical touch to your altered books.

(Pages by Kate Schaefer)

2. Add 1 to 2 inches of green paint across the bottom edge of the page. If desired, use a paint *texture comb* to add detail to the paint strokes. Let the paint dry.

> **Transforming Talk**
>
> A **texture comb** is small triangle-shaped object featuring various decorative edges. You rake the comb over wet paint, leaving decorative marks in the final painted design.

3. Next add the body of your page's main subject by adhering the dress die-cut shape to the left-hand side of your page.
4. Use your rubber stamp and white inkpad to add a face to your subject's body. Position the stamp so the face is directly aligned with the die-cut body. If you make a mistake, simply reposition the die-cut on your page.

You've now added all the necessary elements to your page, and you can finally begin drawing!

This painted page is now ready for decoration.

Be sure to leave plenty of room above and below the dress to add a head, arms, and legs to your figure.

The stamp from Catslife Press provides the perfect head for the die-cut dress.

Hand-Drawn Additions

It's time to start adding the hand-drawn elements to your altered book page spread. Following these steps enables you to create a fun, fairy tale like design. Of course, you can create your page design any way you like.

Use your gel pens to create these elements on your pages:

1. Draw a thought bubble to the right of the girl's head. Write in: "It's so hard to find a good man to rescue you these days."
2. Draw a frightened-looking prince kneeling at her feet.
3. On the right-hand page, outline the shape of a dragon breathing fire at the princess.

Picture This

Remember that your two-page design can go right across the book's spine—no need to stay "within the lines" of the two separate pages. Artist Kate Schaefer did this, and the end result is fantastic.

Don't feel like you have the drawing talents necessary to complete the steps? No worries! Try one of these fun and easy tricks to make your pages stand out:

- Substitute another rubber stamp for one of the hand-drawn elements.
- Find an outline in a child's coloring book or online. Trace the design into your book and use it as a guideline when drawing.
- Search for paper piecing patterns on the Internet, and create your page element from decorative papers. (A great source for finding patterns is scrapbooking.about.com/od/freepatterns.)

If you choose to create your main page elements using stamps or another method, try adding a few drawn items, too. Remember, including your own drawing and writing in your altered books is the same as including a bit of yourself on your pages. There's no better way to reflect who you are in the art you create.

Special Drawing Effects

Now that you've tried a drawing project and are feeling better about your drawing skills, let's get ready for some more doodling and drawing excitement. Try the techniques in the following sections for an even more original look.

Masking

Want to create a resist effect on your pages? What about a fun and funky design full of contrast? If this is your goal, *masking* is the answer. Masking can appear to be a quite complicated technique at first. But it couldn't be simpler.

Transforming Talk

Masking is the act of covering one part of your design prior to applying ink or paint, allowing it to remain free of color to create contrast.

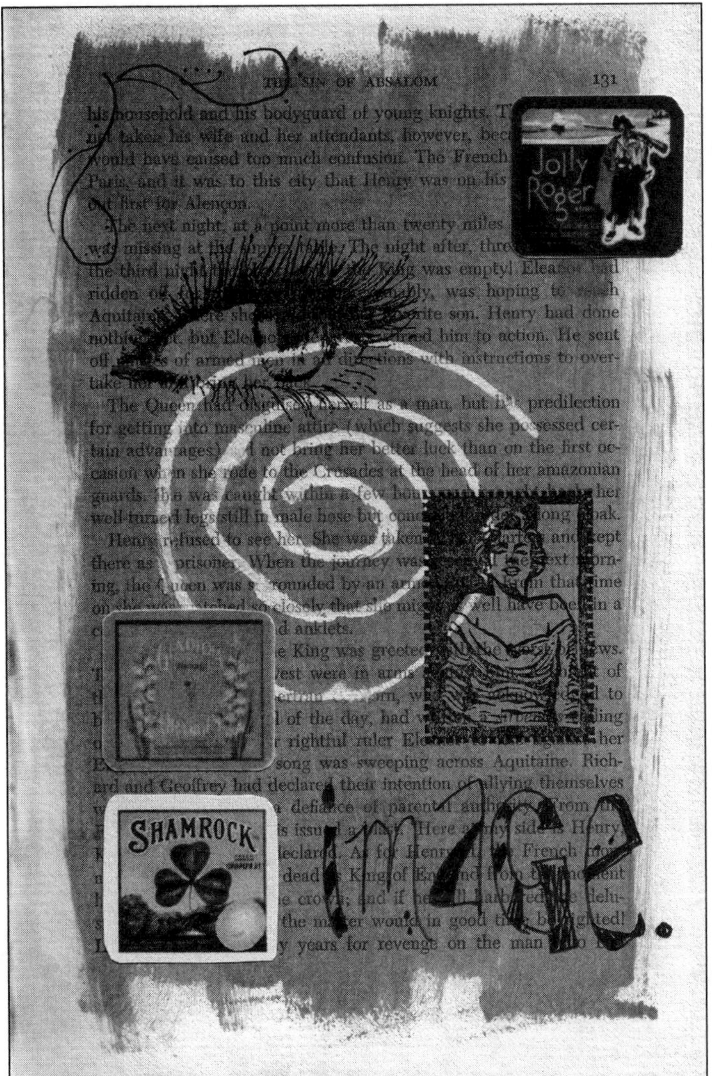

The background of this altered book page was created by drawing a swirl with masking fluid prior to painting the background.

Before you begin to create a masked design in your altered book, be sure you have all the supplies you'll need:

- Book for altering
- Paint or ink of your choice
- Any stamps, photographs, or other items you'd like to use
- *Masking fluid;* preferably a *Masquepen*

Transforming Talk

Masking fluid is a medium that when used on your page, resists paint and ink in the area it is applied. You can find masking fluid at most fine art stores and some paper crafting stores. It comes in many different forms, usually in a small bottle. My favorite masking product is the **Masquepen,** a bottle of masking fluid with a penlike nib tool, which enables you to simply write with the masking fluid.

To create a masked design in your altered book, follow these steps:

1. Use the Masquepen to draw a design of your choice on the background of your page. Let the masking fluid dry completely.
2. Apply paint or ink over your design, and let dry.
3. Gently rub away the dried masking fluid with your finger.
4. Decorate and embellish your page as desired.

Working with masking fluid is a fun and easy process that delivers excellent results.

Altered Alert

If your book pages are especially old or brittle, test the masking fluid in an inconspicuous area before creating your design. On rare occasions, the masking fluid might tear your page. If this happens, pretreat your page by coating it with a thin layer of matte gel medium.

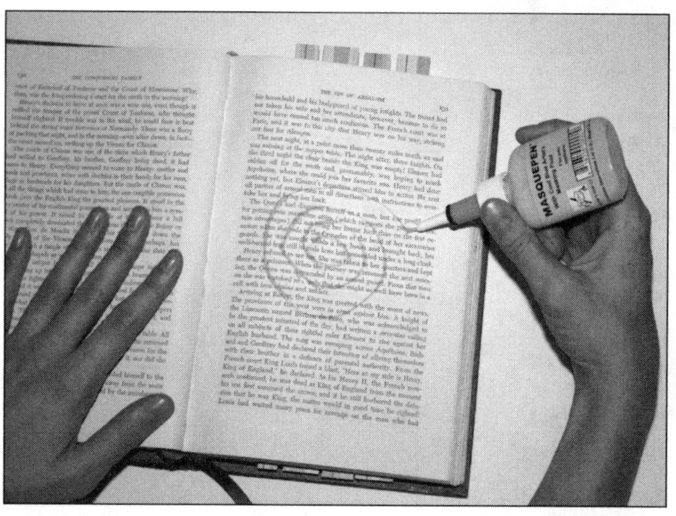

Work slowly with the Masquepen, using even strokes. If you'd like to create a thinner line or other very fine details, use Masquepen's SuperNib attachment.

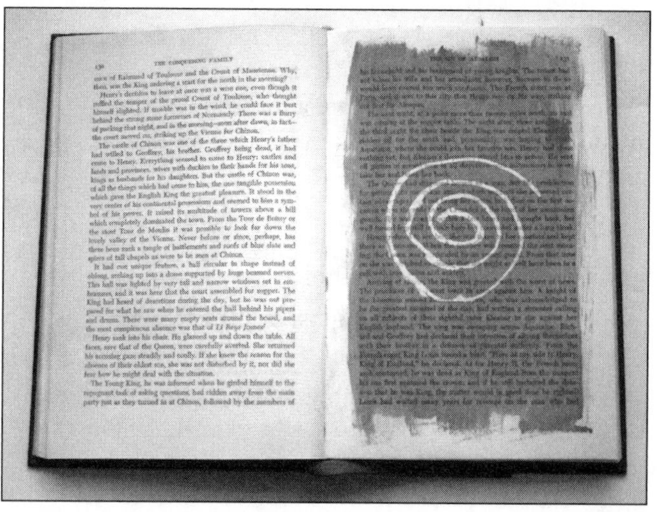

When the masking fluid is rubbed away, your design shines through.

These fun art journal entries were created and drawn with a variety of supplies, including oil pastels, colored pencils, and children's crayons.

(Pages by Nancy Baumiller)

Playing

When it comes to doodling and drawing, don't be afraid to simply forget all the rules and just have some fun. Break out of the box, even when it comes to your supplies. Try creating with any of these tools—or any others you find:

- Colored pencils
- Oil pastels
- Children's wax crayons
- Children's markers
- Artist chalk
- Glitter paint tubes
- Airbrushes
- Felt-tip pens from an office supply store
- Poster paints

Altered art isn't designed to be archival, so experiment. Take the time to create and design just for you. If you're using your altered book to create an artistic journal, as described in Chapter 1, this is an especially great place to try out some fun and unique tools.

Sometimes stepping out of the box and using a creative technique or product is all you need to give a page extra impact and excitement.

The Least You Need to Know

- Many different kinds of pens are available to the altered artist. Experiment and discover which ones you enjoy using the most.
- Don't edit or judge when you're creating. Allow yourself to draw whatever you imagine, and enjoy the process.
- Use masking fluid to create unique resist images.
- Let yourself play with all kinds of drawing tools and mediums. Raiding your children's art supplies can yield exceptionally fun results!

In This Chapter

- Understanding the basics of image transfer
- Learning specialty transfer techniques
- Producing unique image transfers with Polaroid film

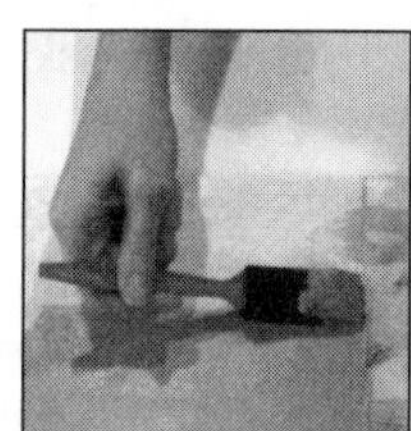

Chapter 8

Image Transfers

So far in Part 2 we've looked at incorporating photographs into your altered art, finding and including ephemera in your work, and adding fun designs to your pages with rubber stamping. We also looked at drawing in your altered pieces, adding personal notes and touches only you can produce. All these techniques can add personality to your altered pages.

But there's more. Now that you've learned all about the different types of creative image sources you can use in your altered books, it's time to discover some unique *image transfer* techniques. Creating an image transfer is yet another great way to add some one-of-a-kind effects to your altered art. In this chapter, I walk you through several image transfer methods. Try them all and decide which one you like the best.

Transforming Talk

Image transfer is the act of literally transferring an image from one surface to another, such as from a paper background to a clear Mylar background. Only the image, not the paper it's printed on, is transferred, creating a semi-transparent effect in the resulting image.

Packing Tape Image Transfer

"Packing tape," you might ask? "To transfer an image?" Yes, you read that right! Using packing tape to transfer an image is by far the easiest image transfer technique and requires no special tools. It's a great method to use for your first attempt at image transfer.

Here's what you'll need:

- Color photocopy of a favorite image, or an image cut from a magazine or book
- Roll of clear packing tape
- Scissors
- Bowl of warm water

Altered Alert

Before you print that photo you scanned or your friend e-mailed you, please note: inkjet prints will *not* work for this transfer method.

Then follow these steps to perform your transfer:

1. Cut your image out so only the part you want to transfer remains. (If your image has a white border, you don't need to cut that part now if you don't want to.)
2. Cover the entire top of your image with clear packing tape.

3. Place your image into a bowl of warm water, and let it soak for 3 to 5 minutes.

4. Remove your image from the water and place it face down on the table in front of you. Using your finger, rub off the paper on the back of the image. All the white paper will come off, leaving only your image remaining.

Unalterable Fact

Completely removing the paper backing from your image might take a while, so don't give up. Your image transfer isn't complete until all the backing paper has been removed.

Your result will be a gorgeous semi-transparent image you can now use as a part of any altered art project.

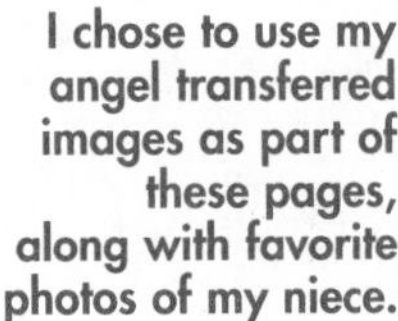

I chose to use my angel transferred images as part of these pages, along with favorite photos of my niece.

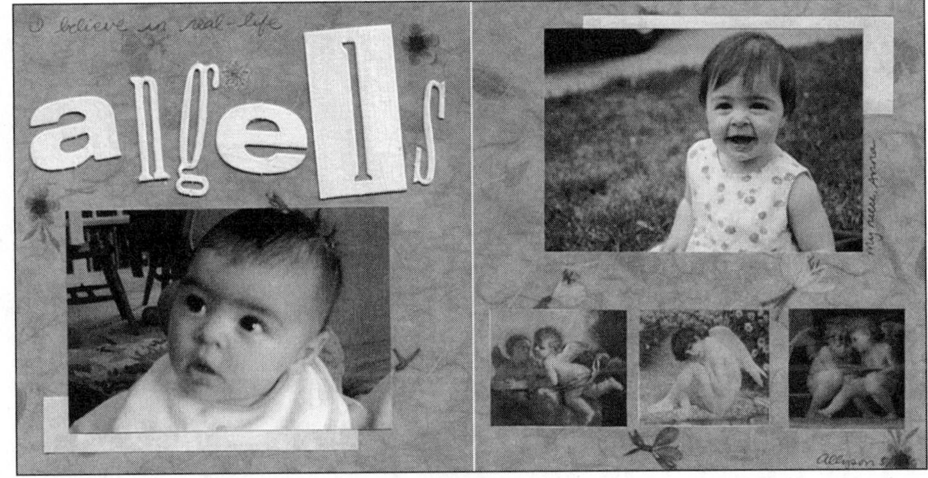

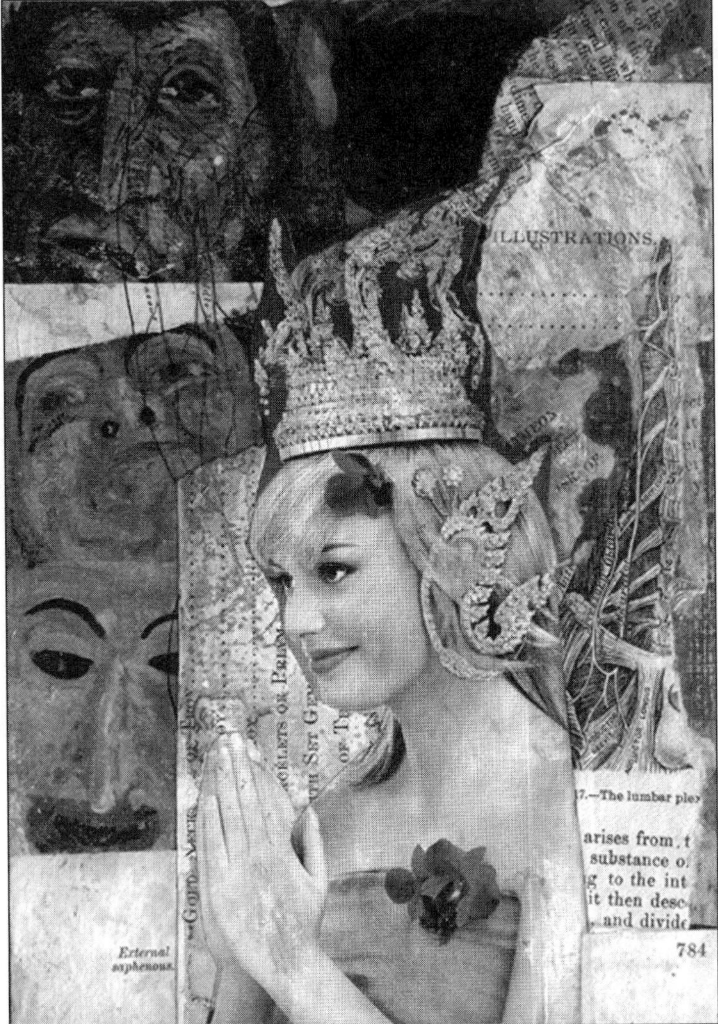

This amazing page uses packing tape transfer with dramatic results.

(Page by Diane Keys)

These gorgeous pages feature caulk image transfers.

(Pages by Diane Keys)

Caulk Image Transfer

Caulk—yes, the same caulk that you purchase at a home improvement store to seal your windows—is the key ingredient in this unique image transfer method. Using caulk to create image transfers yields exciting results!

To create a caulk transfer, gather these supplies:

- Sheet of canvas paper (These can be purchased in tablet form at your local art supply store.)
- Caulk
- Image printed on a laser printer or created with a copy machine

Altered Alert

As with the packing tape image transfer method, inkjet prints will not work with this technique.

With your supplies at the ready, follow these steps to transfer your image:

1. If desired, paint the background of the canvas page using a technique of your choice. See Chapter 2 for some ideas if you need to.
2. Spread caulk over area you'd like to place your image. Keep the layer fairly thin.
3. Lay your image, face down, on top of the caulk.
4. Smooth the image gently, removing any air bubbles. Let the caulk dry completely.
5. Use your fingers to apply a small amount of water on the surface of the paper. Use just enough water to get the image wet—your paper doesn't need to be soaked.
6. Peel away the paper backing. Rub away any residual paper that still remains.

With your image transferred, now you can finish and use the page however you like—maybe as an addition to an altered book or an art journal.

Two different gel medium transfer methods were used to create these nostalgic altered book pages.

(Pages by Diane Keys)

Gel Medium Transfers

As you learned in Chapter 1, gel mediums a great tool for collage and altered artists. In addition, it also makes an excellent choice for image transfer.

To create your own gel medium transfers, you'll need the following supplies:

- Image printed on a laser printer
- Gel medium
- Water
- Credit card or other ID card

Altered Alert

Inkjet prints will not work with this transfer method.

You can transfer images two different ways with gel medium. In the following sections, I give you instructions for both methods.

Gel Medium Transfer—Option 1

If you'd like to transfer your image directly to your book page, follow these steps. This process yields a result that's somewhat mottled but makes a fantastic accent on your pages.

1. Create your background as desired.
2. Brush a thin layer of gel medium onto the surface where you want to transfer your image.
3. Place the image face down on top of the gel medium.
4. Use a credit card or ID card to *burnish* the back of the image very well. Pay extra attention to the center area of your image,

as well as any portions of your image that have a lot of detail. These areas can be the hardest to transfer well. Be careful not to tear your image while you're burnishing it.

Transforming Talk

Burnishing is the act of rubbing the back of an image or element using a blunt edge. A credit card works particularly well. Images should be rubbed thoroughly and with a good amount of strength.

5. Check to see if the image is transferring well by peeling up a bit of the corner. Once the image has transferred, peel off the paper backing, and carefully remove the excess paper by rubbing it off with a small amount of water and your finger.
6. Seal the final image to your page by coating it with gel medium.

Gel Medium Transfer—Option 2

If you'd like your image to transfer more completely to your artwork, or if you'd like to have more freedom with image placement, try this method:

1. Cover the printed image with gel medium. Allow this to dry completely, until clear.
2. Soak the image in a shallow pan of water.
3. Carefully remove the paper backing.
4. Remove the image from the water, and let it dry.
5. Adhere the image to your project with gel medium, and let it dry.

Regardless of how you choose to use gel medium to transfer your images, you'll surely find the results are well worth it.

Polaroid Image Transfers

I still remember the first time I successfully completed a Polaroid image transfer. I was so excited and enthralled by the results as well as the ease of the process. It quickly became one of my favorite artistic techniques for use in both my altered book projects and my scrapbooks.

Polaroid image transfers are easy, but they do require a bit of special equipment. If you're new to the world of altered art and image transfer, consider checking with a local craft or hobby store, as it might have equipment you can try without cost. If you're a seasoned pro (or well on your way to becoming one, by now) you might want to consider making an investment. Initial startup costs for this equipment can run anywhere between $150 to $350, but the rewards well outweigh the cost.

To create Polaroid image transfers, here's what you'll need:

- Daylab Copysystem (I use the Daylab Copysystem Pro.)
- Pack of Polaroid 669 film
- Brayer

UNALTERABLE FACT

Daylab's Copysystem machines create 3¼×4¼-inch Polaroid prints from any image up to 4×6 inches. The system has a multitude of uses, even beyond image transfer. For more information, check out Daylab's website at www.daylab.com.

Armed with the necessary tools, you're ready to begin. These image transfer methods have been perfected by the folks at Daylab, and I am so excited to share them with you here.

Dry Image Transfer

Dry image transfer is the easiest method to use to successfully create with the Daylab system. You'll likely get it right on your first attempt.

1. Begin by selecting an image you'd like to work with. I chose a favorite childhood photograph.

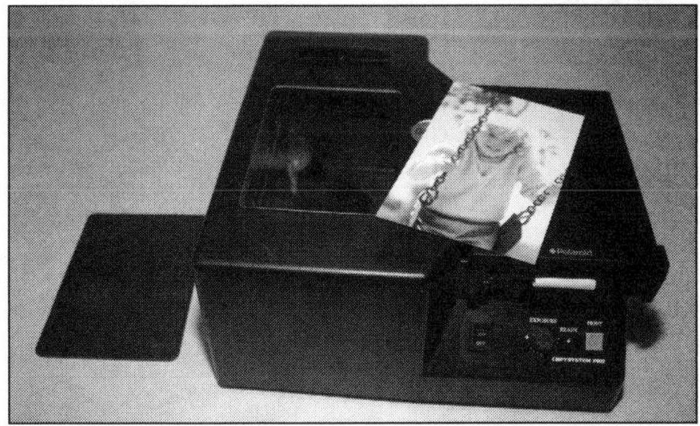

2. Place the photo face down on the Daylab unit's exposure glass. Place the black plastic cover on top of the photo if the glass area is not completely covered.

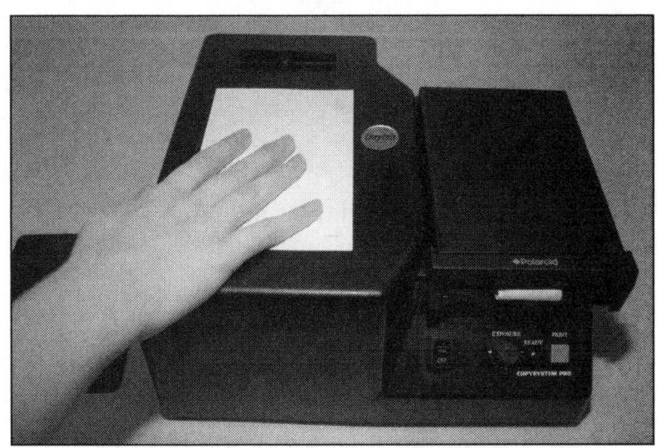

3. Expose the image using the Daylab. (Follow the instructions that come with your Daylab unit if you need additional assistance.)
4. After about 20 seconds of exposure, peel apart the two layers of film.

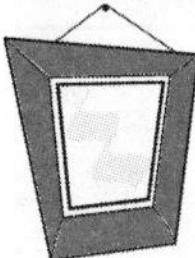

Picture This

Be careful to only handle the film by the edges during this process. You don't want fingerprints on your transferred image!

5. Place the negative side of the film (this is the black side that's covered in chemicals) face down on a paper of your choice. (Cold-pressed watercolor paper works exceptionally well.)
6. Using a brayer, roll over the image firmly for 10 to 20 seconds, being sure to roll over the entire image.

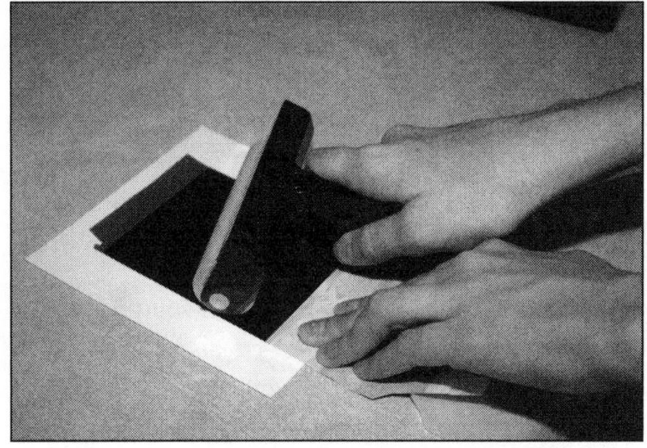

7. Rub the photo and paper together in your hands for about a minute. Be careful to keep the photo and paper together at all times during this process.
8. Gently peel away the film from the paper.

You know have a gorgeous, ghostlike image ready for use in your altered artwork. Consider cutting out the image and adding it to a page or project you're currently working on.

Emulsion Lift Transfer

Image transfer via *emulsion lift* can seem complicated at first. When I first received my Copysystem Pro, I was so excited and performed all sorts of dry transfers. But emulsion lift seemed like it would just be too complicated to be worth it. When I finally tried it, though, I couldn't believe I'd waited so long. The process is easy and almost impossible to mess up. (And if you do make a mistake, you can fix it immediately.) Once you experience the fun of emulsion lift image transfer, you'll never look at images quite the same way again.

Transforming Talk

Emulsion is the goolike coating of chemicals sandwiched between the layers of Polaroid film that allows the film to develop correctly. **Emulsion lift** is the process of separating the emulsion coating from the image itself to perform an image transfer.

For this transfer process, you'll need the following:

- Daylab Copysystem (I use the Daylab Copysystem Pro.)
- Pack of Polaroid 669 film
- Two trays of water, one at room temperature, the other at 160°F
- Vinyl self-adhesive shelf or contact paper
- Brayer
- Sheet of clear Mylar or acetate

Here's how to create your emulsion lift:

1. Following the instructions that came with your Daylab unit, create a Polaroid instant print from the image you'd like to use. Allow it to develop completely.
2. Pull apart the film, and discard the negative half of the image (or use for a dry transfer, as described earlier).

3. Cover the back of your print with shelf paper. (This ensures that the back of your print does not dissolve.)

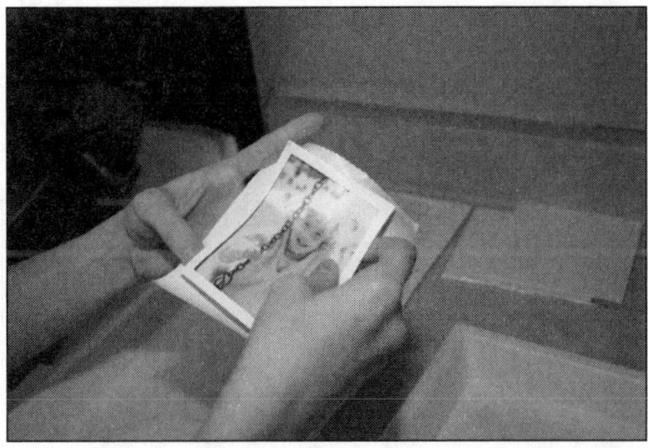

4. Use tongs to place print in tray of water at 160°F. Allow it to soak for 2 or 3 minutes until you notice bubbles appearing across surface of image.

5. Using tongs, move the print to the tray containing the room-temperature water.

6. Once the print is in the water, use your fingers to gently rub the emulsion away from the print so the two layers completely separate.

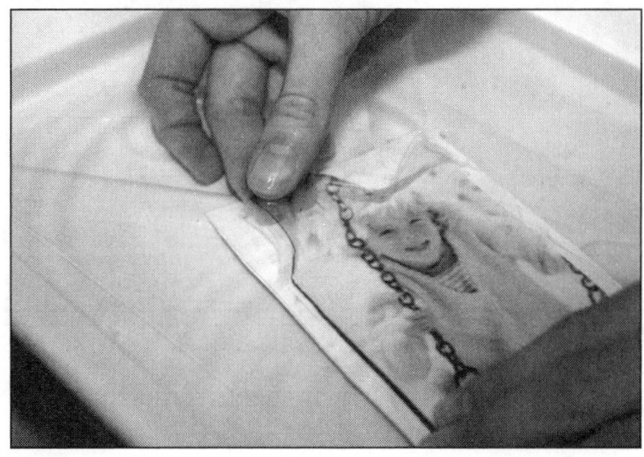

Picture This

Don't worry about ripping the emulsion layer. It's much stronger than it looks, and it's not going to tear!

7. Remove the paper backing from the water. Insert the clear Mylar sheet into the water, underneath the image. Spread the image across the clear Mylar sheet, and carefully lift the image from the water.

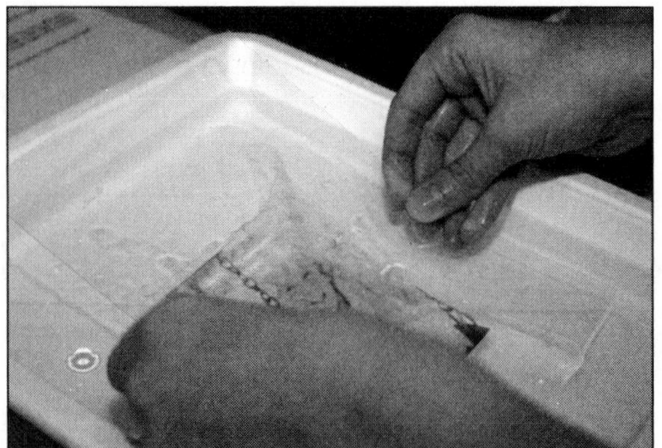

8. Using the Mylar sheet to keep the image spread out, place the emulsion face down onto your book page or other surface.

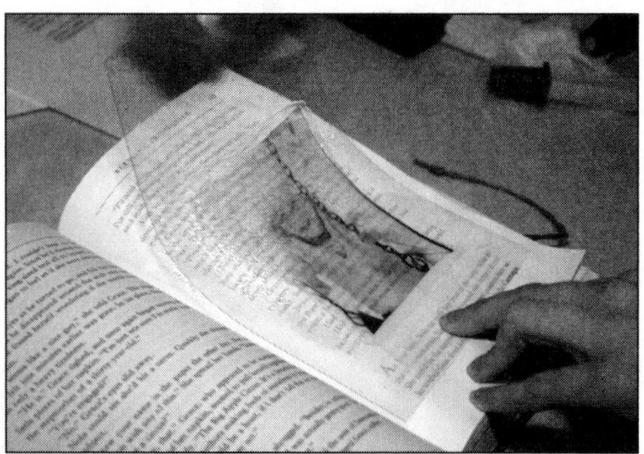

9. Peel away the Mylar sheet from the emulsion.

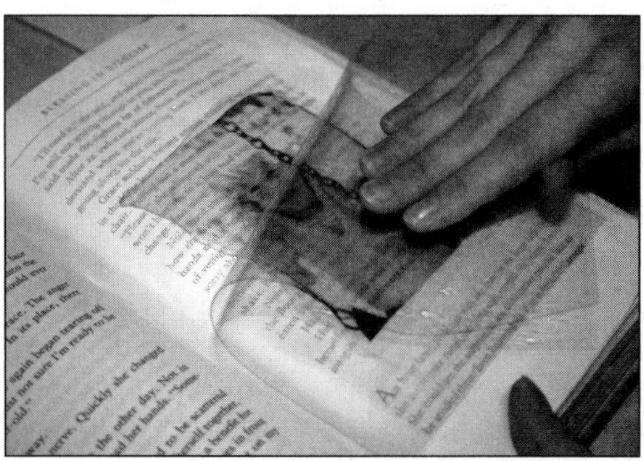

10. Allow the image to dry completely.

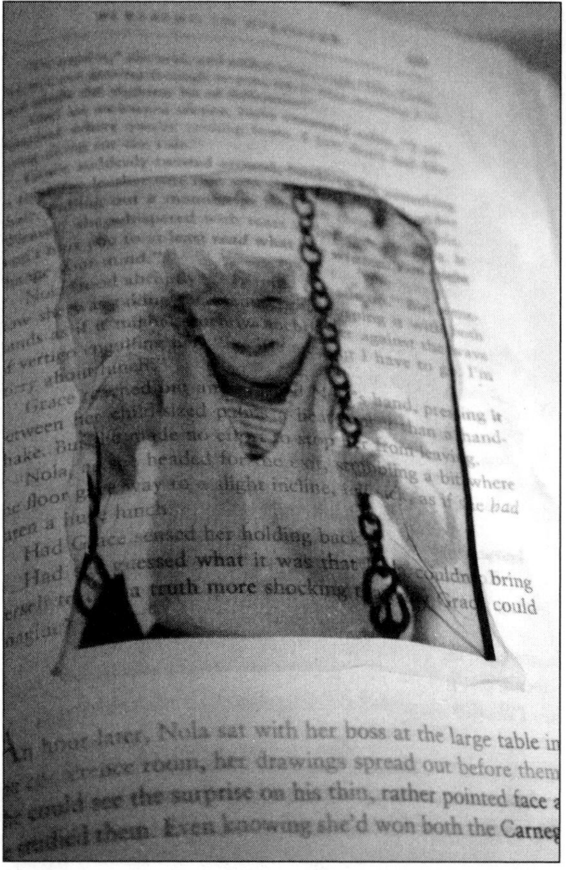

Your image is now transferred to a new surface and has taken on a completely new quality. I love the look this transfer process provides.

Add an accent and some text to make your altered book page complete.

Creating image transfers with a Daylab system is easy, and the look really is unique. Remember that you can use your Daylab Copysystem to transfer images to a variety of surfaces. Try using image transfers on tile coasters or canvas totes for unique gifts. Daylab transfers are a lot of fun, and will add a beautiful touch to almost any project.

The Least You Need to Know

- Image transfer is the process of transferring a printed image from a paper background to another surface.
- Clear packing tape is all you need to perform the simplest of image transfers.
- Caulk and gel medium can be used to create image transfers with beautiful effects.
- Use the Daylab Copysystem Pro and Polaroid 669 film to create dreamy, one-of-a-kind image transfers.

In This Part

Part 3

Fun Additions

One of the best things about altered art is that you can add fun textures and additions to your books and altered projects. In Part 3, you learn how to add fabric, decorative trims, wood, and even pressed flowers to your books. I discuss how to add extra pages and pull-outs to your books, enabling you to create pockets and special hidden elements in your art. Finally, you learn how to create drawers and windows from your book's pages.

Part 3 is sure to help you gain the skills you need to create the perfect addition to any project you can dream of!

In This Chapter

- Adding texture with beads, buttons, and other fabric store findings
- Painting and adding wood accents to your altered books
- Adorning your altered art with floral accessories

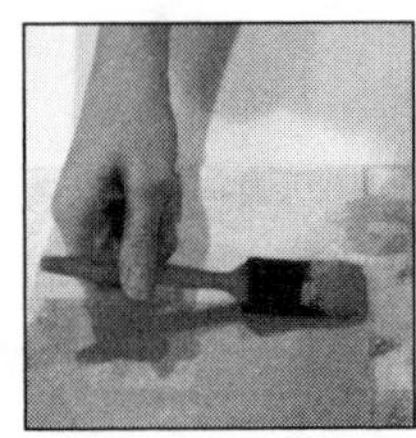

Chapter 9

Total Texture

As you've learned in previous chapters, altered books look phenomenal when embellished with all sorts of photographs, creative images, and more. Now it's time to add some more fun additions that help add texture to your pages, helping them truly stand out. Texture can easily be added to your altered books in a variety of ways, including using favorite items from the fabric store, wooden accents, and even dried flowers.

Buttons, Fabric, Beads, and More

Your local fabric store holds all sorts of fabulous items you can use to add texture and pizzazz to your altered book pages. I love scouring the clearance aisles, discovering what bargain finds I know will be the perfect addition to an altered art project or page.

In the following sections, I give you some examples of finds you can use in your altered artwork, but I'm sure you'll think of more as you browse the aisles.

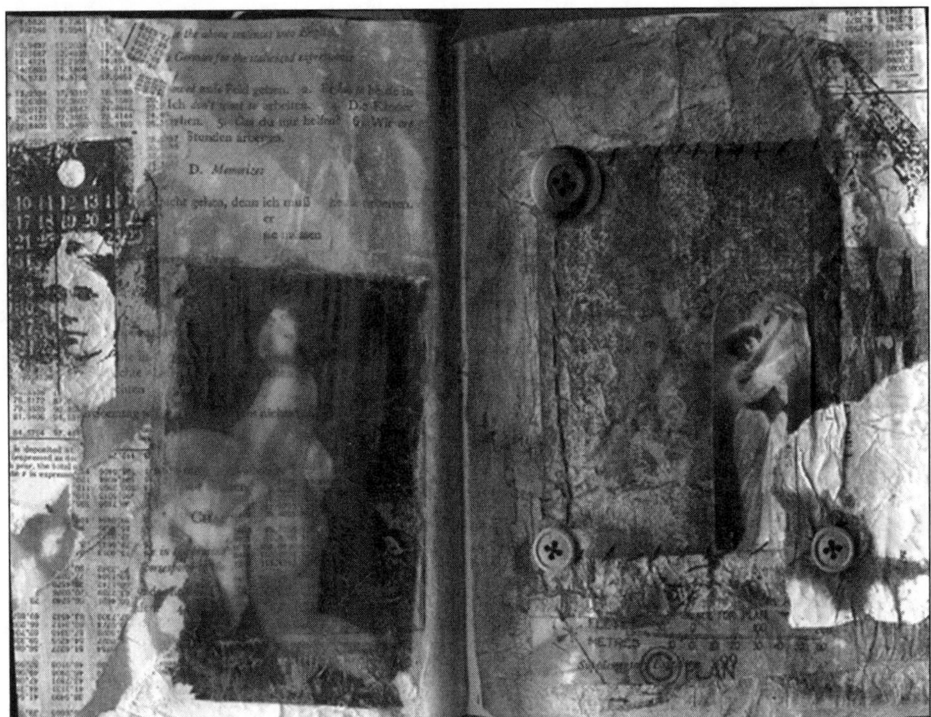

Notice how this artist used just a few buttons to enhance the window shape on her page.

(Pages by Diane Keys)

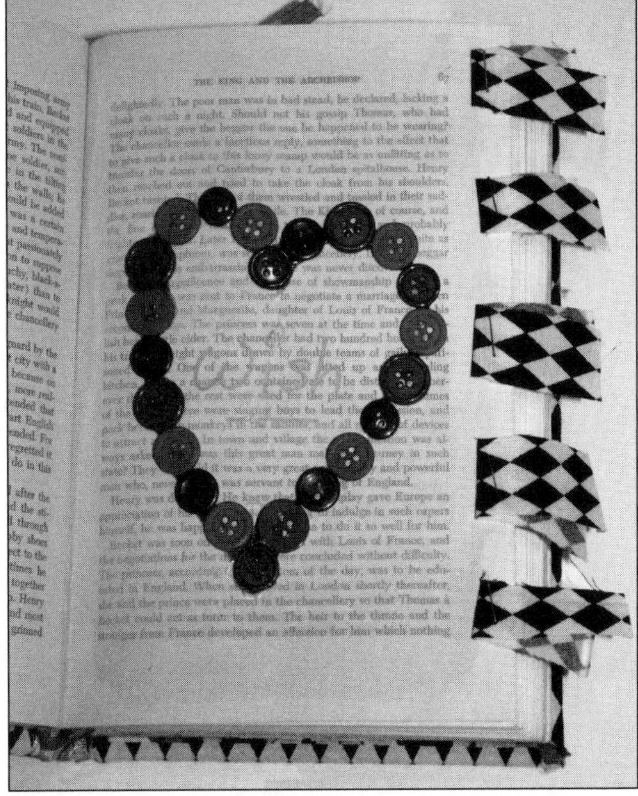

On this page, I used buttons to create a heart shape as the main focal point of my page.

Buttons

Buttons are fantastic for altered art because of the many ways you can use them and the variety of shapes and sizes you can find. You can use buttons to create both soft, nostalgic looks, and fun, playful looks. I love using buttons to make my altered book pages cheerful and bright.

Picture This

Look for buttons at your local fabric or craft store, or try searching at flea markets and antique stores for rare finds.

Fabric and Ribbon

Fabric can also be a great addition to your pages. Fabric cut into strips makes a great decorative edge for any page, as does ribbon. To create the fringe border on my "Heart of Buttons" altered book page, I cut a scrap of fabric into small strips, much like ribbon. I then folded each strip in half and attached it to the book page using a pink staple. I used the same fabric for this decorative edge that I used for my book's cover. The result was just perfect.

Try some of these great uses for fabric and ribbon on your pages:

- Use ribbon to frame a photograph or collage sheet image.
- Weave fabric strips through the book's pages to create a woven background.
- Use ribbon or a fabric strip to tie a decorative element or accent to your page.
- Use ribbon to tie two pages together to create a pocket or other interactive element on your page. (For detailed instructions on this process, turn to Chapter 10.)
- Create a background entirely from fabric or fabric paper.
- Tie a small knot on top of a tag or other element and then attach it to your page.

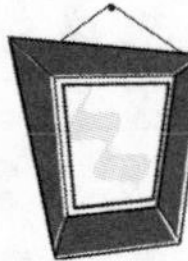

Picture This

Look for fabric remnants and ribbon scraps next time you go shopping. Amazing bargains are often there for the taking.

Beads

Beads are another fun way to add texture and dimension to your page. Beads, like buttons, come in thousands of shapes, sizes, and colors. Try one of these great ideas for using beads on your altered book pages, or come up with a design of your own:

- String beads on a ribbon or piece of yarn and attach to your page.
- Glue beads into a certain shape or form to create a raised element on your page.
- Use large beads throughout a woven background design.

Notice how when the book is closed, the fringe from my page matches the cover.

The artist created this water design on her altered board book page by adhering a cluster of ocean-colored beads across the bottom edge of the page.

(Page by Robin Riley-Wright)

(Book by Carolyn A. Lontin)

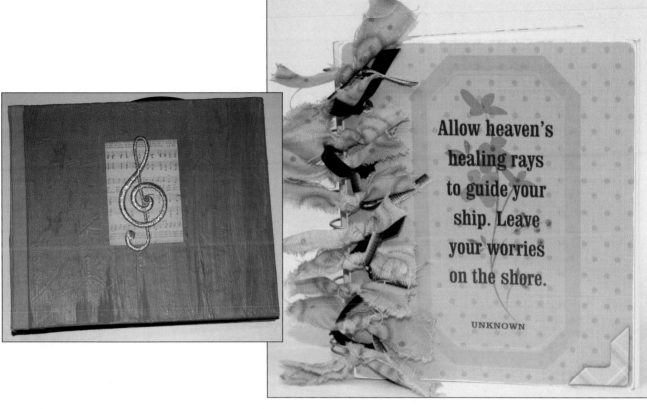

Allow heaven's healing rays to guide your ship. Leave your worries on the shore.

UNKNOWN

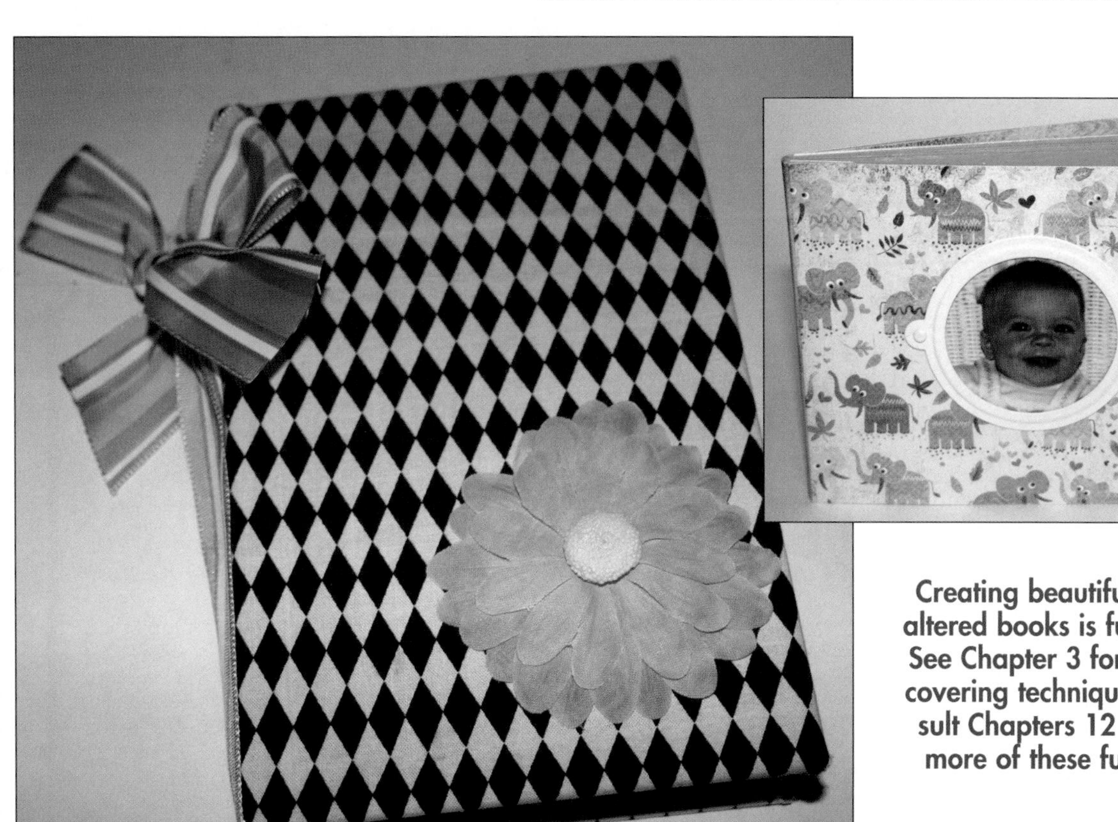

Creating beautifully covered altered books is fun and easy. See Chapter 3 for basic book covering techniques, and consult Chapters 12 and 13 for more of these fun projects.

(Page by Nancy Baumiller)

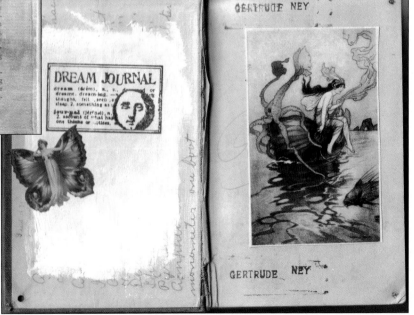

Using ephemera, stamps, Victorian scraps, and other artwork is a great way to enhance the look of your altered books. Visit Chapters 4 through 7 for unique ways to use images on your pages.

Think beyond plain photographs glued to the page! Visit Chapters 8 and 9 to discover unique ways to add image transfer effects and texture to your book pages.

(Page by Diane Keys)

(Page by Mandy Collins)

(Page by Mandy Collins)

Add interactive elements to your altered books with pockets, extra pages, windows, drawers, and more. See Chapters 10 and 11 to learn how.

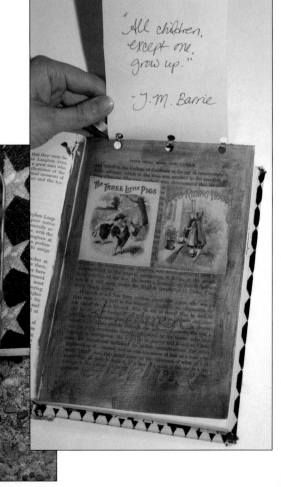

(Drawer by Lynn Anne Cutler)

Part of the fun of making altered artwork is the wide range of items you can alter. Part 4 explores several different types of book structures you can work with.

Use altered art techniques to design and create artist trading cards (ATCs), and share them with artists all over the world. Turn to Chapter 15 to learn more.

And faith in friendship is the noblest part

Oh you, who layest your heavy rays upon my shoulder
To make me shove them forth at every stride
They appear to put on weight as you grow older
And seem to push down harder with all their might
- "Oh You" - Mandy van Goeije

(Cards by Mandy Rentmeester-van Goeije of The Netherlands)

(Card by Julie Richards)

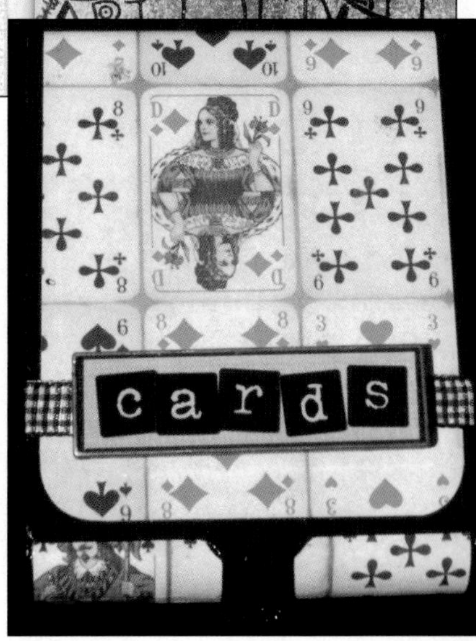

(Box by Tara Daigle)

Altered art for your home? Of course! Visit Chapters 16 and 17 to learn how to create amazing items for your walls, as well as altered boxes, cans, and more.

(Can by Michelle Van Etten)

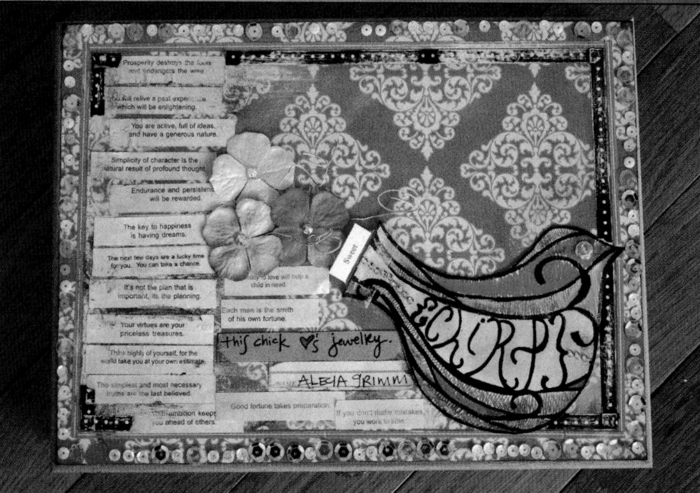

(Box by Alecia Ackerman Grimm)

(Puzzle by Mandy Collins)

Altered frames, shadow boxes, and puzzles are just a few of the fun projects you'll find in Chapter 18.

(Frame by Alecia Ackerman Grimm)

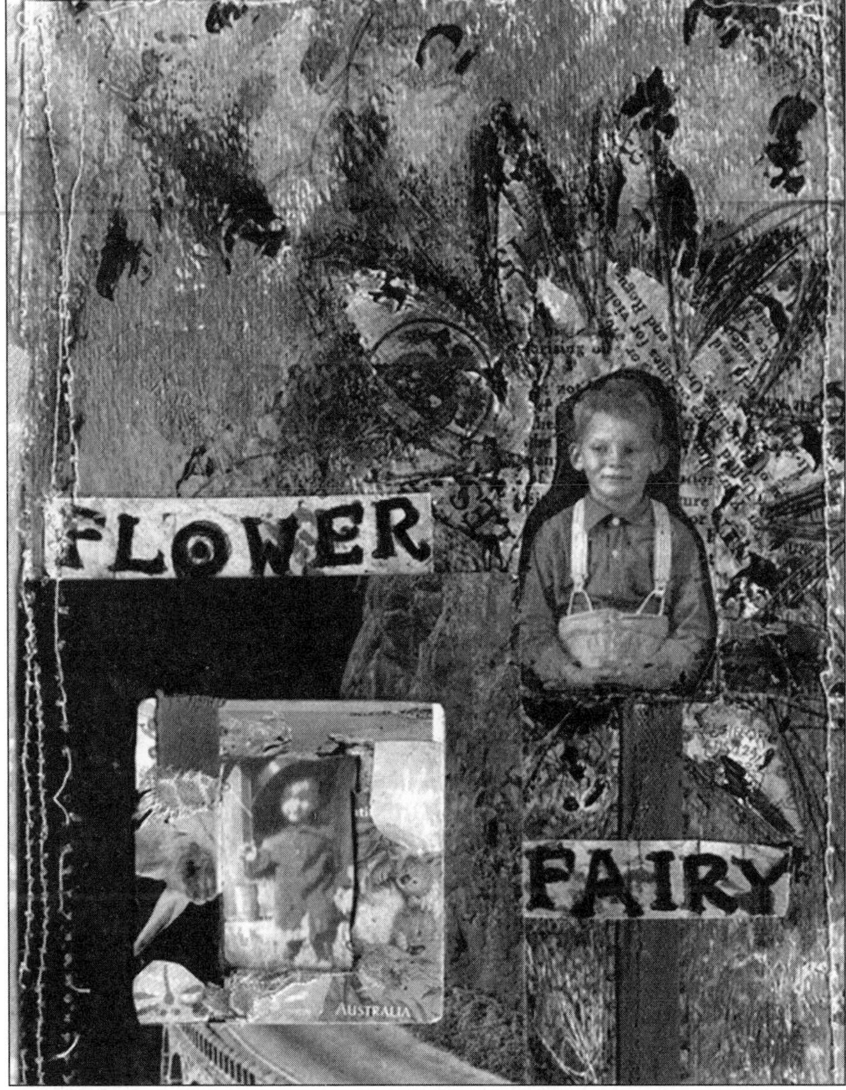

This beautiful page features creative machine stitching on the two outside edges.

(Page by Diane Keys)

Picture This

Don't just be on the lookout for old beads. Robin used a piece of a broken necklace on her whale page. Vintage jewelry is an excellent source of material for your altered books!

Stitching

I love incorporating hand and machine stitching in my altered books. You can do this, too.

If you have previous experience with sewing, simply apply these techniques to paper instead of fabric. And even if you don't have much sewing experience, this won't be difficult for you to pick up. Paper can be sewn just as easily as fabric, both by hand and with a machine.

Don't be afraid to experiment with sewing and stitching on your pages. It's simple and can be quite a bit of fun. Plus, the added texture is simply fantastic.

Altered Alert

When using a sewing machine to add stitching to your altered art, be sure to use a needle designed for denim. This ensures that the needle can easily get through the paper and that your art and your needle remain free of damage.

Other Fabric Store Finds

Don't be afraid to think outside the box when it comes to using unique items in your altered books. Here are just a few of the altered art embellishments I've found at fabric stores:

- Iron-on letters and decals
- Embroidered patches
- Fabric and silk flowers
- Rhinestones
- Yarn
- Zippers
- Decorative jewelry accents
- Fabric paint and dyes

You can use these items and more in your altered books to create dazzling artistic effects.

Wood and Metal Accents

Another neat way to add texture to your altered books is to use wood and metal accents. You can find these at many craft and hobby stores, as well as mass merchant stores. Look in the craft, hardware, and home accent departments to see what you can uncover.

Wooden Accents

I love working with wooden decorative embellishments. These small pieces are generally designed to be used as accents when making shelves, boxes, and furniture; however, they make an excellent addition to your altered artwork as well. Ready-to-finish wood accent pieces are readily available to today's crafter, and they make an easy addition to your altered art.

You have many choices when it comes to using wooden accents. Feel free to paint your accent in a variety of colors, or simply use a single color. If you want, you can even leave it unfinished for a natural look. Use your imagination to create a look that's all your own.

This page uses a painted wooden accent, along with an antique fabric scrap, to make a beautifully textured page.

(Page by Kate Schaefer)

The wooden nautical wheel creates the perfect framework for this altered book page, created over a page of yachting terminology.

(Page by Mandy Collins)

Metal Accents

Metal accents for your altered books can be readily found in a variety of places. Look for metal door and window hardware the next time you're in your local home improvement store. Check to see what metal pieces designed for scrapbooking and other crafts you can at your local hobby store.

For this altered book, the artist used a decorative metal accent to enhance the book's cover.

(Book by Mandy Collins)

No matter where they're from, such metal pieces can make beautiful additions to your altered art.

Elements of Nature

I love bringing texture to my altered books by adding elements of nature to my projects and pages. Including dried bits of nature in altered books is not a new idea, though. During the Victorian era, many individuals dried flowers in handmade flower presses and then added them to their favorite books and scrapbooks. I think they were on to something!

Pressed Flowers and Leaves

One of the most beautiful ways to add floral and leaf accents to your pages is to use dry, pressed flowers and leaves. You can still find traditional flower presses at many craft and stationery stores. They're easy to use and yield excellent results. The only problem is that using a traditional flower press requires weeks of drying time. This poses a problem to the altered artist who wants a natural accent but with instant results.

For this reason, I love to use the *Microfleur*. The Microfleur enables me to create hand-dried flowers and leaves in my microwave in just a fraction of the time it would take to dry and press them naturally.

Transforming Talk

Beeline Products' **Microfleur** is a form of flower press that works in the microwave, yielding natural-looking dried flowers and leaves in minutes. Check out www.microfleur.com.au for more information.

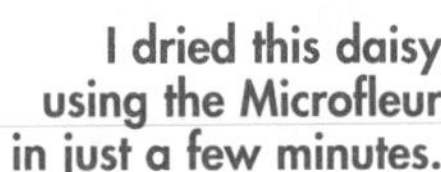

I dried this daisy using the Microfleur in just a few minutes.

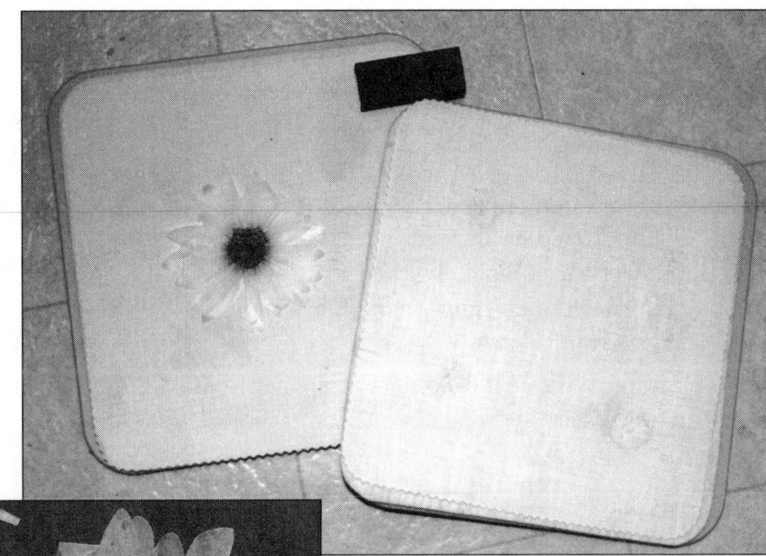

Dried flowers are the focal point of this altered book page.

(Page by Kate Schaefer)

To press your own flowers and leaves with the Microfleur press, follow the manufacturer instructions. Be sure not to overheat the press when you're working, as it can cause the flowers to burn.

After you've dried your flowers, adding them to your altered book pages is a breeze. Be sure the flower has completely dried to a thin, papery texture and then simply adhere it to your book using a strong adhesive.

Don't want to use real flowers? Faux paper or fabric flowers are an excellent alternative and can be just as lovely.

Additional Elements

You can use natural elements on your pages in infinite ways. Take a walk outside or visit your local hobby store to find some of these items:

- Seashells
- Small starfish and seahorses
- Small pebbles and rocks
- Tree bark and wood pieces
- Butterfly wings (both real and faux)

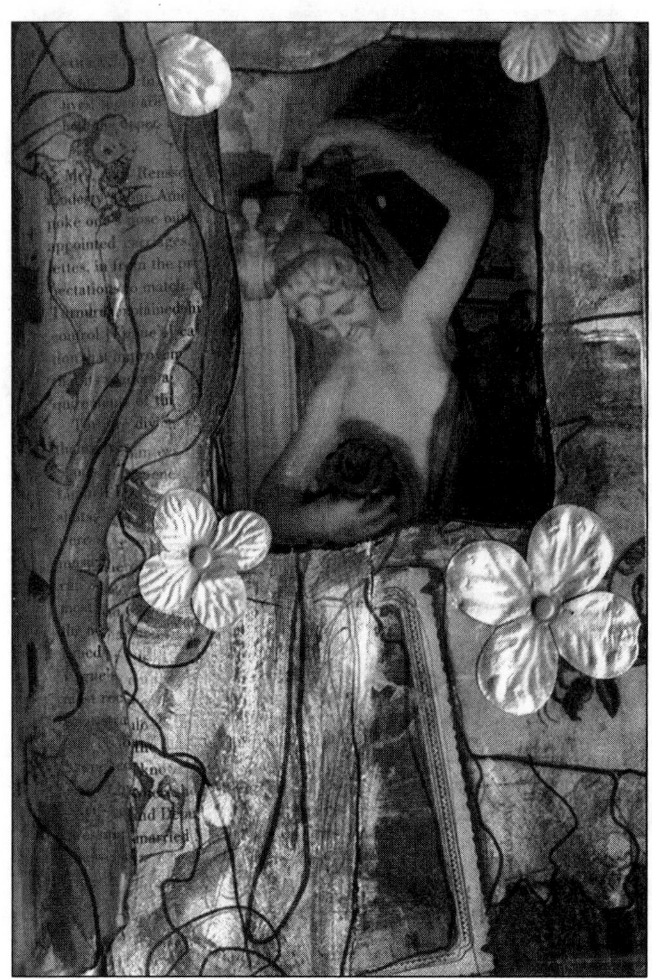

This beautiful page uses pink paper flowers to add color and texture.

(Page by Diane Keys)

A closer look at this page shows the small starfish and shells the artist added to the wooden wheel to enhance the page's theme and texture.

(Page by Mandy Collins)

Altered Alert

While it's certainly fun and beautiful to use natural elements on your pages, be sure you do so in a way that's friendly and respectful of the world around you. Tree bark makes a fantastic addition to your page, but be sure you pick it up off the ground—don't pull it straight from the tree!

The Least You Need to Know

- Beads, buttons, and other fabric store finds make perfect additions to your altered book pages.
- Wooden and metal accents are fun ways to add texture to your altered art.
- Pressing flowers and leaves in the microwave enables you to get completely natural results in just a few minutes.
- Feel free to use elements of nature on your pages, but respect the environment throughout the process.

In This Chapter

- Creating pockets in your book pages
- Incorporating envelopes as pocket pages
- Adding hinged elements

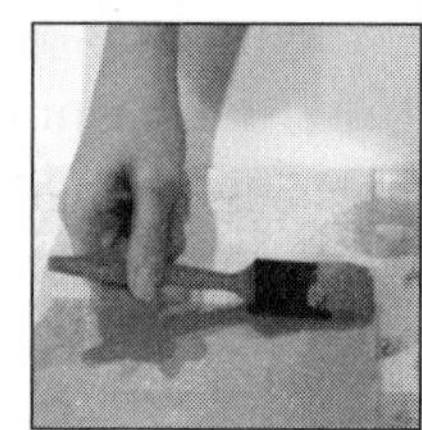

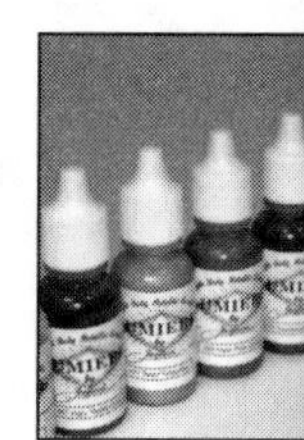

Chapter 10

Pockets and Moveable Pages

The altered book pages you've made so far are fantastic. You've added a great variety of creative images and even some bits of texture. Now it's time to take it one step further—by adding pockets, tags, and even small hinged pages to your altered book creations. By doing this, you'll be creating an interactive element in your altered books, making them really stand out.

Fun with Pockets

Adding pockets to your altered books is one of the easiest ways to create an interactive page. Pockets are simple to make, and you can add them to your book in a variety of ways.

UNALTERABLE FACT

Books with pockets have been around for ages. As a child, you likely read books that had fun flaps you could lift up and see fun animals hiding underneath. Adapt this same idea to your altered books, but with a more artsy feel.

Creating the pocket is just the first step, though. Once you've added a pocket to your page, you can fill it with any sort of treasure you can imagine:

- Tags containing quotes or journaling
- Ticket stubs or other modern ephemera
- Vintage ephemera
- Photographs

These are just a few ideas of what you can put in your book's pockets. The choice is really up to you. Look around and see what interesting items you can find to surprise someone as they pull it out of a pocket.

Picture This

Altered books with pockets are excellent gifts. For a memorable gift, give an altered book in place of a greeting card, and hide a gift card, cash, or upcoming event ticket in a special pocket.

Creating a Pocket Page

Creating a pocket page in your altered book is simple, and adds an interactive element to your pages. When you add pockets to your altered book pages, things don't have to be what they seem. Try adding a pocket to one of your existing altered book pages, or create an entirely new page, using a pocket as its centerpiece.

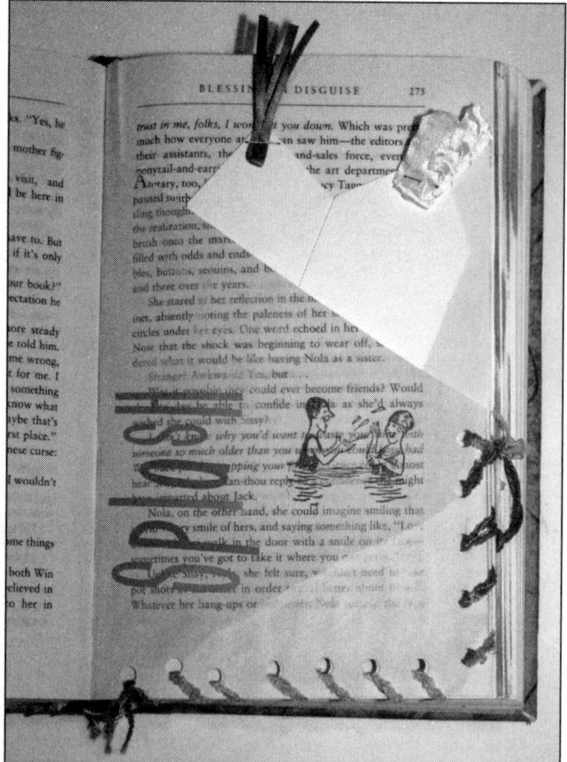

This pocket page has a fun, summery feel. The tags inside the pocket are just waiting to be embellished.

To create a pocket page like this inside your own altered book, you'll need a few supplies:

- Book to alter with at least 4 consecutive unaltered pages
- Scissors
- Hole punch
- Yarn or decorative thread of your choice
- Paint and embellishments for page design

When you've gathered your supplies, follow these steps to create your pocket page:

1. Begin by gluing two pages together to create a page with a double thickness. Then, glue the two following pages together as well. You should have a set of two double thick pages, immediately one after the other.

2. Paint the first page and let it dry.
3. Use scissors to cut away the top part of the painted page at an angle.

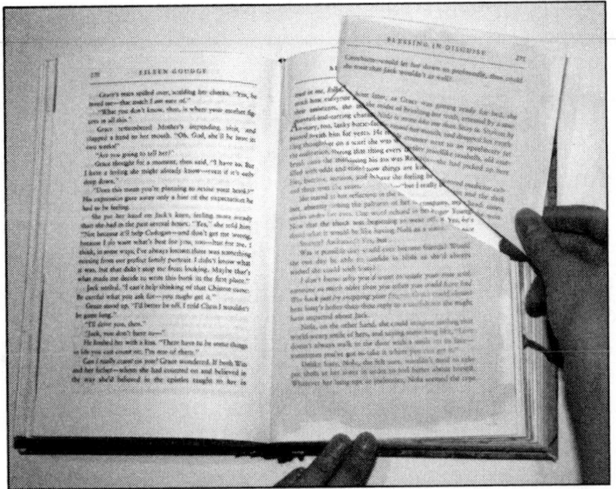

4. Hold the cut pages and the following two glued-together pages together. Punch holes along side and bottom edges of both sets of pages.

5. Thread yarn through the holes, stitching the pages together.

6. Secure the edges of stitching by tying a knot at each end or securing the loose ends to the back of the page using a strong tape adhesive.
7. Embellish the pocket and page as desired.
8. Fill the pocket with items of your choice.

Now that you see how easy it is to create a pocket page in your altered books, you might want to make a lot more. Go for it! Here are some other ideas to try:

- For a softer look, tear the page edge instead of cutting it.
- Use a thin decorative ribbon in place of yarn or fiber for a feminine look.
- Create a page with two pockets by working with three pages instead of two and cutting the pockets at varying heights.
- Consider using decorative-edge scissors to cut your pocket page, or try cutting your pocket in a curved or triangular design instead of a simple angle.

Creating a full-page pocket is a great way to add interest and surprise to your altered book pages. Hiding notes, tags, or small treasures inside is a fun way to create an interactive element in your book.

Including Small Pockets on Your Pages

Sometimes you'll want to add a pocket or two to your book without creating an entire pocket page. The easiest way to do this is to simply glue a small pocket or envelope directly to your page design and then fill it as you like. All these items make great pocket additions to your pages:

- Coin envelopes
- Small string-closure envelopes
- Library card pockets
- Small mailing envelopes
- Gift card envelopes
- Small envelopes from children's valentine cards

This page uses a small glassine envelope with a string closure to add a pocket to the bottom left corner of the spread. The artist chose to slip a playing card inside.

(Page by Diane Keys)

When attaching envelopes and pockets to your pages, be sure to use a strong adhesive designed for paper. This ensures that your pocket stays put, regardless of what's kept inside.

Altered Alert

Be careful when gluing envelopes and pockets into your book. It's very easy to accidentally glue the opening shut!

Adding Pockets as Pages

Another fun way to add pockets to your altered books is to allow the pocket itself to serve as an extra page in your book. When you first went through the process of thinning out your book (see Chapter 1 for more information if you need it), you were left with several 1-inch pages sticking out of your book's binding. These small striplike pages are perfect for adding pockets to your book.

All you need for this process is a pair of library pockets (I chose pink ones manufactured by Bazzill Basics) and a strong adhesive. Here's how to add your pockets:

1. Use adhesive to glue the bottom of the pocket to the top of the page strip. Press down firmly, and allow the adhesive to dry. Turn the pocket so it's facing away from you.

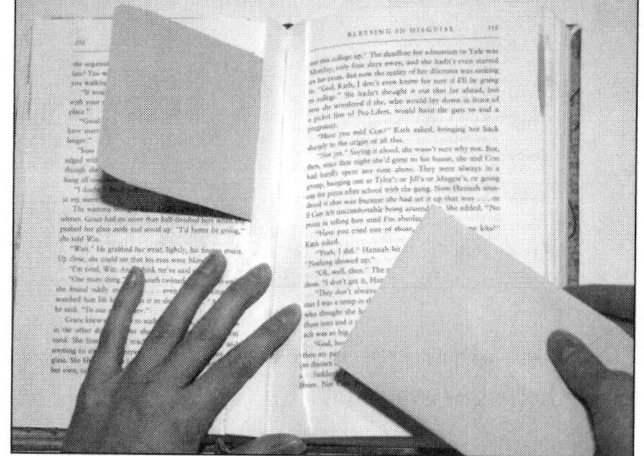

2. Glue the second pocket at the bottom of the second strip page so the two pockets don't overlap.

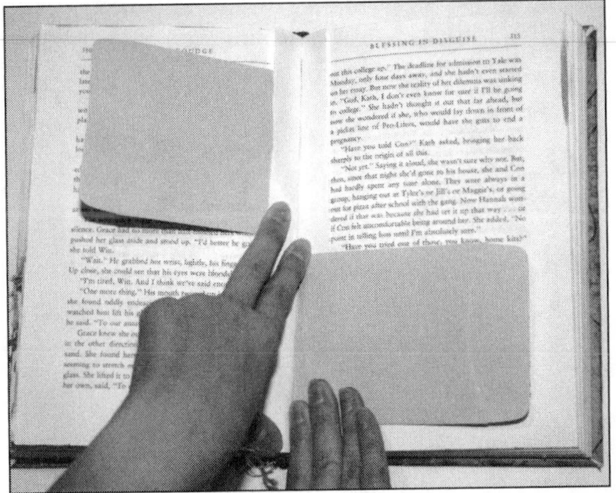

3. When the adhesive is dry, add tags or other fun items to your pockets.

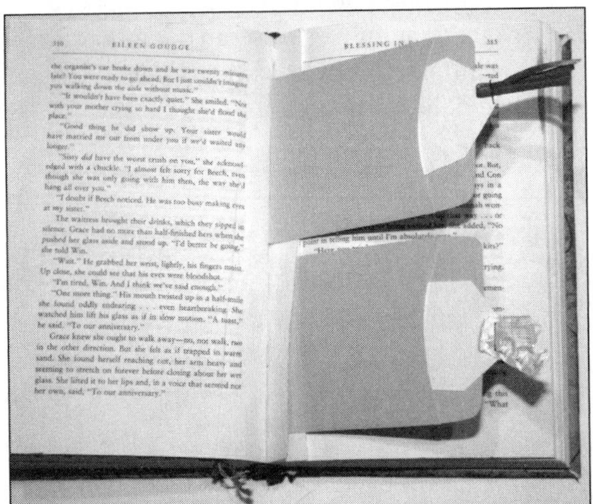

Because pockets like these aren't part of any other page in your book, they really take on a quality of their own.

Feel free to embellish your added pockets, along with the pages that surround them, for a beautiful look.

These altered book pages, showcasing a variety of seed packet images, feature a pocket page in the middle containing a pull-out tag. The final product is simply stunning.

(Pages and pocket by Mandy Collins)

Altered Alert

Smaller and more rounded items might fall out of the pockets, so it's best to store flat items in pockets with a side opening so they don't get lost.

Getting Interactive: Moveable Pages

One of the most fun ways to add interactivity to your altered books is to add additional pages to the book—namely moveable flaps. You can do this a variety of ways; my favorite is by tying and sewing.

Here's what you need to add movable pages to your altered book:

- Book for altering
- Paper image, book page, or photograph you want to add as an extra page or flap
- Hole punch
- Ribbon, yarn, or decorative trim
- Paint, embellishments, and other accents to decorate your page as desired

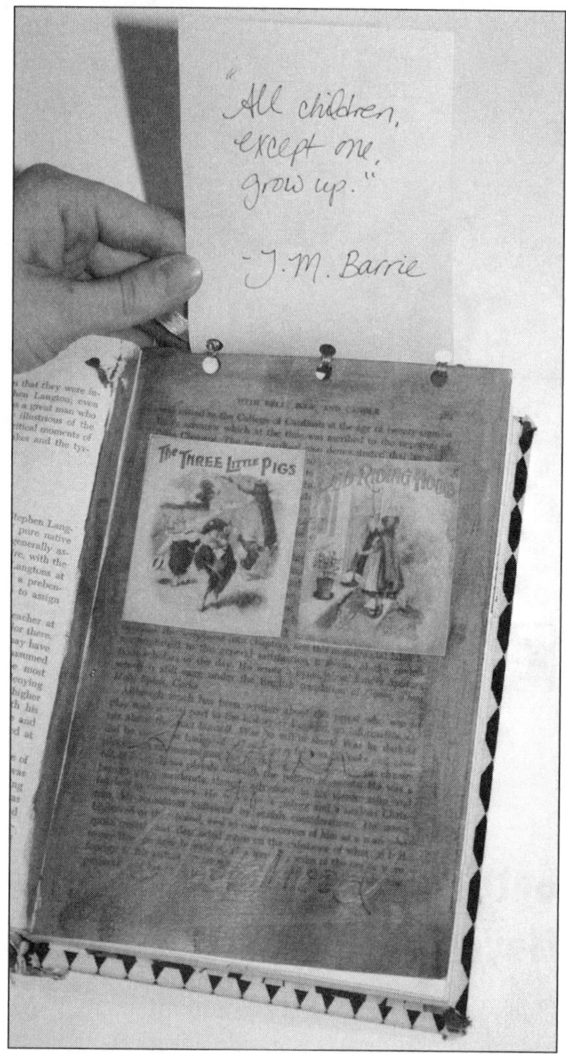
"All children,
except one,
grow up."
-J.M. Barrie
The Three Little Pigs

A small page flap lifts up to reveal a favorite quote, adding to the charm of this altered page.

When you have your supplies, you're ready to create your pages. Here's what to do:

1. Be sure you're working with two pages that have been glued together for extra strength.
2. Decorate and embellish your page as desired.
3. Position the element or paper you want to add to your page in the desired position, aligning one edge of the element with an outside edge of the book page.
4. Holding the item to be added and the page together, punch holes along the common edge.

5. Use ribbon or decorative trim to tie the two items together. You can stitch them together, as you did to create the pocket page, or simply use a scrap of ribbon for each hole, finishing with a simple knot, as I've done here.

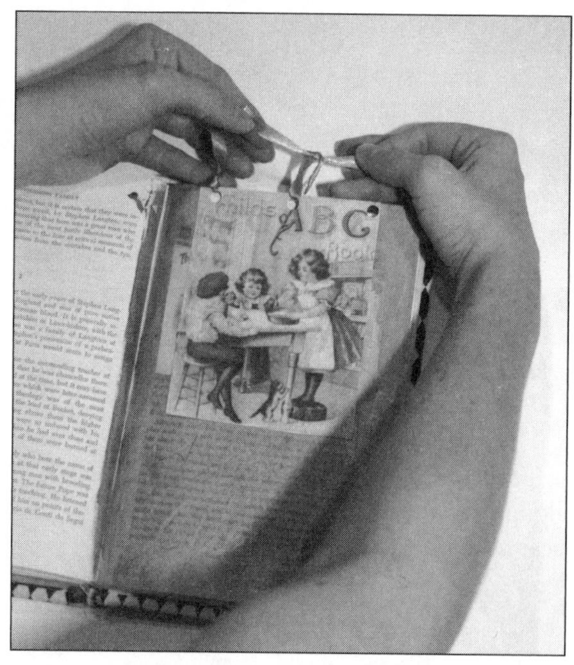

When your new element is secured to your page, lift the added element to reveal the page underneath. This technique can be used with any size item, on any page edge.

Picture This

Want to add a flap to the middle of your page instead of its edge? Consider using adhesive to attach part of your flap to your page and then simply lift up to view the page underneath.

Try using this technique to create some of these fun effects:

- Hide a favorite quote, song lyric, or special message.
- Cover up a favorite photograph.
- Add a title or phrase to your added element and then lift it to see the corresponding artwork.
- Use different types of ribbon and trim for each punched hole to create a fun frayed edge that sticks out of your book and adds to its visual appeal.

Moveable page flaps add dimension and interest to your book pages and allow you to create two versions of the same altered book page—one with the flap closed, and a second design when the flap is opened. Try adding a moveable flap to one of your altered book pages for a different look.

The Least You Need to Know

- Creating a pocket page by stitching two pages together is a fun way to get a large pocket that can hold a variety of items.
- Use small envelopes to add pockets directly to your altered book pages.
- Pockets can be added directly to your book, allowing them to stand alone as pages.
- Add extra pages to your book by sewing and tying them to pages already secured in your book's binding for an interactive effect.

In This Chapter

- The fun of interaction in altered books
- Cutting a window through your book pages
- Creating a hidden drawer in your altered book

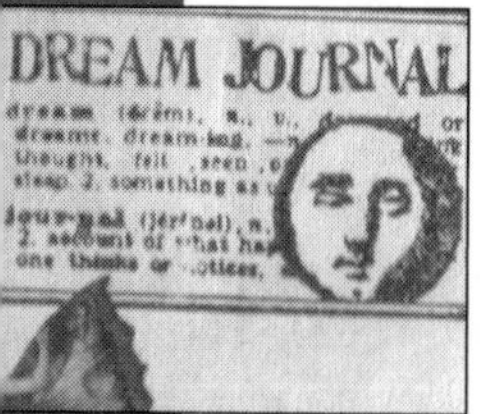

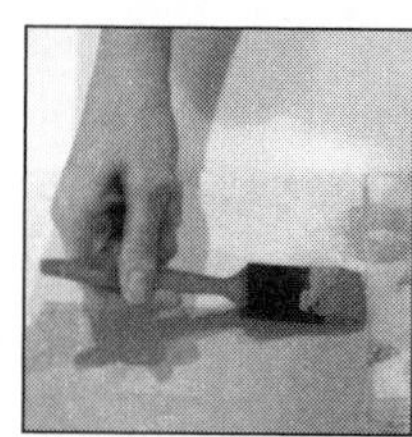

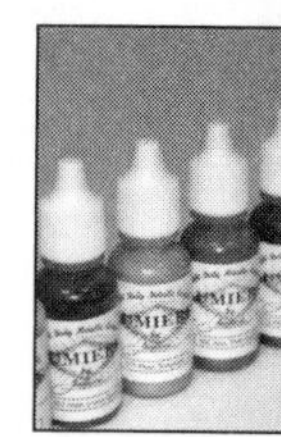

Chapter 11

Windows, Drawers, and More

As you learned in Chapter 10, one of the most exciting things you can do with your altered books is to make them interactive. In this chapter, we build on that idea and you learn how to cut windows and niches into your altered books. These fun windows allow you to hide secret treasures inside your altered books, making them even more exciting and unique.

But there's more! In this chapter, you also learn how to create a pull-out drawer right in the middle of one of your books.

The Cutting Edge

Before you can start adding unique dimensional items into your books, you'll need to learn the basics of constructing windows and drawers. To start, let's cut a *niche* into one of your altered books.

Transforming Talk

A **niche** is a shallow opening in an altered book that can be filled with small dimensional items such as seashells, metal charms, and more.

To cut a niche into your book, you first need to decide if you want to create an open niche or a closed niche. With an open niche, you cut all the way through the paper so you can see through the niche completely and it becomes a window inside your book. With a closed niche, you leave the final few pages of the niche intact, creating an enclosed space in which you can hide objects and more.

To create a niche, you need the following supplies:

- Book you want to alter with at least 30 to 50 consecutive pages available for alteration
- Gel medium or decoupage glue/finish
- Craft knife and cutting mat
- Metal-edged ruler
- Foam brush
- Binder clips or other clamps

When you have your supplies, follow these steps to create your niche:

1. Clamp several pages in your book together. I recommend working with a group of pages that's about $1/8$ to $1/4$ inch thick.
2. Use a foam brush to coat the page edges with gel medium. Let this dry completely.

Be sure to apply an even coat all the way around the page edges. Don't forget to work underneath the clamps!

3. Using a metal-edged ruler and a pencil, outline the area of your book that you'd like to cut out.
4. With a few clamps still in place, hold your ruler in place on the edge of your cutting line, and slowly cut out the pages. If you're creating an open niche, cut all the way through the entire block of pages. If you're creating a closed niche, leave the final few pages in place for a background.

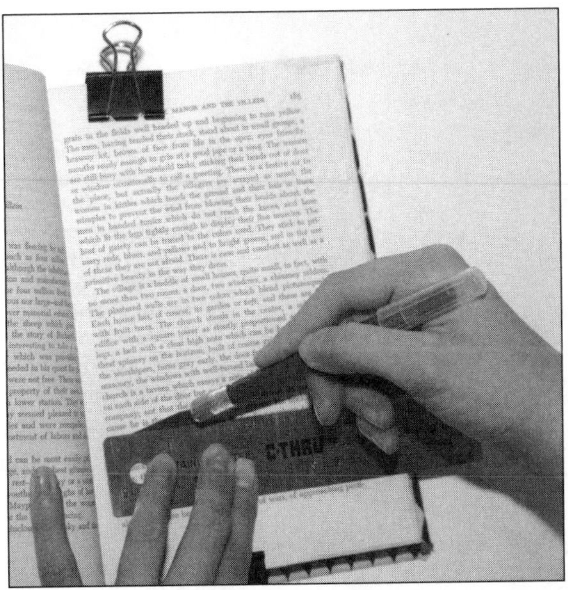

Cut through just a few pages at a time until the entire block of pages is cut out.

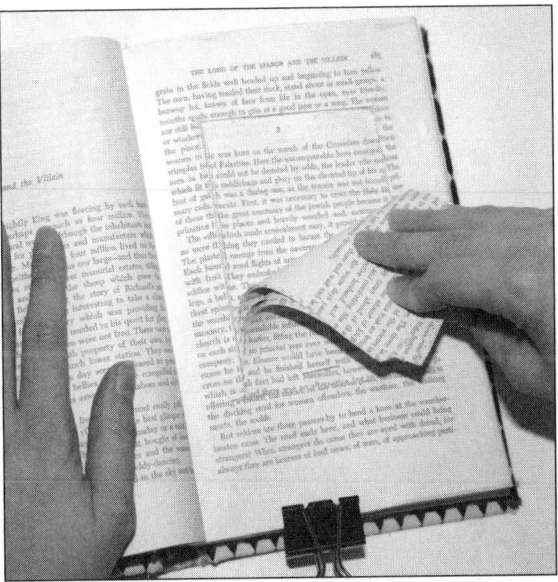

Be careful not to tear your book's pages when removing the cut-out portion. If your knife didn't get all the way through, go back over the missed area until it's completely cut out.

Altered Alert

Don't try to cut out your niche without a metal-edged ruler. If your knife slips, you could end up ruining your book or possibly cutting yourself. Neither are good outcomes.

5. Carefully pull out the cut pages, removing them from your book.
6. Coat the inside cut edges of your niche with gel medium, and let it dry completely.

Your book now has a niche that's ready to be filled, embellished, and altered until it becomes a completed, beautiful page in one of your altered books.

Niches are so fun to work with, you'll likely want to try creating a niche or two in one of your altered books. When it comes to this technique, practice definitely makes perfect. Follow these simple tips to help ensure success:

- Begin small. Niches can be any depth, but the deeper they are, the harder they can be to cut out. Start with a niche that's only about $\frac{1}{8}$ inch thick. You can always cut deeper later on.
- Use a scrapbooking or shape template to help ensure that your cutting area is completely straight and even.
- Allow ample drying time for each step. If the pages have not dried completely, they might start to pull apart as you're working.

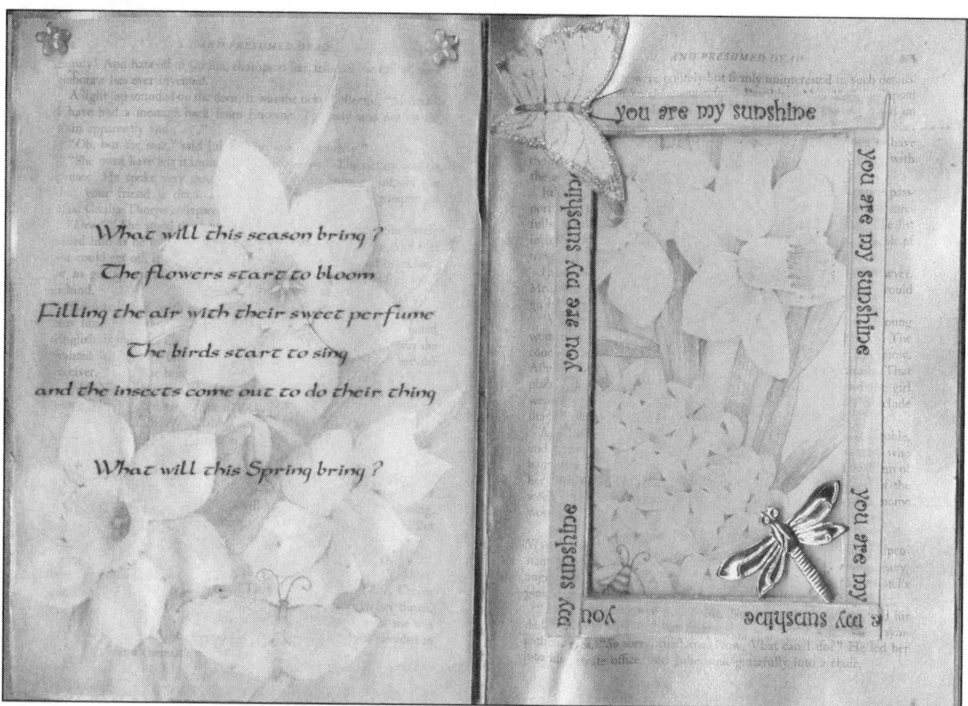

This spread uses a niche beautifully—it allows the flower patterned paper to really "pop" through and holds the dragonfly charm quite nicely.

(Pages by Mandy Collins)

To create a windowlike effect on these pages, the artist used a rubber stamp with a window opening.

(Pages by Sandy Wisneski)

This stamped window design showcases the inside image quite well.

(Page by Sandy Wisneski)

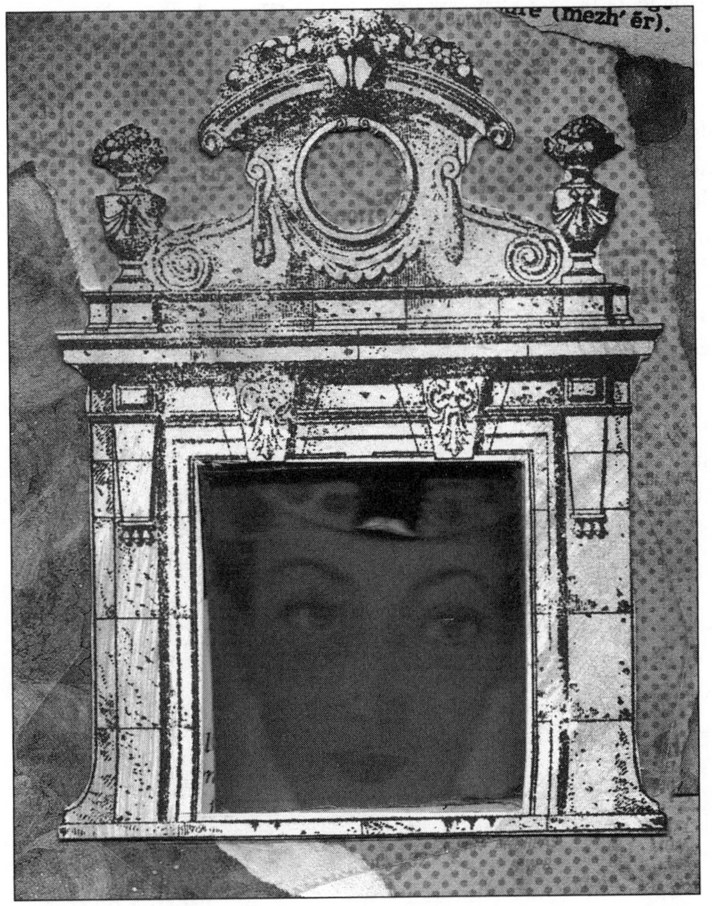

This altered book page incorporates actual watches as part of its design, the perfect complement to the page's title, "Time is on your side."

(Page by Jackie Baxted)

Don't be discouraged if your first niche doesn't turn out exactly as you wanted. Try again and notice how it gets easier and easier every time.

Niche Uses

Okay, so you've created a niche in your book. Now what? How do you use it? What can you put in it? In the following sections, I offer a few common techniques for using the niche, but really, when it comes to possibilities for the niche, the only real limit is your imagination.

Windows

One of my favorite ways to use niches in my altered book creations is to use the niche as a window. If you've created an open niche, this is easy, as your window is already in place. Try one of these fun ideas:

- Create two altered book page spreads next to one another in your book, with the window between. Allow the window to let the reader peek through one side of your page spread to the other.
- Place a portion of a message in the windowed area, so that only when the reader flips the page can she read the entire passage.
- Create your altered book pages as usual, placing a favorite element in the window area. Turn the page, and incorporate that element into a new book page.

If you've created a closed niche in your book, you can still obtain the window effect in your book. Plus, you won't have to worry about positioning new artwork behind the window, so you have the fun of a window without all the extra work.

Creating an effect like this on your own altered book pages is quick and easy. Gather your book and niche supplies, along with a rubber stamp featuring a window opening you would like to use and some paper or cardstock. Then, follow these steps:

1. Stamp image onto your paper or cardstock.
2. Use a craft knife to cut out the opening of the stamped design.
3. Use the opening cutout to determine the size of your niche. Trace the opening on your book pages.
4. Create your niche by cutting along the line you traced around the opening.
5. Embellish your page.
6. Adhere the stamped image over the window opening.

There are many different ways to dress up your window niches. Try one of these suggestions:

- Adhere ribbon or decorative trim around the outside of the niche to "frame" it.
- Use a stamp or sticker featuring a window design over the window's opening.
- Scan or take a digital photograph of the view from a window in your home, size it to fit your book, and print. Use it as the backdrop in your niche.

These are just a few ideas to get you started. What else can you think of?

Treasure Chests

In addition to adding depth and space in your altered book pages, you can use niches to add extra special items and charms in your books. The niche is deep and can hold some larger items, so you don't have to worry about the weight of these objects harming your book pages. Plus, you'll always be sure your book will close when it's complete.

Jackie's page is the perfect example of using a niche to hold a treasure. This page was created as part of an altered book she made for her niece upon her graduation.

Jackie's page also shows us that there's more than one method that can be used to create a niche. Jackie opted to use spackle instead of gel medium. This created a unique finish to her pages and enabled her to create a one-of-a-kind distressed look. To create the same effect on your pages, you'll need these supplies:

- Book you want to alter
- Watches or other objects for your window(s)
- Spackle
- Inkpad of your choice
- Glue stick
- Craft knife
- Sandpaper

Follow these steps to create your own niche:

1. Gather a chunk of pages that's the same depth as the item you wish to house in your niche.
2. Draw out the size and shape you need on the first page of your niche.
3. Clamp your pages together.
4. Cut through the pages, 3 or 4 at a time, until you've cut out all the pages of your niche.
5. When you've reached the desired depth and shape, use sandpaper to smooth out any rough edges.
6. Glue the pages together using a glue stick.
7. Use spackle to cover the page. Grab a putty knife or just go ahead and get your hands dirty.
8. Cover the top of the page and all three of the outer edges with spackle. This ensures that the pages stay together. Let your book dry completely, at least overnight.

9. If your niche is open, glue 3 or 4 pages behind the niche together and then adhere those to the back of your window page so your niche is closed and you have a nice backdrop to your windows.
10. If desired, paint the inside of your window. Embellish your page as desired.
11. Add items to your niche and adhere with strong adhesive. Let this dry completely.
12. To add a finished look to your page, run an inkpad lightly across the surface of the paper. Watch the ink fill in the nooks and crannies left by the spackle. The results are really something.

Regardless of what you choose to place inside your niche, the look of the final page will make you proud of your work.

Picture This

Working with spackle is quite messy! Be sure to cover the rest of your book with plastic wrap to keep it clean and protected.

Altered Drawer Book

It's time to take the niche one step further. This process enables you to create an altered book containing a pull-out drawer. Sound complicated? Don't worry. Now that you've mastered the art of cutting niches, creating an altered book containing a drawer should be quite simple.

First, you'll need to select the book you'd like to alter. It's important that it be large enough to accommodate a drawer, which will made from the bottom half of a small tin, such as a breath mint or candy tin. It's also a good idea to choose a book that you haven't previously altered. This book project requires quite a bit of useable space to accommodate the drawer, so it's best to start with a clean slate.

When you've selected your book, gather the rest of the supplies you'll need:

- Small tin without lid
- Gesso
- Strong liquid adhesives
- Craft knife and cutting mat
- Hammer and small nail
- Craft wire
- Beads of your choice
- Chalk ink
- Collage sheet images on paper and transparency
- Embellishments of your choice

This altered book contains a fun drawer full of surprises inside!

(Altered drawer book by Lynn Anne Cutler)

Then, follow these steps to create your project:

1. Open your book. Clamp together the book pages you want to use to create the opening for your drawer. You can use as many or as few pages as you'd like; just be sure your gathered pages are at least as tall as your tin.
2. Place your tin on the top book page in the place you'd like it to be inserted, aligning one edge of the tin with the edge of the book page. Trace $1/4$ inch around the three inside edges of the tin.
3. Using a craft knife, cut through all the pages to create a rectangular space in which to insert the drawer.
4. Coat the edges and the inside of the cut pages with gel medium or decoupage glue, adhering them together. Let these dry completely, preferably overnight.
5. To create the tin drawer, punch two holes in one side of the tin using hammer and nail. String craft wire with beads and then thread the wire through the holes and tie them to the tin to secure. This forms the handle of the drawer.

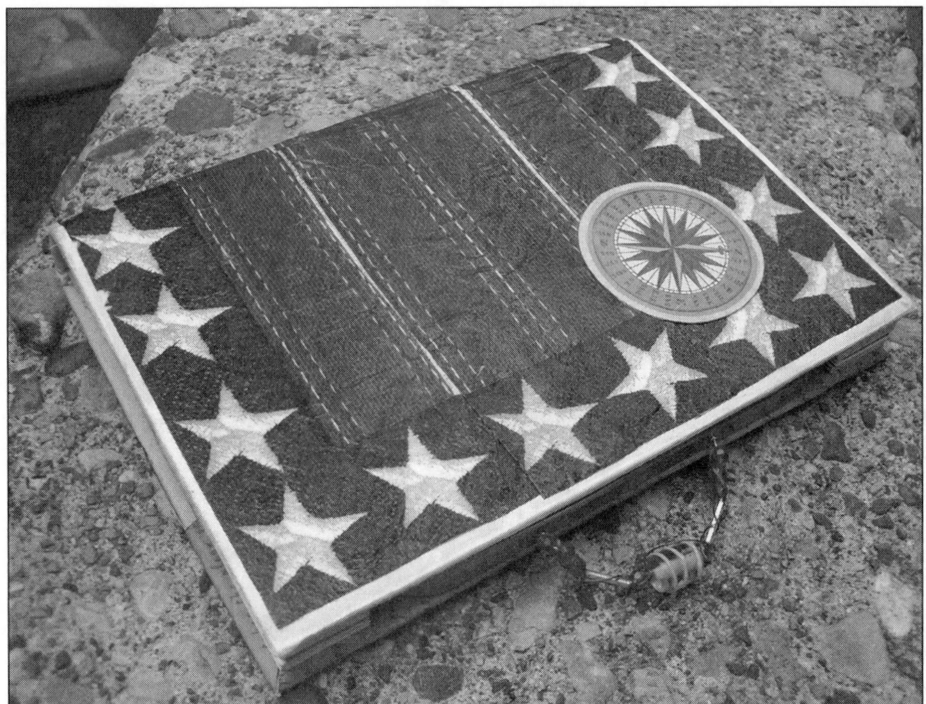

When your book is closed and the drawer is fully inserted, only the drawer's handle gives you a glimpse of the treasure inside.

(Altered drawer book by Lynn Anne Cutler)

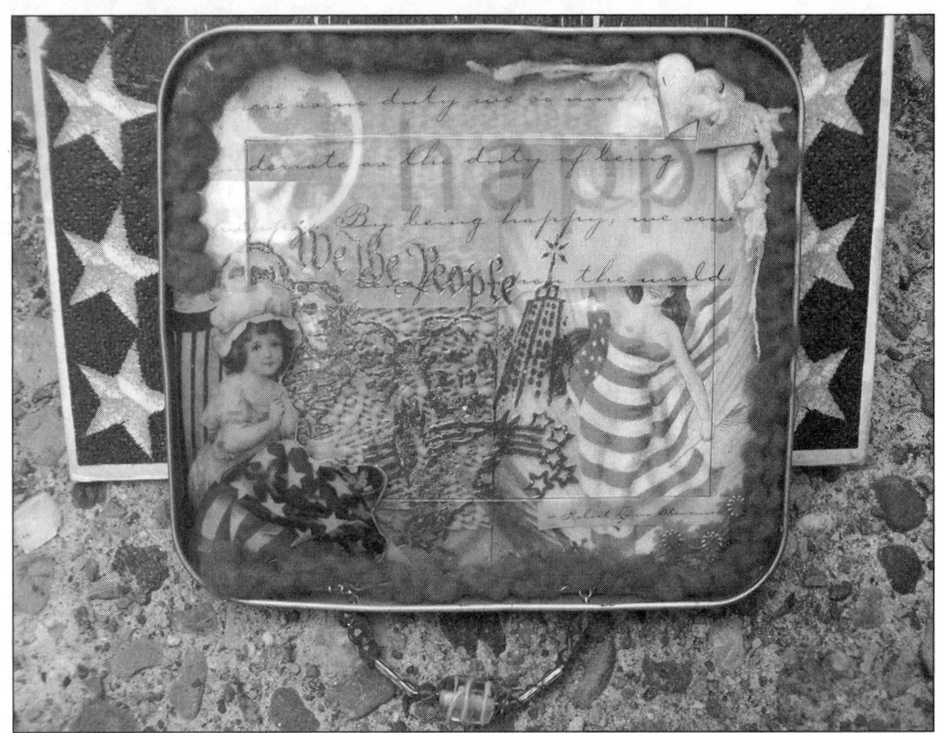

The beautiful interior of this drawer surprises and delights whoever encounters it.

(Drawer by Lynn Anne Cutler)

6. Cover your book using any method you choose, as described in Chapter 3. Lynn chose to use a decorative paper napkin for her book's cover.
7. Embellish your book's cover as you wish.
8. Embellish the inside of the drawer as you like. Creating an image collage, along with a few dimensional touches, can be an excellent technique choice.
9. Insert the drawer into the book.

Altered drawer books can be created to celebrate almost any theme. Consider celebrating your patriotism, as Lynn did, or select another topic that appeals to you.

The Least You Need to Know

- Creating a window in your altered book is a fun way to provide an interactive touch to your books.
- Cutting a niche in an altered book is easy and allows you to add unique dimension to your book projects.
- For extra interaction, consider creating an altered drawer book.

In This Part

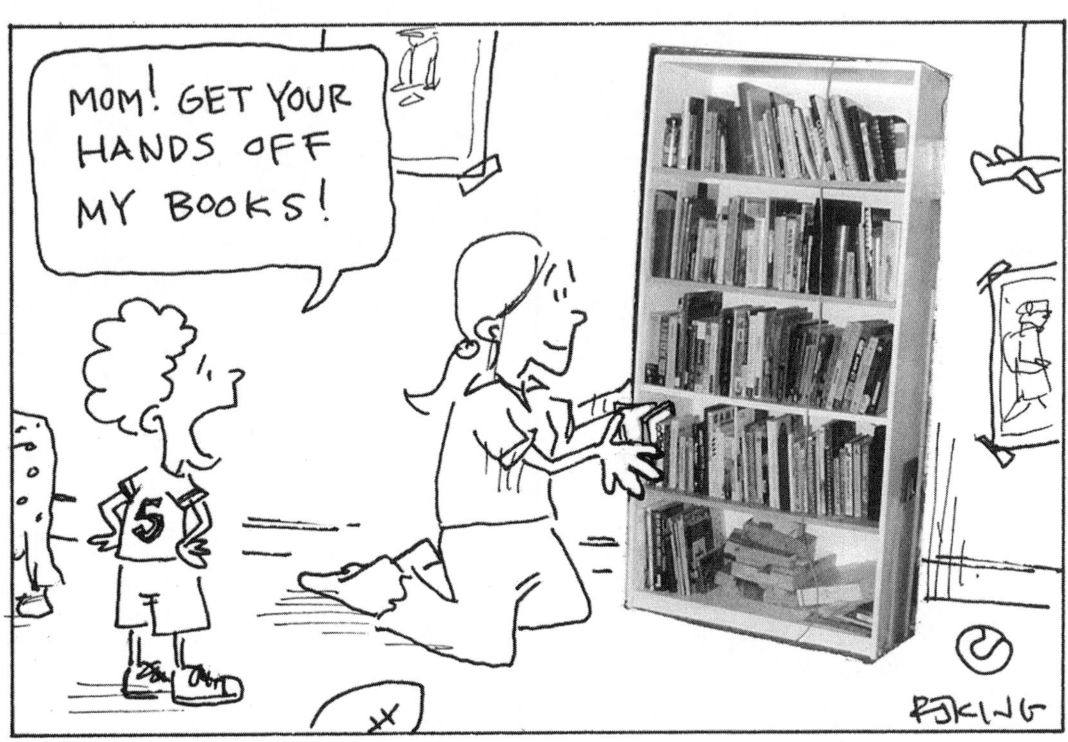

Part 4

Unique Book Structures

The techniques you've learned so far work with almost any project, but of course there are some exceptions. Certain book structures require special treatment and consideration. That's where this part comes in. In Part 4, I discuss altering children's board books, what makes them unique, and how to create a project that will last. You learn how to alter collector's albums and scrapbooks, too—creating a beautiful altered record collection album along the way. Finally, you learn how to create your own books by altering office supplies and other common throwaway items from your home.

These projects and techniques will take your altered art to the next level, enabling you to create and explore with new surfaces and textures.

In This Chapter

- Learning what makes board books unique
- Preparing a board book for alteration
- Creating a beautiful altered board book to celebrate baby

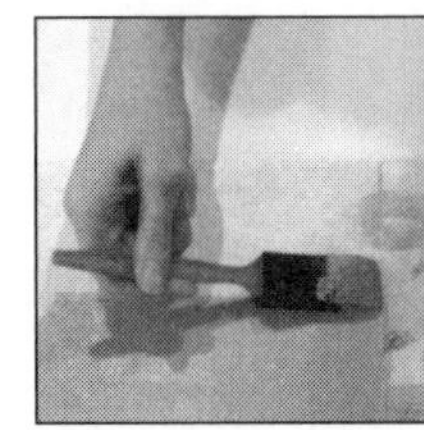

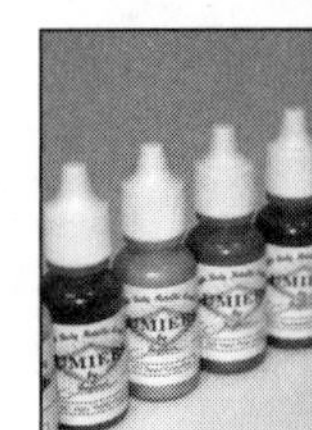

Chapter 12

Board Book Basics

By now, you're nearly an altered book pro. You've learned tons of great techniques, and maybe you even created a few of your own designs. Now it's time to take a look at your first unique book structure—the board book. Board books are great fun for the altered artist because they provide a ready-made strong surface, have a limited number of pages, and come in all sorts of unique shapes and sizes.

Look for board books in the same places you find other books to alter—garage sales, library sales, and secondhand stores.

Why a Board Book?

You might be wondering what makes altering a *board book* any different from working in a book with standard pages. At first glance, it might seem that it would be just as easy. And while it is easy, you need to consider a number of factors before making plans to alter one of these unique books.

Transforming Talk

Board books are small, sturdy books made from heavy-duty cardboard. They're typically produced for very young children and feature bright, colorful designs.

Board books are made from stiff, thick cardboard. This makes it nearly impossible to simply tear out a page to allow room for bulky embellishments. Plus, board books are usually coated with a thick, glossy finish. If you simply apply paint or paper to this slick surface, it's not going to stick well, resulting in frustration and making it nearly impossible to obtain the final product you're envisioning.

You might be thinking that it's just too hard to alter a board book and decide to move on to another project. Wait! Altering board books is still fun and easy. It just requires a few different preparation steps.

Preparing Your Board Book

The following preparation steps guide you through preparing a board book for alteration with a smooth, easy working surface throughout. By the end of this section, you'll be ready and able to create a fantastic-looking project in no time.

When selecting a board book to alter, look for a book that is in fairly good condition. Books that have pages with severely worn edges or a binding that's very weak won't hold up to alteration very well. Choose a book in fairly good condition.

When you've found a board book you'd like to alter, simply grab a few basic supplies:

- Your chosen board book
- Sandpaper or sanding block
- White or black gesso
- Paint, decorative paper, or other finish of your choice

Follow these steps to prepare your book:

1. Sand each page of your book to a clean finish, including the front and back covers, to remove all traces of the glossy coating. Quite a bit of the design and text of the book may also rub away. Don't worry, this is completely normal.

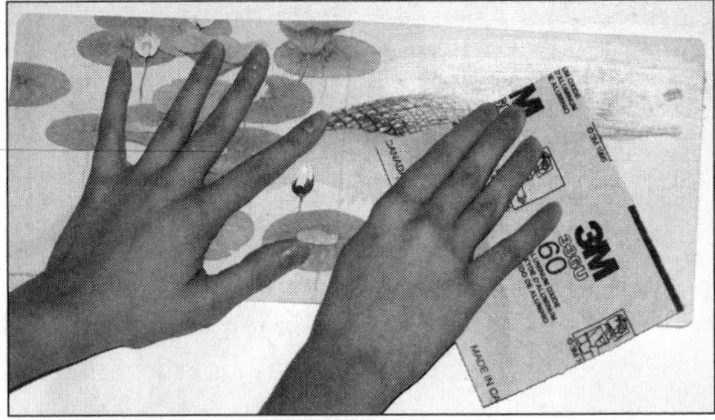

For the fastest results, use coarse sandpaper when sanding your board book.

Picture This

Properly sanding the pages of your book can be a lengthy process. Don't be afraid to take your time. This step is the most important part of the entire preparation process, as it gives your pages the surface necessary to hold paint, glue, and whatever else you choose to add.

2. Wipe away any dust that remains on the surface of your book with a paper towel.
3. Coat each page of your book with a white or black gesso, and let it dry completely. This ensures a smooth work surface when you begin to alter your book.
4. Apply acrylic paint, decorative paper, or any other background of your choosing to each page of your book.

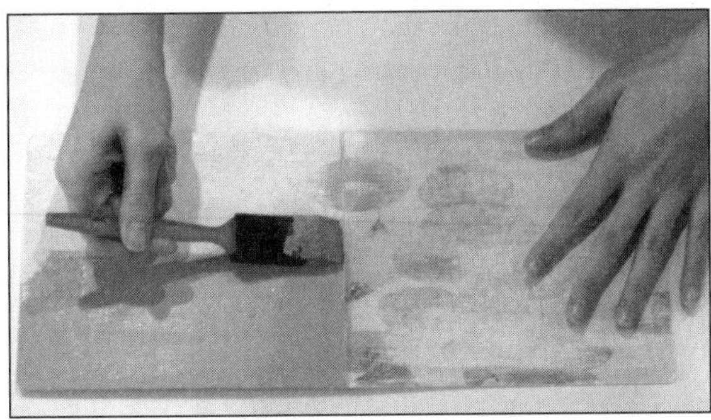

Use wide, long strokes to get the best paint coverage.

Picture This

If you're going use acrylic paint for your page backgrounds, feel free to skip the gesso—as long as you're using a thick-bodied acrylic paint and you've completely sanded away all traces of glossy coating. Apply two or three coats of paint to ensure strong, even color.

Your board book is now prepped and ready to alter. Feel free to add images, text, and other alterations to your heart's content!

Keeping It Flat

As I've mentioned, board books have thick pages, so thinning out your book isn't an option, as it would completely destroy your book's binding. You'll be working on every single page in your book, so it's a good idea to stick with alterations that keep the book's pages as flat as possible. This ensures that the book still closes when it's complete.

What kind of alterations will help you keep your altered board book flat? Painting and rubber stamping are excellent techniques, as they enable you to add fabulous texture and detail without adding too much bulk. Thin decorative papers and stickers also work well.

These board book pages have been made beautiful by adding metallic paper, transparent collage sheet images, and hand-drawn designs—all ensuring that the book will lay flat when closed.

(Pages by Kate Schaefer)

Be sure to leave the area closest to the binding untouched. You can paint and add paper in this area, but it's best to keep stickers and decorative items about $\frac{1}{4}$ inch from the inside bound edge of the book. This helps ensure that your book closes when completed and also helps prevent the book's binding from breaking apart over time.

Picture This

Avoid using dimensional items on the inside pages of your book. If you'd like to add a charm or other accent, consider using it on the book's cover. Or consider cutting a window in a facing page to allow the item to fit inside your book without adding bulk. (Turn to Chapter 11 for help with cutting a window. It will be a bit more difficult because you're working with cardboard pages, but the process is basically the same.)

Baby Board Book

One of my favorite uses for altered books is to transform them into mini-scrapbook-style albums containing family and heritage photographs. Because board books are small-scale in nature, contain a limited number of pages, and are already sturdily constructed, they're an ideal choice for this type of project.

For this altered book adventure, I chose to alter a child's board book and use it to feature some favorite photos from my first year of life, as well as some personal ephemera. You can also complete this project to celebrate a special baby girl in your life, or change it up to honor a young boy or another someone special in your life.

Deciding on Photographs and Ephemera

Enjoy the process of choosing which photographs and ephemera you'd like to include in your altered baby book. There is no right or wrong number to include, and it's entirely up to you to select the types of photos and items you'd like to use.

For your photographs, consider one of these options:

- Photos that span a specific time period, such as 1 week, 1 month, or 1 year in baby's life (For my project, I elected to use several different photographs from my first year.)
- An entire set of photos from a single professional (or home) photo shoot
- A series of photos in the same place or featuring the same behavior but at different times
- A group of photographs showing baby's different moods throughout the year

When selecting the ephemera you'd like to include try incorporating any of these items:

- Birth certificate
- Newspaper from baby's day of birth
- Hospital documents: record cards, ID bracelets (baby and Mom)
- Birth announcement
- Newspaper announcement (if available)
- Church documents: baptism certificates, cradle roll certificates

Altered Alert

When choosing to work with important items such as birth and baptism certificates, work with copies. You'll likely need the originals someday, and you don't want them stuck inside an altered book!

Gathering Your Supplies

When you've selected your photos and ephemera, you'll need to grab a few more things to complete your project:

- Child's board book of your choice
- Photographs and ephemera to include in your book
- Sandpaper
- White gesso
- Soft pink acrylic paint
- Decorative patterned papers (Oh, Baby! Girl Collection by BasicGrey)
- White jumbo circle bookplate (BasicGrey)
- Alphabet, quote, and image stickers (Memories Complete)
- Black pens for journaling and doodling (Sakura)

With all the supplies you need in hand, you're ready to begin creating your project.

Picture This

The amount of decorative papers and paint you need for this project depends on the size of the board book you're altering. Measure your book and count its pages before heading to the store, and you'll be sure to have enough supplies to fully complete your project.

Altering Your Book

With this project, you'll want to start by working on the interior pages of your book first:

1. Sand away all the glossy coating and interior designs of your book.
2. After you've sanded the pages, paint each page with a coat of white gesso, followed by a coat of pink. (If you want, skip the gesso and opt for two or three coats of pink.) For best results, be sure to let each coat dry completely before applying the next.

Next, it's time to alter your book's interior pages. There are a number of ways you can do this, and the final results are really up to you. I recommend starting with the first spread in your book, but you can work on pages in any order.

For my first pages, I chose to include a favorite portrait and some birth statistics. I also added one of the birth announcements my parents sent to close family and friends.

Feel free to begin your board book exactly as I did, or try a completely different approach. You might want to include your photos in chronological order or simply add them as you see fit. You can construct each of your pages in the same manner as the first or try a completely different design on each page. Whatever you can imagine works!

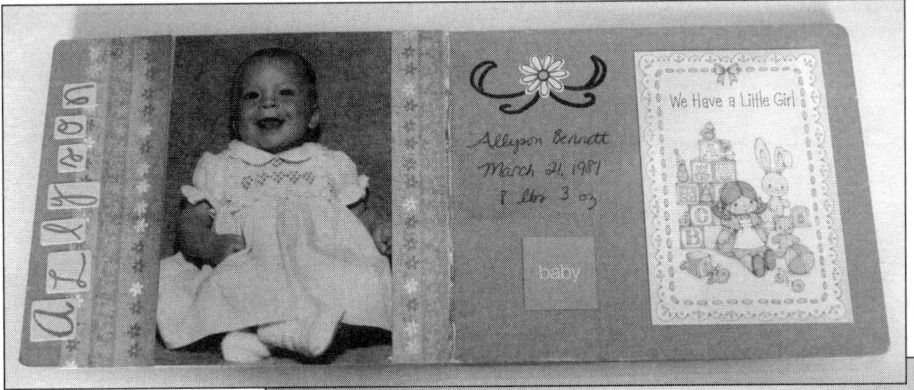

This opener combines cute patterned papers with stickers and doodled designs.

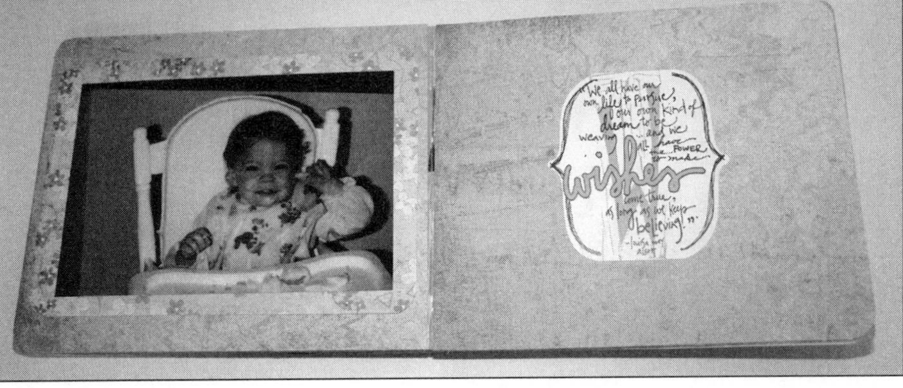

I chose to end my book with a photo from my first birthday, along with an inspiring quote from Louisa May Alcott.

The design of this patterned paper sets the tone for the contents inside my altered board book.

This completed cover perfectly suits my altered book.

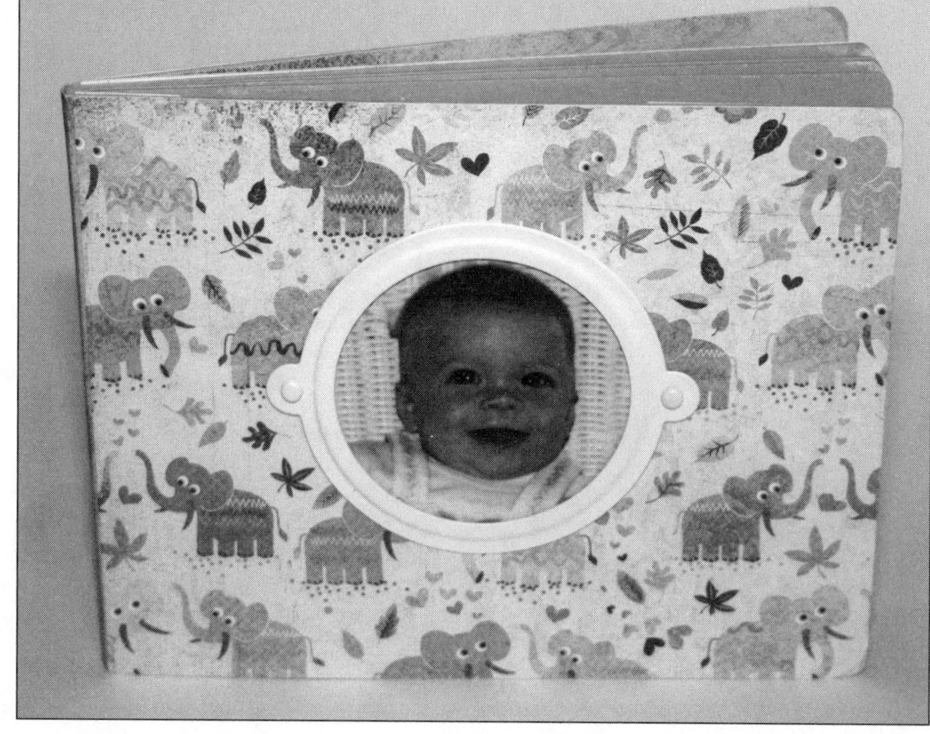

Covering and Finishing Your Book

After you've designed your book's interior pages, it's time to decorate the cover. Begin by covering the entire outside of the book with decorative paper. (Turn to Chapter 3 if you need assistance with this.) For the front and back covers, I chose an elephant print paper that coordinated with the other patterns inside my book. I used a solid pink for the book's spine. Bookbinding tape isn't necessary for board books, so I simply covered my book's spine with patterned paper.

After your book is covered, you can add the finishing touches. Follow these simple steps for a beautiful final product:

1. Crop a favorite photo to fit the window of the jumbo bookplate.
2. Adhere the photo to your book's cover.
3. Using a strong adhesive of your choice, attach the bookplate to your cover so it frames your photograph.

Altered Alert

Bookplates generally come with brads that can be used to attach it to various projects, but board books are too thick for this type of application. Be sure to use a strong adhesive instead. If you want, insert the brads through the holes simply for decoration, as I did.

4. *Optional:* If you want to make your book even more durable, consider coating your cover and decorated pages with a thin layer of decoupage finish. This keeps your pages protected and allows them to be enjoyed safely by little fingers.

That's all there is to it! Your altered board book is now a photograph-filled keepsake, ready to be enjoyed!

The Least You Need to Know

- Altering a board book is a great special project.
- Sand away the glossy coating on altered book pages prior to alteration so your designs will stick.
- It's important to keep your altered pages flat when altering a board book.
- Creating a board book to honor a special infant in your life is a simple way to make a personalized keepsake.

In This Chapter

- Discovering different kinds of books for altering
- Altering vinyl records (remember those?)
- Celebrating your favorite music with an altered record album collector's book

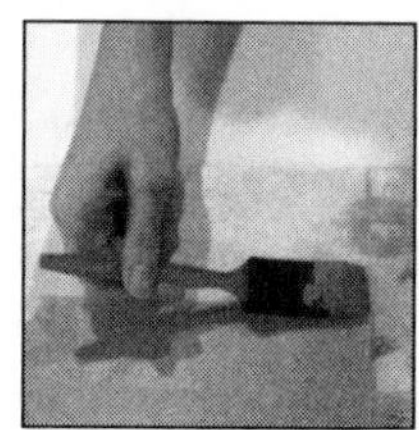

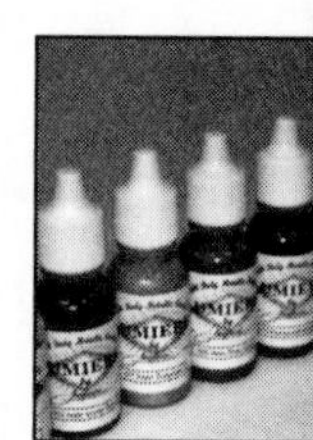

Chapter 13

Special Collector's Albums

Want to create an even more unique altered book? Seek out a one-of-a-kind book structure or specialty collector's album. These albums, while sometimes a bit harder to come by, make the creativity of altered books even more prominent.

In this chapter, I walk you through the steps of altering an album designed to hold vinyl records (we also learn how to alter the records themselves, but let's not get ahead of ourselves). But that's just the tip of the iceberg! With so many different books available for the altered artist to work with, it's hard to pick just one.

Different Kinds of Books to Alter

We've altered hardcover books. We've altered spiral-bound books. We've altered board books. In the next chapter, we make and alter books made from office and mail supplies. But never-ending options are available to you, the altered artist. Don't believe me? Try altering one—or more!—of the following kinds of books:

- Coin collector's album or tabletop coin folder
- Postage stamp collector's album
- Vintage photo album
- Oversize vintage scrapbook
- Wallet photo holder

Where can you find such books? Try these resources:

- Yard sales
- Flea markets
- Antique stores
- Online auction sites, such as eBay
- Hobby stores (for collector's albums)

Try a new and different book structure for your next project. No matter what you choose, you'll be glad you took the opportunity to try something a little bit different from the books we've already explored—and expand your altered art resumé in the process!

Altered Record Collector's Album

About a year ago, I came across a small vintage record album at an antique store. Filled with 10 45 rpm records, it seemed like it was just begging to be altered.

Altered Alert

Be sure not to alter records that have sentimental or monetary value; choose ones that would otherwise be discarded. Your mother's prized collection of Beach Boys albums is *not* a good place to start!

After letting it sit in my studio for quite some time, I realized that the album would make a perfect showcase for my love of music. I could pay tribute to each genre and my favorite songs, and thus the idea for the altered record album was born!

This album was an exciting find—I love it when items like this cross my path.

Rounding Up Your Supplies

To create your altered record collector's album, you'll need a few supplies:

- 45 rpm record collector's album, with at least 10 records inside
- Gesso
- Decoupage glue/finish
- Acrylic paint
- Decorative patterned paper of your choice
- Rubber stamps and ink of your choice
- Permapaque markers in a variety of colors (Sakura)
- Treble clef iron-on patch (Wrights)

For the most part, you can create this album with items you have in your stash already. There's no need to go out and buy any special supplies or papers. I used scraps for most of my decorative papers. If your art supply area is fairly stocked with the basics, you should be all set. The most important part of the project is the album, so focus your efforts on finding one that's perfect for you.

The embroidered treble clef patch is the perfect touch for this album cover.

Preparing and Covering the Album

The record album I purchased was not in excellent condition. The binding was slightly ripped, and the cover was quite scuffed. So to prepare my album for alteration, I had a bit of work to do. If your album is in similar condition, or if you just want to create a beautifully fun album cover, try these steps:

1. Paint your book's front cover, back cover, and spine with a thick layer of gesso, and let it dry completely. Repeat if necessary. (My album needed about three coats.)
2. Paint your album any color you want.
3. Use bookbinding tape to repair any tears in the spine and secure the binding. (See Chapter 3 if you need assistance with this process.)
4. Embellish your cover as desired.
5. Cover the album with a thin layer of decoupage finish to seal your design.

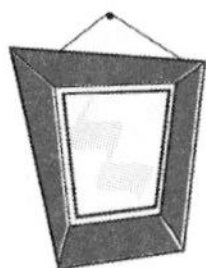

Picture This

Want a different look for your album cover? Try printing copies of your favorite CD covers and using them to create a collage on the front of your album.

Your album's cover is now complete. Now let's look inside, and see what fun we can have in there!

Planning Your Album's Interior

Creating an altered book with so many pages requires a little advance planning. My album had 10 pockets and records for a total of 20 pages. I chose to create one page each for a variety of musical genres. Each pocket and record celebrates two different types of music, one on each side. Before you begin any alterations, figure out which musical genres you'd like to highlight as part of your altered record collector's album. Here are the 20 categories I used:

1. Pop
2. Country
3. Rock 'n' Roll
4. Urban and Rap
5. Rhythm and Blues
6. Classical
7. Folk
8. Traditional
9. Children's
10. Show Tunes
11. Dance
12. New Age
13. Soundtracks
14. Hard Rock and Metal
15. Contemporary Christian
16. Vocal/Opera
17. Indie Girl Rock
18. The British Invasion (Then and Now)
19. Power Ballads
20. My All-Time Favorites

As you can see from my list, I enjoy almost all types of music! If you're the same way, this list of musical genres might work for your altered album layout. You can also try one of these other options for your altered album's organization:

- Theme your album around one single genre, with a page and record for each of your favorite songs.
- Create an album focusing on your favorite artist or musical group, and use a different song on each page. Celebrate what each song means to you, and why it's so special.
- Create your album with a "through the years" theme—using a page and record to celebrate your favorite songs at different stages throughout your life.

You can choose to celebrate any music you want in your altered album. It's your project, so the important thing to remember is to choose music you love!

Decorating Your Album's Interior

Altering the pages of your album is one of the best parts about this project. For each page, you'll need to select background papers and collage elements that fit the mood of that particular page. Then you're ready to begin.

Altered Alert

Before you begin, remove the records from the album pages. You don't want to accidentally damage a record while you work with excess glue or cutting!

This page is just waiting to be altered.

For my British Invasion page, I chose to use part of an old atlas as a background.

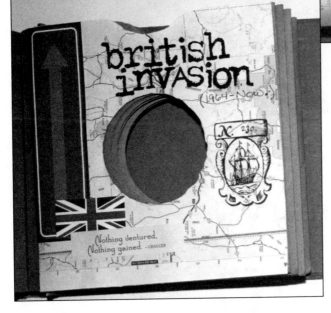

The stamp from 100 Proof Press and collage embellishments add the perfect finishing touches to this page.

1. Turn to a blank album page.
2. Measure the page's dimension, and cut background paper to fit it. Adhere the paper to the page.
3. Use scissors to cut out the middle of the page (where the record label shows through) and the top lip of the page.
4. Add collage elements, stamping, or any other techniques you'd like to use to finish your page.

Repeat this process for each of your remaining pages.

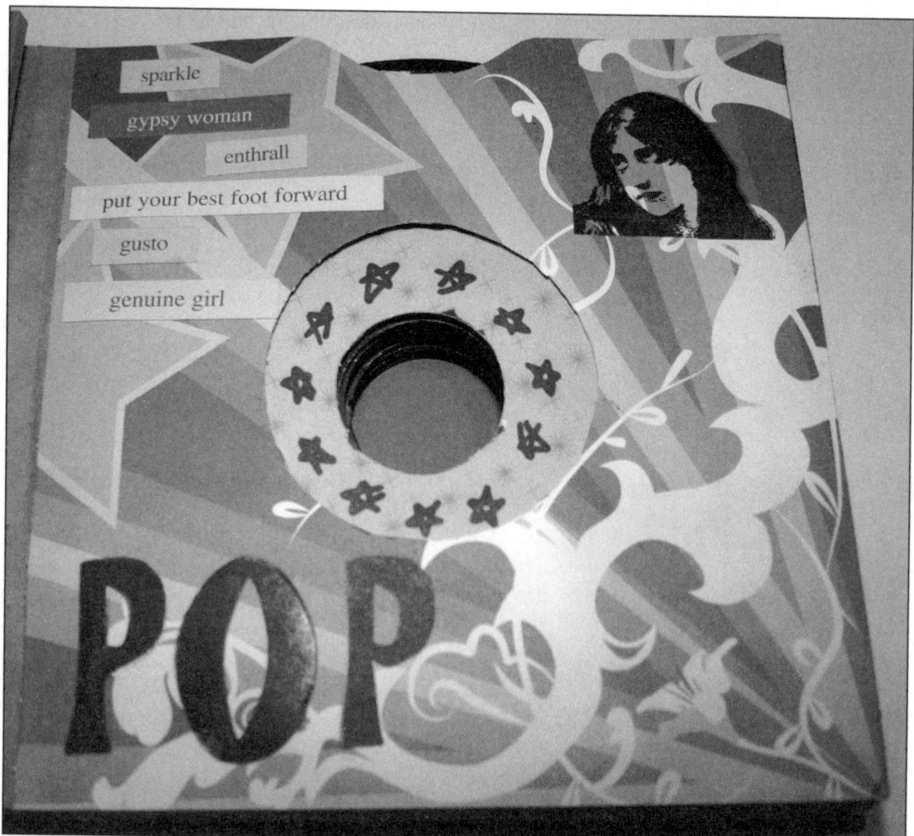

This fun page celebrates my love of pop music—my favorite genre.

Embellishing the Records

With your interior pages complete, there's only one step left—to alter the records themselves! This is my favorite part of this altered album project.

To embellish and decorate each record, you'll need a few supplies:

- A set of Permapaque markers
- Some patterned paper
- Glue stick

Remember, you'll embellish one side of each record for each musical genre or song you've chosen to celebrate in your album. Choose your patterned paper and colors to match the interior album page you've already altered.

1. Be sure your record is clean and dust-free before you begin to work with it.
2. Cut a scrap of patterned paper just larger than your record's label.
3. Cut your paper into a circle, and adhere it to the record's center.

Picture This

To correctly size your paper for the interior circle, lay your paper over the top of the record label. Use your finger to burnish the edges of the label area onto your patterned paper. Because the record label is raised, it leaves an indent in the paper all the way around the circle. Use this as a cutting guide, and you're all set.

Begin with a clean, plain record.

This record celebrates many of my favorite pop songs.

4. Cut out the record's center circle from the paper.
5. Using the Permapaque pens, embellish the label with a doodled design of your choice. (Turn back to Chapter 7 for some design ideas.)
6. Using a white Permapaque pen, write the names of a few favorite songs around the edge of the record. Repeat so you have two lines of song titles going all the way around the record.
7. Using a colored Permapaque pen, write a few phrases describing what you enjoy about the genre around the innermost circle edge.

Repeat this process for all your remaining records.

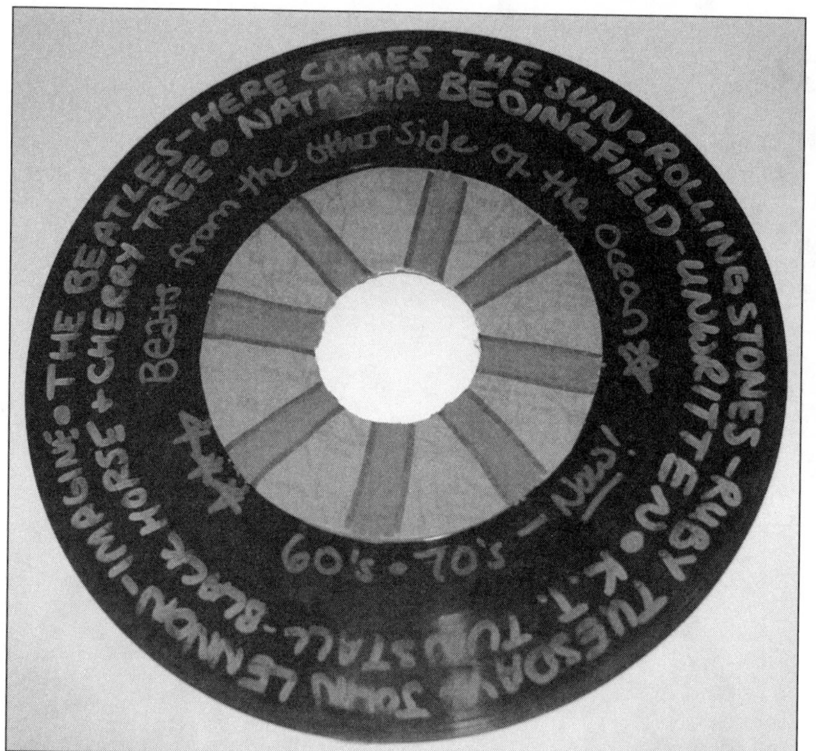

This altered record coordinates well with its matching page, celebrating the British Invasion.

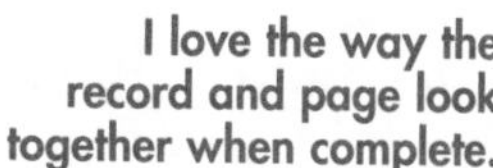

I love the way the record and page look together when complete.

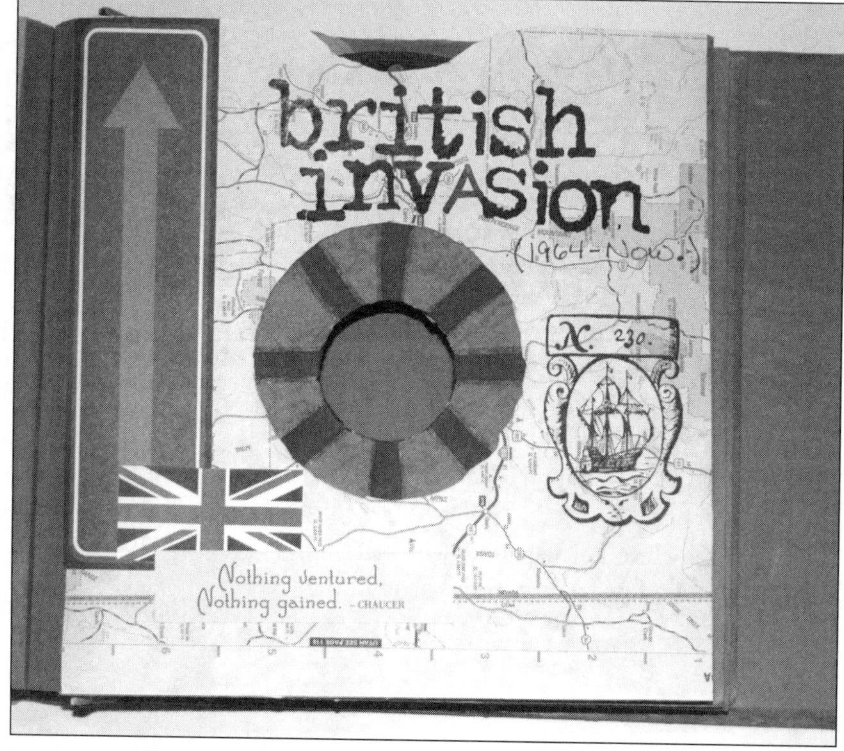

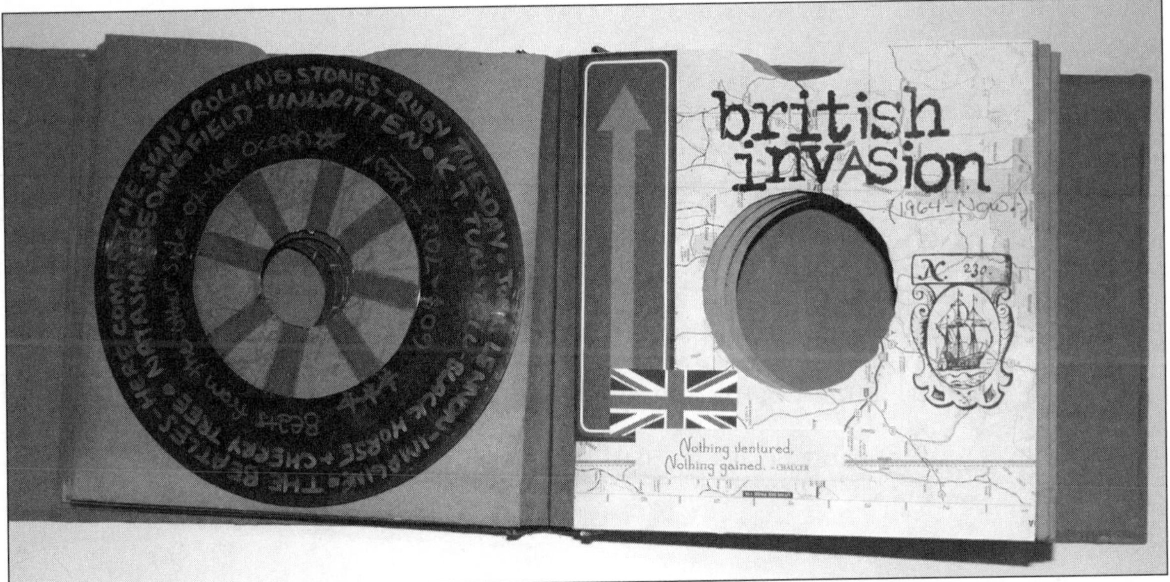

Pull out the record for a cool surprise!

Altered Alert

Remember that your records and pages are two-sided. Be sure the two sides of each page match the same two sides of each record. This ensures that all your records match up perfectly when they're inserted into the pocket pages of your album.

Putting It All Together

Your album is nearly complete. All you need to do now is add your records to their pocket pages and you have a fun and funky musical tribute.

That's all there is to it. Pull out this album any time you need a musical pick-me-up or just want to reflect on the tunes that make you happy.

Picture This

Use a computer and software program to burn a CD containing all the songs celebrated in your altered album. Hide it in one of the pockets for an extra-special treat.

The Least You Need to Know

- Altering uniquely structured albums, particularly collector's albums, results in a very interesting altered art project.
- Consider creating an altered collector's album to celebrate your favorite songs in a variety of genres.
- You can alter more than just album pages! Altering records or other album contents creates an altered book that's full of surprises.

In This Chapter

- Creating faux postage
- Making an amazing altered envelope book
- Creating books from ID badges, tags, and file folders

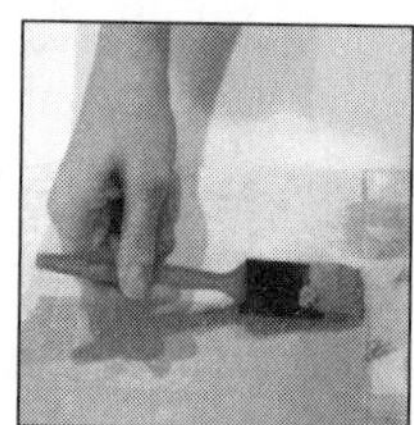

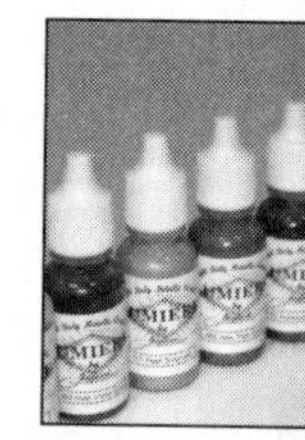

Chapter 14

Altered Books—Mail and Office Style

Believe it or not, your local office supply store can hold a wealth of goodies for the altered artist. Envelopes, file folders, shipping tags, and more can all become the foundation for amazing altered artwork. Add these great supplies to the tools already available through some of the best rubber stamp and art companies, and you have fantastic art just waiting to happen.

The Postal Look

One of my favorite ways to create unique altered art looks is by using postage stamps—both real and imagined. Adding postage stamps to my art provides a one-of-a-kind look—and it's quite a lot of fun. I can create altered art that appears as though it's been sent through the mail, without the hassle of heading to the post office.

But before you can use postage on your altered art, you have to gather some!

Real Stamps

Using postage on your altered book pages is fun and easy. All you need to do is round up some cancelled stamps and you're good to go. Cancelled stamps arrive in your mailbox every day. Simply cut them off of envelopes you receive, and they're ready to add to your altered creations.

Unalterable Fact

Older or international stamps can add a vintage feel to your art. So many different styles and themes are available, it can be worth the extra effort it takes to find them.

If you don't like any of the cancelled stamps that come to you in the mail, try one of these sources to find some:

- Antique stores
- Online auction sites, such as eBay
- Hobby and craft stores
- Specialty online stamp stores

Finding the perfect postage stamp can sometimes be a challenge, but the results of your search will be well worth it.

Notice how the postage stamps used on this altered book enhance the overall page design.

(Page by Jackie Baxted)

Picture This

Remember to seek out old postcards in addition to postage stamps, as they often still have postage on them. You get ephemera and postage for one low price!

Rubber Stamps

Can't find a real stamp with the design you want? One of the easiest ways to get a postage look is to use faux postage rubber stamps. Creating a unique postage look is easy when you have rubber stamps already designed to appear like postage.

These stamps from 100 Proof Press and Catslife Press are just a few of the choices available to today's altered artist.

To create faux postage using these stamps, simply stamp the image in a favorite ink color on a solid sheet of white paper or cardstock. Then cut out the image. Add decorative edging if you like!

Picture This

Faux postage rubber stamps aren't just limited to the stamps themselves. Visit Ma Vinci's Reliquary (reliquary.cyberstampers.com) for great stamps featuring postmarks and cancellations.

Altered Envelope Book

I love projects that are simple, yet still beautiful. One of my favorite altered books is one made entirely out of envelopes. When I discovered this spiral notebook already filled with envelopes, I knew I'd found something great.

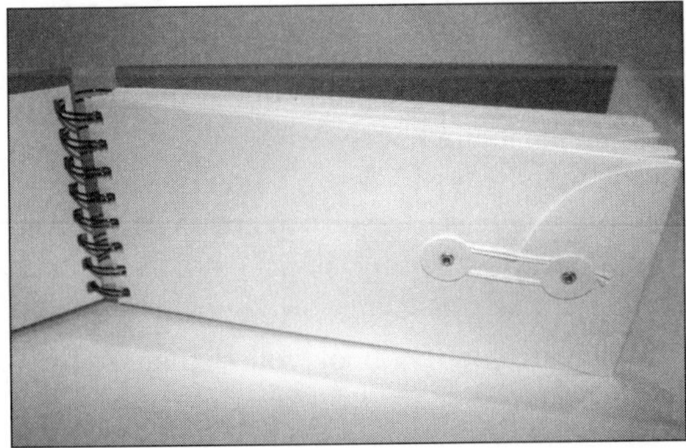

This envelope book by 7gypsies is just begging to be altered.

I decided to alter my envelope album to hold all my special keepsakes from my relationship with my husband. Movie ticket stubs and notes he's written me are just a few of the treasures you'll find inside each envelope. Decorate your envelope to hold whatever strikes your fancy!

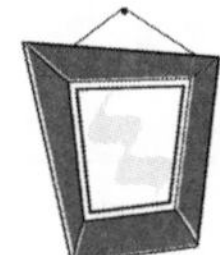

Picture This

Want an envelope album made entirely by hand? Easy:

1. Gather a pile of standard envelopes.
2. Punch two holes on the left side of each envelope.
3. Tie a ribbon through the holes to bind all of the envelopes together.

Now you've got an album ready to alter!

Envelope Book Supplies

To embellish your altered envelope book, you'll need a few supplies:

- Four sheets decorative patterned paper of your choice
- Glue stick or other adhesive
- Faux postage, which you've already created
- Mail and postmark rubber stamps of your choice
- Any other embellishments (optional)

Let's get started.

Thinking Outside the Envelope (Book)

You'll want to make more than one of these fun envelope books to document many areas of your life!

1. Begin by covering your front and back covers with patterned paper as described in Chapter 3.
2. Embellish and decorate your cover as desired.

This album cover uses a bookplate and paper flower to complete the design.

3. Embellish the front side of each envelope in your album any way you like.

Let your personal style shine through your decorated envelopes, and allow your design to reflect the contents of each envelope.

4. Embellish and decorate the back side of each envelope in your album to resemble a mailed letter.

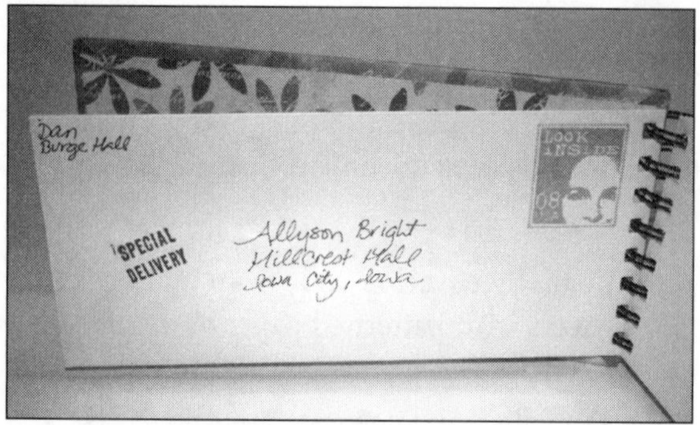

By using a faux postage rubber stamp, I was able to gain an authentic look for this envelope.

That's all there is to it. If you want, add some additional embellishments or finishing touches to your album. You now have an entire album full of customized envelopes just waiting to hold your personal treasures, whatever they may be.

Albums from Office Supplies

You can make altered books and albums from more than just envelopes. After I discovered envelope albums, I was curious to see what other items could be made into altered books and scrapbooks. Turns out, your local office supply store is full of them! Check out the amazing projects in the following sections.

Shipping Tag Books

Manila shipping tags can be an excellent foundation for an altered book. They are uniform in size, making them easy to bind, and quite inexpensive. Head to your local office supply store and grab a package of shipping tags. Pick out a few favorite papers and embellishments, and get ready to start creating!

You can create and embellish your tag album any way you want. This album was created with a kit manufactured by Sweetwater Scrapbook. Inside was the book's cover, binding, and all the shipping tags necessary to create a fantastic mini-album celebrating special days. Seek out a similar kit, or create your own book design.

To create your tag book, follow these steps:

1. Punch two holes in the left-hand side of each tag.
2. Stack the tags on top of one another, all facing the same direction.
3. Use posts and screws or decorative ribbon in the two holes you punched to bind your tags together into a mini-book.
4. Embellish each tag to your liking.
5. Attach ribbon to the hole in each tag.

Altered Alert

When creating tag books, be sure to bind your tags together first! If you don't, it can be easy to accidentally design a tag upside down or backward and then it won't fit quite right when you go to bind your album.

I covered the right-side tag with patterned paper, accents, and a favorite photo. The left-hand tag holds some text and additional information.

Repeating the same design throughout your tag book provides continuity.

Adding ribbon to your tags helps them stand out.

This ID badge mini-book is full of fun photographs and patterned papers.

(Book by Rachael Giallongo)

ID Badge Book

Believe it or not, a bunch of ID badges can also make a great mini-album. These badges are usually used for holding nametags at major events or as identification for company employees, but why not use them to make a fun altered mini-book? Look for these in bulk at your local office supply store.

To create this great book, simply gather up a pile of ID badges and the papers and products you'd like to use. Then you're ready to start creating:

1. Measure the insert size for your album, and cut papers to fit inside.
2. Decorate and embellish the inserts however you like, and add the inserts to the name badge sleeves.
3. Bind the badges together using decorative ribbon.

See how easy that was? And the result is a cute mini-album you'll be happy to show off to all of your friends and family.

File Folder Album

Another item that makes a great mini-book is the basic file folder. These come in a variety of sizes, colors, and textures.

The world of scrapbooking has recently become obsessed with altered art and office supplies, and many companies are responding to the overwhelming demand for products that easily lend themselves to altered art and book creation.

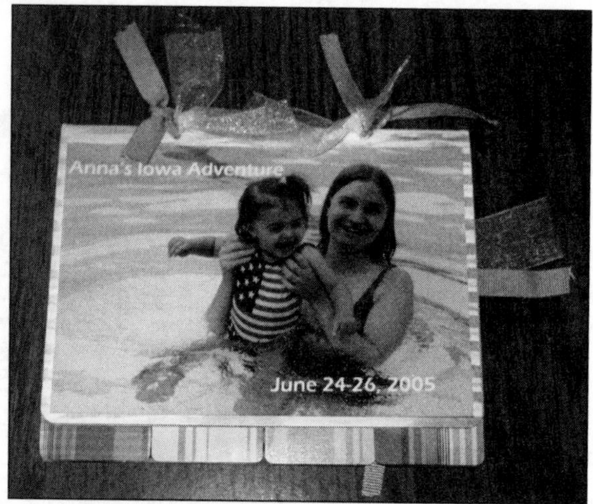

This mini–file folder album was created from a kit manufactured by Daisy D's Paper Company.

Whether you choose to create your book from a kit or simply use file folders from the office supply store, creating a mini-book made from file folders couldn't be easier. You just need a few file folders and some decorative ribbon. Here's how you do it:

1. Determine the number of folders you'd like to use to create your book. Three or four is generally a good number.
2. Bind the file folders together by punching 2 or 3 holes along the spine of the folders, stacking them together, and securing with ribbon.
3. Add your altered artwork to the pages of the folder book as you like.

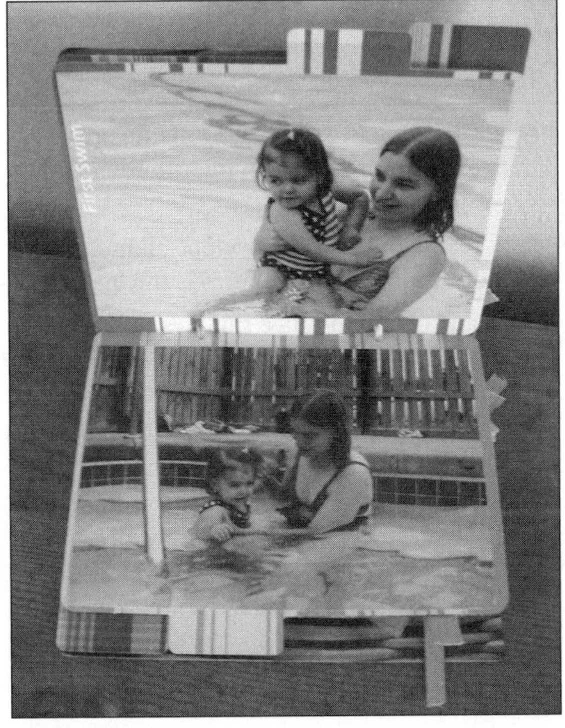

4. Add any finishing touches you want to include.

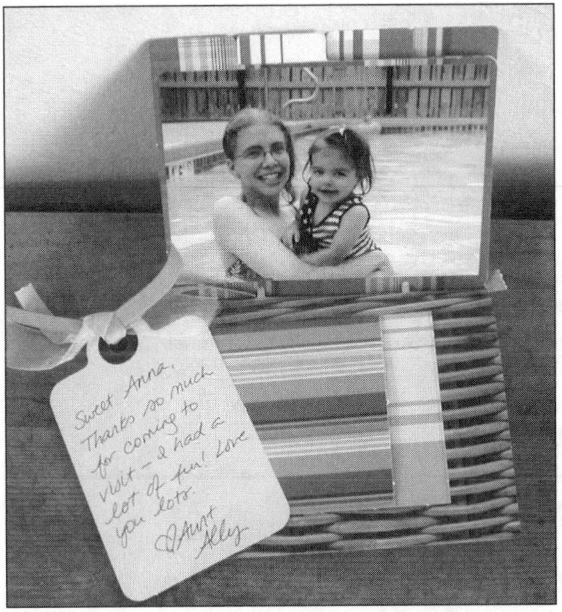

I enjoyed adding a pocket containing a message to my niece in the back of this mini-book.

Putting It All Together

When it comes to making mini-books and albums from office supplies, your imagination is the only limit. Try combining techniques and products for even more unique looks. Altered artist Wendy Malichio designed this fun project using shipping tags and handmade envelopes. Create this project for yourself, or combine two different products to design an album project on your own.

To create a book like Wendy's, you'll need these supplies:

- Patterned Paper, Fibers, and Letter Stickers (Fiber Scraps)
- Walnut ink (Fiber Scraps)
- Shipping Tags
- Binder clip
- Additional embellishments of your choice

This album cover uses a binder clip for an embellishment, taking the office theme one step further.

When you have your supplies, follow these steps:

1. Trim a piece of 12"×12" patterned paper in half to create the base of the booklet, folding it in half and then folding the edge over to create the "pockets" for the tags.
2. Sand and ink the paper for a distressed look.
3. Add your photos and accents as desired.
4. Ink the shipping tags, and add your journaling. (A cute idea is to have your subjects write a note on the tags as well.) Add fibers, and slip the tags inside the pockets of the tag booklet.
5. Secure together with an office clip.

No matter how you choose to create a mini-book, using office supplies can be a fun and inexpensive way to create new and fabulous looks for your altered art!

The Least You Need to Know

- Using postage stamps—authentic or faux—can provide a unique addition to your altered artwork.
- Creating an altered envelope album to hold your special treasures is fun and easy.
- Many common office supplies, including shipping tags, ID badges, and file folders, make an excellent foundation for creating mini-books to showcase your altered art and photographs.

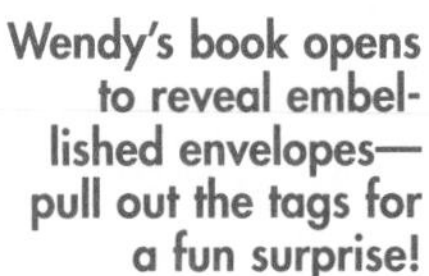

Wendy's book opens to reveal embellished envelopes—pull out the tags for a fun surprise!

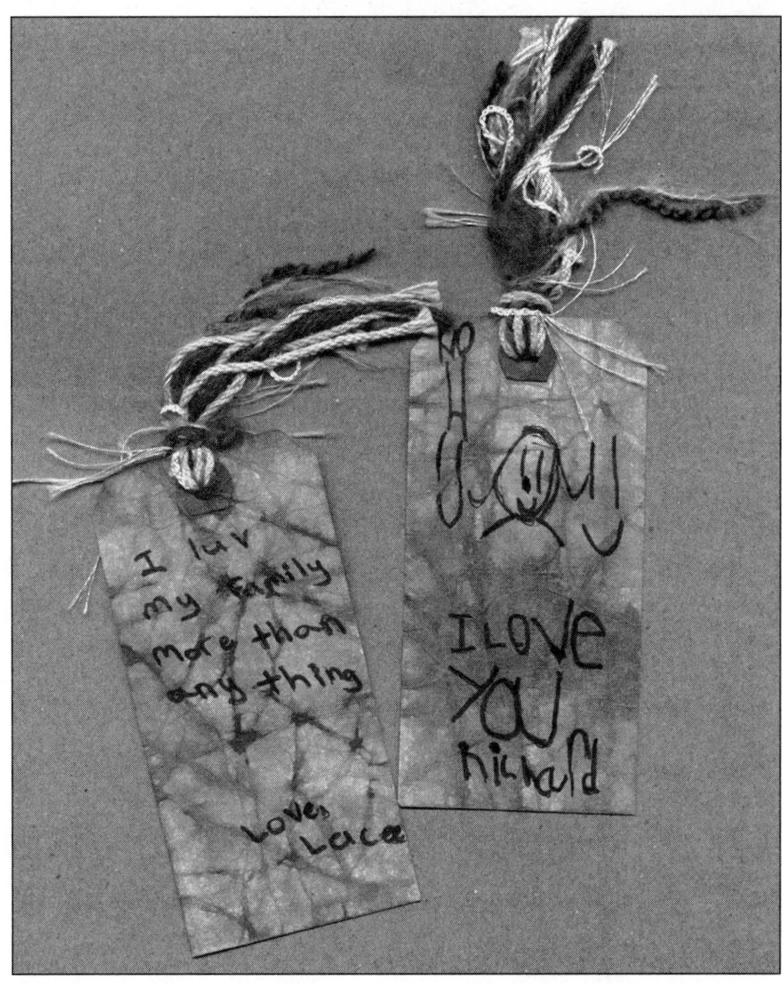

Wendy had her children each write a note on a tag—a fun way to include their perspectives.

In This Part

Part 5

Beyond the Book

Now that you've mastered the art of altered books, a world of possibility awaits you. It's time to think "outside the book" and explore new projects. In Part 5, you learn how to create artist trading cards (ATCs), as well as decorative wall canvases. You also discover how to alter boxes and tins and create small decorative touches for your home.

After completing this part, you'll have created a variety of unique projects to decorate your living space or give as one-of-a-kind gifts. You'll have conquered the basics—and beyond—of altered art.

In This Chapter

- A short history of artist trading cards
- Creating artist trading cards
- Tips on ATC trading
- Storing and displaying your cards

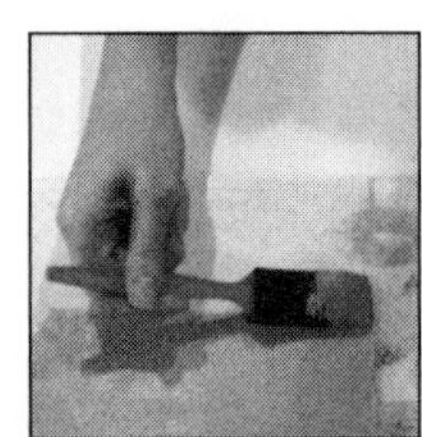

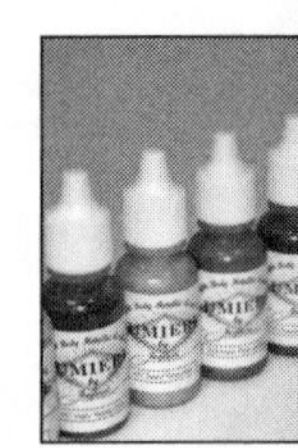

Chapter 15

Artist Trading Cards

By now, you're an altered book pro. You've worked on all sorts of altered book pages and even created some books with unique structures. Now it's time to move outside the book into a very exciting world: the world of artist trading cards.

Introducing Artist Trading Cards

The concept of *artist trading cards* (*ATCs*) is still a relatively new one in the world of altered art, although it is quickly gaining momentum.

Transforming Talk

Artist trading cards (ATCs) are miniature works of art, sized the same as traditional sports trading cards. They're usually one-of-a-kind originals and are created to be traded, never sold.

The idea was introduced by Swiss artist M. Vanci Stirnemann. In 1996, he created the world's first ATCs—in fact, he created 1,200 of them! In 1997, he put them on display at a local art gallery and then encouraged artists to design their own cards and bring them in to trade. This was an entirely new concept—one which delighted the art community.

Since then, card swaps continue to occur regularly at the gallery where Stirnemann first exhibited his ATCs, as well as at other galleries and meeting places all over the world.

UNALTERABLE FACT

To learn more about the initial exhibit of ATCs, or to learn how to contribute your own cards to the ongoing collection, visit www.artist-trading-cards.ch.

ATCs are designed to be very similar to other trading and playing cards, except they're handmade. Usually colorful and full of creative techniques, ATCs are fun for artists to create, share, and trade.

The ATC Rules

When it comes to ATCs, a few non-negotiable guidelines exist that every artist should follow. All styles of imagery, technique, and product are allowed, as long as the following card specifications are met:

- Cards should be $2\frac{1}{2} \times 3\frac{1}{2}$-inches in size.
- Cards should be traded, never sold.
- Cards should always be signed on the back by the creator.

Of course, art by nature is designed to break rules. So why is it, then, that ATCs have a set of guidelines everyone must follow? Because ATCs are designed to work in a system. By having artists create pieces that are all the same size, collectors can store, display, and enjoy their collection with ease. Plus, it gives new ATC creators quite a bit of freedom. The canvas size has already been decided. All they have to do is create and go!

ATCs were developed to make art accessible to everyone. With just a quick trade, anyone can own real, one-of-a-kind pieces of art. This is why cards should always be traded, and never sold.

In the world of ATCs, all artists are worth celebrating. No single artist is "better" than any other. True, some cards will inevitably end up among your favorites and other pieces won't necessarily strike you in quite the same way, but regardless, every artist is unique and has a statement to make and art to share. By signing your cards, you're making yourself—and your art—accessible to the world. This is what ATCs are all about.

UNALTERABLE FACT

Nothing quite beats the feeling when you get a random e-mail from someone who has crossed paths with your card. It's quite a joy!

Creating Your Own ATCs

Ready to jump on the ATC bandwagon and create your own cards? Let's get started. All you really need is a piece of cardstock or lightweight cardboard and the tools and embellishments of your choice.

Gathering Your ACT Supplies

Let's create a simple ATC—we begin by rounding up a few supplies:

- $2^1/_2 \times 3^1/_2$-inch piece of cardstock or lightweight cardboard
- Gold metallic paint
- Butterfly fairy rubber stamp (Catslife Press)
- ATC signature stamp (Catslife Press)
- Butterfly stickers (Violette Stickers)
- Wide ribbon scrap (Strano Designs)
- Fine point pen (Pigma by Sakura)
- Adhesive of your choice
- Blue pigment inkpad (Memories by Stewart Superior)

You can create this card using these exact materials, or you can substitute with stamps and stickers already in your collection.

Making Your First Card

When you have everything you need, follow these steps to make your very own ATC:

1. Cover both sides of your card with metallic gold paint. Let this dry.

2. Adhere the ribbon scrap to the bottom-right corner of the card, trimming at the edges of the card.

3. Add a stamp in top-left corner of the card.

4. Add stickers to right-hand edge of card, overlapping the ribbon if you like.

5. Using a fine-point pen, add any text you like to the front of your card.
6. Now, for the back: flip the card over and add the ATC signature stamp to the back of the card.

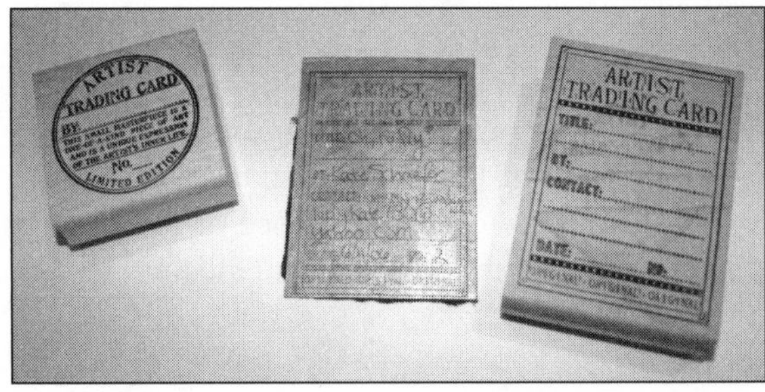

7. Use a pen to fill in the details on the back of the card.

The front of your card is now complete and almost ready to share!

(Card by Kate Schaefer)

Now that you've created your first ATC, the possibilities are endless. You'll discover that creating in this size and format is quick, simple, and rewarding.

Exciting ATC Tools and Products

With the recent surge of ATC popularity, several manufacturers have begun offering products and papers specifically designed to help you create ATCs quickly and easily. These products aren't necessary to create quality ATCs, but they can sure make the process quite a bit more fun!

Hands down, my favorite ATC product is the series of ATC Paper Pads manufactured by Memories in the Making. These miniature pads of paper are already cut to $2\frac{1}{2} \times 3\frac{1}{2}$ inches, eliminating the need for a ruler or cutting tool. Each pad contains 20 different papers, and you get 2 of each design for a total of 40 papers in each pad. The pads come in many different themes: Sewing, Oriental, Architecture, Jungle Animals, Botanicals, and Calligraphy, just to name a few choices available.

These paper pads provide ready-made artwork you can use either as a background image or as a focal point on your ATCs.

I love working with these paper pads because they're an easy source of fun and beautiful images that look amazing both on my ATCs and as part of my other altered art projects. Plus, I love that they fit in my on-the-go art bag. While the papers aren't sturdy enough to serve as the card itself, they fit perfectly on top of a piece of cut cardstock, creating a fabulous background. Images can also be cut out from the individual paper pads and added to the cards.

This artist trading card was created using these paper pads, and the result is fantastic!

Another fun ATC tool is the simple playing card. Playing cards are great for altering into ATCs, as they're already the correct size and shape. Playing cards also have a background image already on the card. You can buy designer sets of playing cards created just for alteration from companies such as Memories in the Making, or feel free to alter any playing cards you lying around.

This ATC was created simply by altering an old playing card.

Picture This

Altered playing cards make excellent gifts for those who enjoy poker and other card games. Consider creating an entire series of cards themed around your friend's favorite games!

Finally, I love the ATC packs of *Stampbord* from Ampersand Art Supply. Stampbord is a very forgiving surface. Plus, its special thickness allows for excellent results, every time.

Transforming Talk

Stampbord is a specially designed stamping surface, similar to cardboard, but thicker, stronger, and with a clay coating designed to hold ink and deliver amazing stamping impressions.

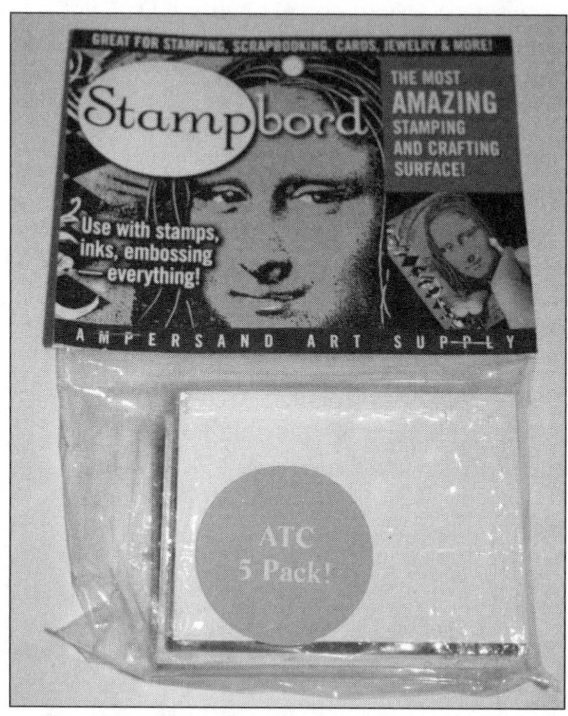

These Stampbord pieces are perfect for creating ATCs when you want to do a lot of stamping or use heavier-weight materials.

With so many different ways to make ATCs, no matter which techniques and products you elect to use, your cards are sure to be a success! Try using some of the techniques you learned earlier in this book, or make up your own completely new ideas.

This ATC was created using Stampbord as a base. Notice the clean stamp impressions as well as the excellent dimension of the card.

(Card by Julie Richards)

Time to Trade

Now that you've created a few different cards, you're ready to trade with other artists. There are many ways to trade cards with artists all around the world, regardless of where you live.

First and foremost, I recommend trading cards in person at least once if you can find the opportunity. Trading in person allows you to meet the creators of the cards you'll be getting, which can be a great experience. Plus, it's fun to be able to see all the different cards in each person's collection and decide on your trades together.

Picture This

To find or start a trading group in your area, check out MeetUp.com. This site enables individuals all over the globe to connect via common interests. To find an ATC group in your area, visit artisttradingcards.meetup.com.

If you can't meet in person or just want to trade with artists who live a bit farther away, a number of options are available. Try visiting one of these websites for more information on online and mail trades:

- www.artist-trading-cards.ch
- www.atcards.com
- groups.msn.com/Paint-n-ThingsATCs
- www.atcquarterly.com
- community.livejournal.com/artist_cards

One of my favorite parts of trading with other artists online is the variety of cards I receive and the various locations they come from—all over the world! I currently have cards from several different countries and continents in my collection.

Taten
seines
Angel

I love these ATCs by Claudia Hafner of London. Her use of texture and dimension is amazing!

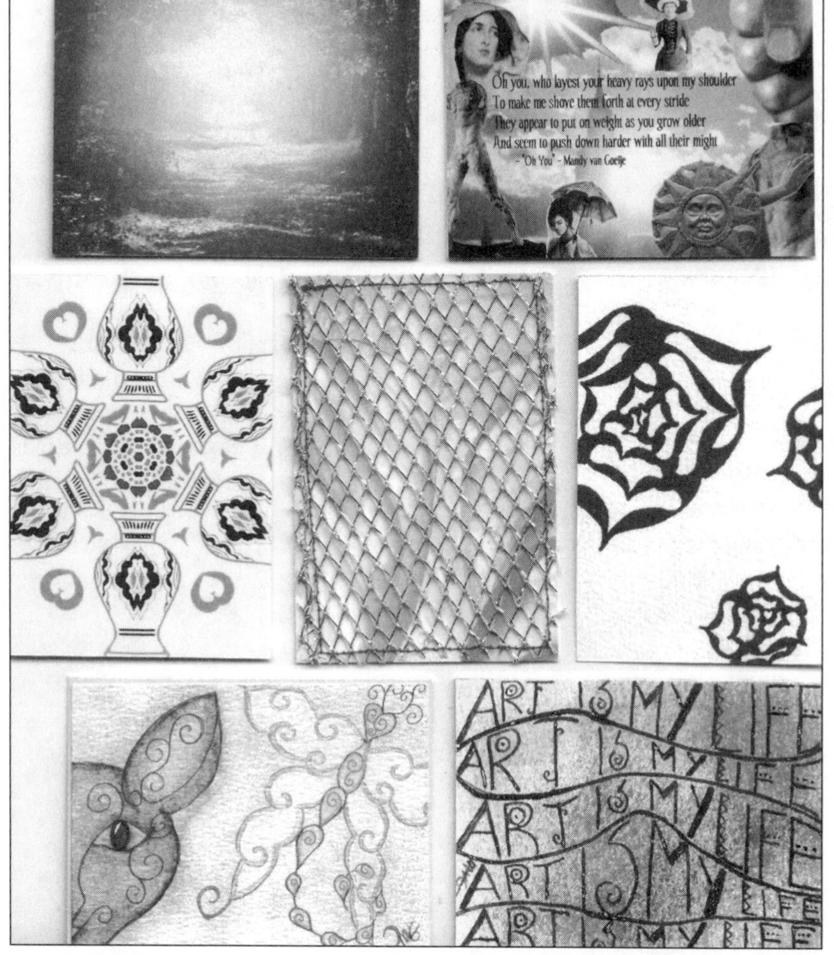
Oh you, who layest your heavy rays upon my shoulder
To make me shove them forth at every stride
They appear to put on weight as you grow older
And seem to push down harder with all their might
- "Oh You" - Mandy van Goeije
ART IS MY LIFE
ART IS MY LIFE
ART IS MY LIFE
ART IS MY LIFE
ART IS MY LIFE

These are just a few of the cards sent to me by Mandy Rentmeester van Goeije of the Netherlands. Notice how she uses techniques ranging from digital collage to hand-drawn paintings on her cards.

Storing and Displaying Your Cards

There are so many different ways to store and display your cards from albums to boxes and more. It's important to find a system that works for you and enables you to access and enjoy your cards whenever you want.

Albums

Storing your cards in an album is probably the easiest way to display your cards. Because artist trading cards are designed to be the same size as sport and other trading cards, any album designed for this purpose works fine. You can even use a simple three-ring binder from your local office supply store. Fill it with page protectors designed for trading cards, add your cards, and your work is done.

Altered Alert

If you have cards in your collection that are very bulky or heavy, an album might not be the best storage choice, as standard trading card page protectors are designed to hold flat, thin cards.

You could also use an album designed specifically for ATCs, such as those manufactured by Memories in the Making. These albums contain pocket pages that allow open access to all cards inside. Each album holds 72 cards to start and can be expanded to accommodate additional cards.

Albums such as this one are beautiful and make an excellent home for your ATC collection.

(Cards by Belinda Spiwak)

Boxes

You could also simply showcase your cards in a beautiful storage box. Boxes of ATCs are great conversation-starters for your coffee table, and storing your cards in boxes ensures that they stay free of dust and protected from the elements.

Any box or case designed for playing cards will hold and protect your ATCs. Try searching thrift stores for vintage playing card cases. Or if you want something really fancy, consider purchasing an engraved silver playing card case from a specialty store, such as Things Remembered. No matter what case you find, you'll be sure to have something to keep your cards safe and sound.

If you'd like your card box to have a little more personality, why not decorate a box for your cards? Consider creating a design to match the theme of your cards, or to match the décor of the room in which you plan to store your box. To learn the basics of altering wooden objects, and for more decorative ideas, turn to Chapter 17.

This wooden box by Walnut Hollow is designed to hold cards and can be decorated in any way you want.

Another fun storage option is to use a tin playing card case. You can buy these ready to embellish from Pinecone Press, Memories in the Making, and a few other major manufacturers. Simply decorate to your heart's content, insert your cards, and you're ready to go.

This tin is perfect for holding your ATCs.

(Tin by Tara Daigle)

Opening the tin lets you to access the cards inside. Use it for playing cards or your ATC collection.

(Tin by Tara Daigle)

To learn more about working with altered tins, turn to Chapter 17.

Handmade Displays and Storage Options

Sometimes your cards are so beautiful, and you just can't find the perfect display option to properly showcase them. If you're crafty—and I think you are if you've gotten this far in the book—why not create an album or showcase completely from scratch? All the techniques and book structures you've learned so far in the book can be adapted to hold and display artist trading cards. Consider these ideas:

- Cut a drawer into an altered book and fill it with ATCs.
- Add envelopes to your altered books, each containing a different ATC.
- Sew your ATCs directly into an altered book (Be careful when choosing this option if you'd like to be able to remove the cards later.)
- Create a file folder or envelope book to store your ATCs.

You can even create storage options to match your card collection.

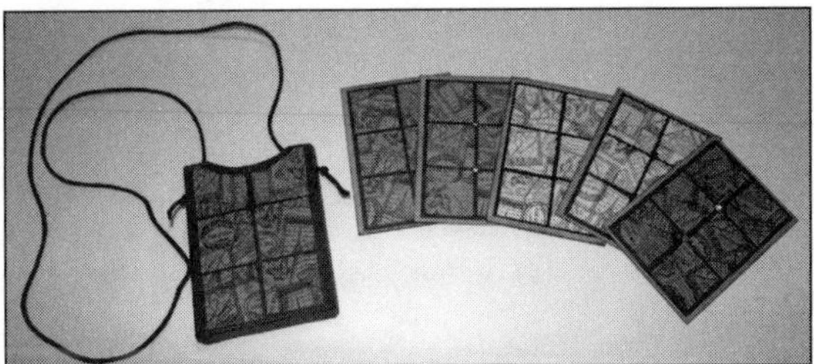

This artist chose to create an amulet to hold her series of postal-themed cards. Notice how the card holder and cards are all designed to match.

(Cards and amulet by Yvonne Thistle-Brewer)

To create a project like this one, simply design a pocket thick enough to hold all your cards. Decorate the pocket to match the cards you'd like to include. Then add silk cord to the top of the pocket. For assistance creating a pocket to hold your cards, turn to Chapter 10.

Another way to store and display your ATCs is in a handmade star book. This amazing project, designed by Chris Chapman, is perfect for your ATCs.

When your star book is closed, it looks like any other album. Open it for an ATC-filled surprise!

(Album by Chris Chapman)

This beautiful star album is a great showcase for ATCs.

(Album by Chris Chapman)

Feeling adventurous? Why not create a star book of your own? The Internet has a variety of excellent resources to help you. The San Diego Museum of Art has an excellent tutorial online at www.sdmart.org/pix/starbook.pdf. Or search the Internet for bookbinding structures, and you'll be presented with even more great ideas.

No matter how you choose to showcase your ATC collection, your results are sure to be memorable.

The Least You Need to Know

- Artist trading cards (ATCs) are a fun and unique way to share your art with others across the globe, as well as obtain original art for your collection for no monetary cost.
- ATCs should always be $2\frac{1}{2} \times 3\frac{1}{2}$ -inches, signed by the artist, and traded, not sold.
- Many unique products are available to help you create ATCs. Use your imagination to see what fun cards you can create.
- You can display your ATCs in an album, in a box, or in a unique handmade book. Or you could get really creative and think of another ATC display, such as an amulet.

In This Chapter

- Creating altered wall décor
- Altering block letters
- Creating art on canvas

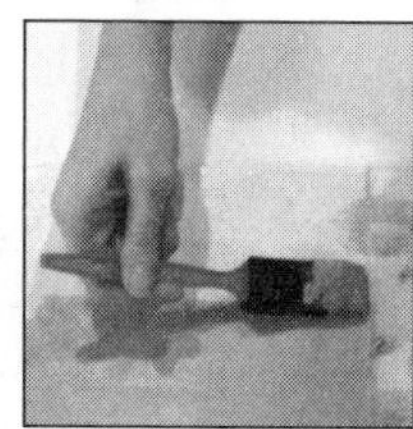

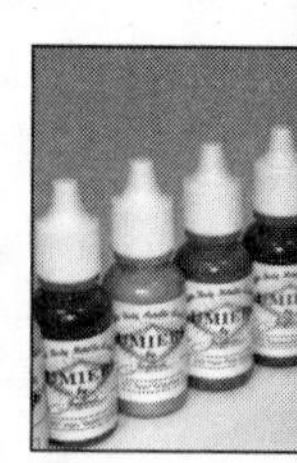

Chapter 16

For Your Walls

Altered art isn't limited to books and trading cards. You can apply the same principles and techniques you've used throughout this book to create fantastic items for your walls, too. From words to photos, wood to canvas, the possibilities are only defined by your imagination.

Altered art décor makes for excellent gift-giving as well. Next time someone you love celebrates a special occasion, why not surprise him or her with a unique item for the home?

Altered Block Letters

Altered block letters are one of the biggest crazes to hit the art world in recent years. Usually made from wood, altered letters are easy to make and look beautiful as part of your home décor.

You can purchase letters for altering individually or in sets, and you can spell out anything your heart desires. You'll want to get solid wood letters, and look around for the size and font you prefer.

Picture This

If you plan to spell out a short word or a series of initials, larger letters are perfect. If you plan to spell out a longer word or even a phrase, smaller letters are best.

Look for wooden letters at your local craft, hobby, or scrapbooking store. If you can't find the letters you're looking for, try searching online with one of these great retailers:

- www.adornit.com
- www.craftcuts.com
- www.woodenletters.biz

To the Supply Closet!

When you have all the letters you plan to alter, gather a few supplies:

- Your wooden letters
- Patterned paper of your choice, enough to cover all letters
- Decoupage glue/finish (Mod Podge or Aleene's Instant Decoupage)
- Foam brush
- Craft knife and cutting mat
- Sticklers foil stickers (Sakura)
- Soufflé pens (Sakura)
- Ribbon scraps
- Small alphabet stickers of your choice
- Sandpaper

I chose to alter the word *imagine* for my art studio wall. Carolee's Creations (www.adornit.com) offered this word as a set of letters, so I was ready to go. I chose patterned papers manufactured by American Crafts.

If you're using a different patterned paper for each letter, take a moment to decide which pattern will go on which letter. Pay attention to what patterns and colors sit next to each other. For example, you don't want to have three striped patterns in a row, followed by three circular-patterned papers. Mix things up to keep it interesting!

Altering the Letters

When you've decided on the order of your patterned paper and letters, you're ready to begin. Pick up your first letter, and follow these steps:

1. Using a foam brush, coat the entire top of the letter with decoupage adhesive.
2. Lay the letter upside down on the *wrong* side of the patterned paper. Press firmly and let dry.
3. Place a cutting mat underneath your patterned paper, and cut around the outside of your letter to remove the excess patterned paper.

4. Use sandpaper to sand away the edges of the paper, leaving your letter edges clean and smooth all around.

Your letter is now covered in patterned paper and ready to embellish.

Picture This

Depending on where you purchased your letters, the edges may be unfinished wood. If you want, paint the edges white, or cover them in patterned paper. For a natural feel, simply leave them as is.

5. Apply a foil sticker to your letter.

6. Color in the foil sticker with Soufflé pens.

Altered Alert

Soufflé pens are designed to work with foil stickers, leaving an opaque, raised finish. Using another pen might not yield the same results. When in doubt, test first on a scrap of extra paper, with a sticker you don't plan to use on your project.

Work slowly with the Soufflé pens for best results.

You now have your first completed letter! Repeat steps 1 through 4 for each additional letter you plan to display. Then, decorate all the letters with foil stickers, or mix it up and use a combination of stickers, ribbon, and other embellishments. I chose to use a combination of items to decorate my letters, and I was delighted with the results.

When you've created all your letters, it's time to put them on display. I chose to showcase my letters by simply leaning them on the wall, but you can hang your letters if you prefer. If the letters you're working with already have a hole in the back for hanging, simply add a nail to the wall, hang your letter, and you're all set. If not, add a small picture hanger to the back of each letter and then hang them on your wall for display.

These letters look great sitting on a bookshelf, leaning up against the wall.

Altered Alert

Letters not hanging straight on your wall? Try moving them just a bit off-center. If one side of your letter is heavier than the other, due to ribbon or extra embellishment, you'll need to place your picture hanger accordingly.

Creating on Canvas

Creating on canvas is much like creating in books, except your workable space is significantly larger, and the end result goes on your wall instead of your bookshelf. Try one of the fun canvas projects in the following sections to enrich your home décor.

Nature's Beauty Canvas

Nature photographs look amazing in almost any home because of their natural appeal. Try using a favorite photograph to create a wall canvas for your home. This beautiful wall canvas, designed by April Derrick, is simple to create and looks gorgeous in almost any room.

This stunning canvas is sure to be the center of conversation in any home.

(Canvas by April Derrick; photo by Kris Duvall)

To create a beautiful canvas like this for your own home, gather these supplies:

- 12×12-inch-stretched canvas (Canvas Concepts)
- 12×12-inch-*Life Noir* patterned paper (7gypsies)
- 12-inch-wide nature photograph of your choice

- Purple and black cardstock
- Rub-on letters
- Estate Sale Cream letter stickers (Sonnets by Creative Imaginations)
- Clear dot sticker
- Black bias tape
- Black acrylic paint
- Decoupage glue/finish

Now it's time to get crafting.

Picture This

While priming the canvas with gesso first isn't necessary for this project, it can help with paint adhesion. Opt for black gesso and get a dramatic result.

1. Paint the entire canvas surface, as well as the sides, with black acrylic paint. Let dry. Apply second paint coat if necessary.
2. Adhere the photo to the black cardstock using decoupage glue.
3. Trim the patterned paper and purple cardstock into strips. Adhere the strips to the canvas with decoupage glue. Let dry. Be sure to smooth out any air bubbles as you're gluing the papers.
4. Apply rub-on letters and alphabet stickers to the cardstock strip.
5. Glue a small strip of bias tape on the right-hand side of the cardstock strip.
6. Add a clear dot sticker to the bias tape.

You now have a beautiful wall hanging that can be enjoyed in your home for many years to come!

At the Beach Wall Canvas

You first saw this canvas in Chapter 1; now you can create it for yourself! I love this project because it's fun and whimsical—every time I look at it, it makes me smile. What more could I ask for when it comes to wall décor?

First, you'll need a few tools and supplies:

- Black-and-white photograph of you and your significant other (or another special couple in your life)
- 12×12-inch wall canvas
- 12×12-inch beach scene patterned paper (Poppets designed by Claudine Hellmuth, manufactured by Lazar StudioWERX)
- Die-cut male and female body shapes (Poppets designed by Claudine Hellmuth, manufactured by Lazar StudioWERX)
- Male and female arms stamps, male and female feet stamps, and thought bubble stamp (Poppets designed by Claudine Hellmuth, manufactured by Lazar StudioWERX)
- Black archival inkpad
- Black fine point pen
- Decoupage glue/finish
- Fine-point scissors

With your supplies in hand, follow these quick steps to create your canvas:

1. Use scissors to cut both heads from the photograph. Adhere these to the patterned paper.
2. Adhere the die-cut body shapes underneath the corresponding heads onto patterned paper.
3. Use the stamps to add the arms, legs, and feet to each body.

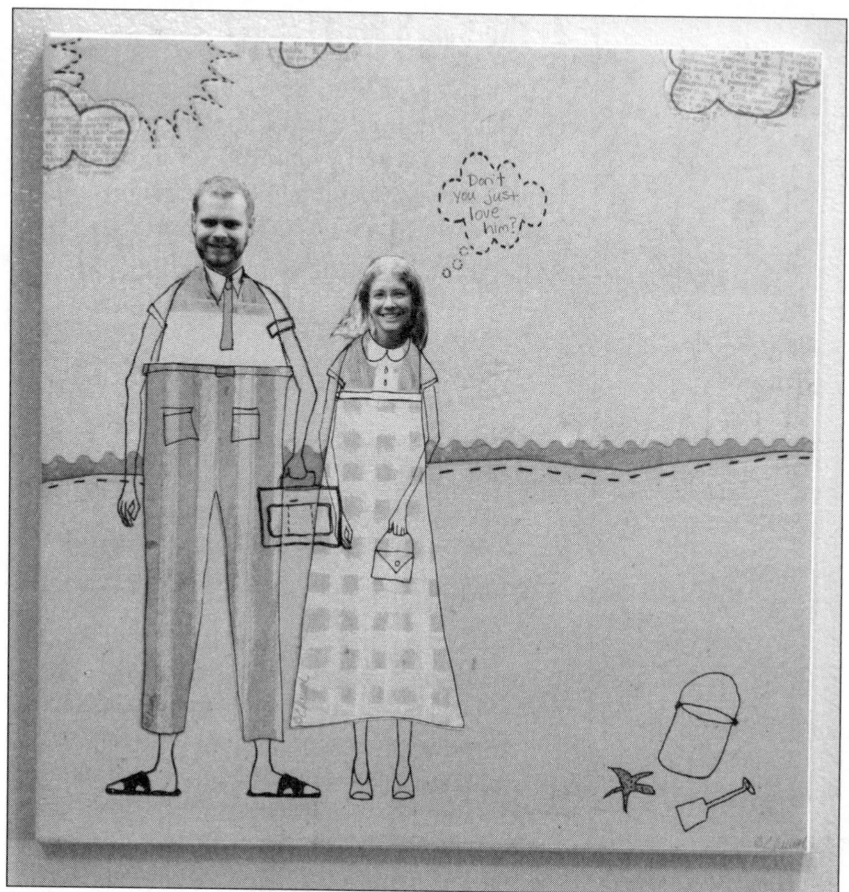

This canvas design is sure to brighten and lighten any room.

4. Use the stamp to create a thought bubble for one person on your paper.
5. Write a thought inside this bubble using the fine-point pen. I wrote: "Don't you just love him?"—a thought I often have about my husband.
6. Adhere the patterned-paper page to the canvas with decoupage glue.

Now display your new canvas with pride!

More Canvas Projects

Your mind might be spinning with ideas of what you can create after reading through the preceding projects. That's great! Go create and have fun with it! No matter what you choose to create and how you choose to create it, remember that altered canvases should reflect your personality and style.

Try one of these ideas as an altered canvas project:

- Create a series of canvases displaying your favorite locations.
- Make a canvas for each season of the year, displaying a view from a window in your home.
- Design a large canvas with a monogram letter for your child's bedroom.
- Celebrate a special interest or hobby by creating a themed canvas.
- If you're a scrapbooker, adhere a favorite 12×12-inch scrapbook page to a canvas and display year-round.

Canvas creations are perfect for your home—no matter what your style of décor. Create projects that match your own home and celebrate the things and people you care about. When you're finished, be sure to display your new canvas with pride!

The Least You Need to Know

- Altering block letters is fun and easy. Create a word or monogram that reflects your personal style.
- Creating a nature-themed wall canvas is a great way to add beauty into your home.
- Consider creating a whimsical wall canvas for a fun touch to add to any room.

In This Chapter

- Altering wood and other kinds of boxes
- Creating altered vases and cans
- Designing see-through altered cans

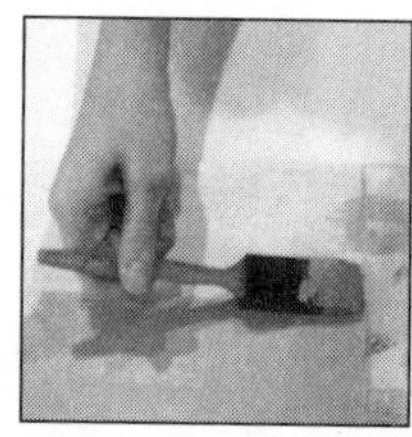

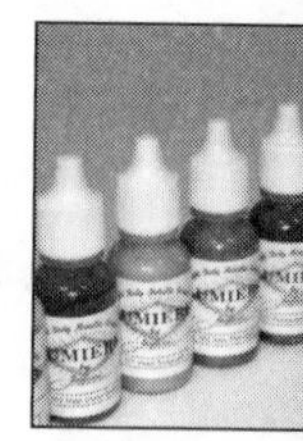

Chapter 17

Altered Boxes, Tins, and More

It's time to get dimensional. By now, you're a master at altering the flat surfaces of books, ATCs (artist trading cards), and canvas. Now you're going to try your hand at altering in three dimensions. In this chapter, we look at altering lunchboxes, tins, paint cans, and more. Many of the techniques you've learned from previous chapters can be applied to three-dimensional objects and alterations—making these projects simple, but still quite a bit of fun. Ready? Welcome to the world of the curvy.

Altered Tins

Tin boxes have been around for hundreds of years. My grandmother uses them to pass out holiday cookies to friends and family. A friend of mine uses them for pouring candles. When I was in grade school, we turned them into pencil cans. As it turns out, pencil cans are still cool, even for grown-ups. Take the time to turn a tin from ordinary to extraordinary with one of these great projects.

Altering tin boxes is a great way to create unusual keepsakes. With hundreds of different ways to alter tins, let your imagination go and see what you can come up with!

Altered Lunchboxes

For many of us, lunchboxes bring back happy childhood memories. I still remember picking out a new one each year as part of my back-to-school shopping. Well, metal lunchboxes are back in a big way, and ready for your creative touch.

This altered lunchbox is perfect for the artist's extensive collection of poems and quotes.

(Tin by Michelle Van Etten)

Creating an altered lunchbox of your own is easy! You'll need these supplies:

- Metal lunchbox (Provo Craft)
- 3 or 4 sheets of 12×12-inch patterned paper (BasicGrey)
- Rub-on letters (Rusty Pickle)
- Flowers, rhinestones, and leaves (Prima Marketing, Inc.)
- Ribbon (Sheer Creations)
- Glitter glue
- Gel medium, decoupage glue, or other strong adhesive of your choice

When you have your supplies, you're ready to begin altering your lunchbox:

1. Measure each side of your lunchbox, and cut patterned paper to fit. Allow an inch or 2 for overlap, to ensure that your lunchbox gets completely covered.
2. Adhere the patterned paper to the lunchbox using decoupage glue. Be sure to smooth out any air bubbles that form while you're adhering the paper. Let this dry completely.
3. Cut tags from a new sheet of patterned paper. To the tags, add rub-on letters to form words of your choice. Adhere the tags to the lunchbox.
4. Adhere the flowers, leaves, and rhinestones to the lunchbox.
5. Tie short ribbons all around the handle.

That's all there is to it! Altered lunchboxes are fun and can be used for a variety of purposes. Try altering a lunchbox using one of these ideas:

- Create a lunchbox for your daughter's hair accessories.
- Design a lunchbox featuring you or your child's favorite celebrities, TV personalities, or other famous friends. (Try searching the Internet for photographs if you don't have any of your own on hand.)
- Create a music-, movie-, or sports-themed altered lunchbox to hold all your ticket stubs.
- Cook up an altered lunchbox to store your favorite recipes.
- Create an altered lunchbox to use as an address book.

Altering lunchboxes is fun and rewarding, and the end result is second to none! And I'm sure the more you make, the more you'll find the perfect use for them around your home or to give as gifts.

Tin Shadow Boxes

Lunchboxes aren't the only tins worth altering. Take a look around your kitchen, especially in the pantry. See any tins in there worth altering? Tins come in all shapes and sizes, carrying all sorts of products, from tuna to SPAM or other canned meats to breath mints. Whether you choose to get your tin from the pantry or find one at your local craft store, have fun altering it!

Altered Alert

If you choose to alter a tin that originally held food, be sure to clean it completely and thoroughly before alteration. If not cleaned properly, acids and other chemicals from food may react with your paper and cause damage to your artwork.

Take a moment to flip through Parts 1 through 4 of this book. What techniques featured in those chapters did you love? What creative imagery caught your eye? Try employing some of those same altered book techniques while creating an altered tin. The results are well worth it.

To create her altered tin, Jennifer opted only to use the base of the tin, discarding the lid. (This is a great technique when you find yourself with a damaged or missing tin lid.) She created a collage inside the tin using some favorite collage items. The result is a beautiful tin that makes a charming addition to any tabletop.

Altered Alert

When working with tins—especially tins that have been opened with a can opener—watch out for sharp edges. Be sure any jagged edges have been thoroughly sanded to ensure that your art is safe to handle.

This tin is altered using a combination of vintage imagery, ephemera, and found objects.

(Tin by Jennifer Kinton-Bailey)

Don't be afraid to think outside the box—or should I say, outside the *tin*—and try your favorite paper techniques on metal. As we've learned over and over again, so much of altered art creation is allowing yourself the freedom to play and experiment with your creations. Try that in an altered tin today!

Wooden Boxes

I briefly touched on altering wooden boxes for holding your ATC cards in Chapter 13, and we explored altering wooden letters in Chapter 16. Now it's time to take that knowledge one step further and have some fun altering a wooden box to create a fun and funky jewelry box.

I love altering ready-made wooden boxes and shapes. It's simple, and I know the result will be a sturdy product I can enjoy for many years to come. You can find plain wooden boxes in many places. The best source I've found are craft and hobby stores, which often carry wooden boxes as well as other unfinished wood pieces—perfect for altering and sharing with others. My favorite boxes to alter are manufactured by Walnut Hollow.

This wooden box has been altered to showcase the artist's love for jewelry and art.

(Box by Alecia Ackerman Grimm)

To alter a wooden box to hold your jewelry or other treasures, you'll need a few key items:

- Wooden box of your choice
- Gel medium or decoupage glue/finish
- Decorative papers, embellishments, and ephemera to suit your style

UNALTERABLE FACT

As with much of altered art, few guidelines exist for you to follow when creating an altered jewelry box. The most important thing is to remember to allow your creative style to shine through.

Follow these steps to get an altered jewelry box ready to decorate:

1. Cover the box's outer surface thoroughly with decoupage glue.
2. Adhere decorative papers and collage elements of your choice all over the box.
3. Cover the entire surface with decoupage glue a final time. (This will dry hard and clear, giving your box a strong finish.)

Now, how you decorate your box is entirely up to you. For her jewelry box, Alecia used a combination of items, including the following:

- Patterned paper (SEI)
- Fortune cookie messages
- Decorative tape (Heidi Swapp)
- Rhinestones
- Sequins
- Paper flowers (Mermaid Tears)
- Bird die-cut shape (Poppy Ink)

Feel free to use similar items, or seek out your own products and ephemera according to your own interests. Remember, in altered art, you decorate and create to express *you*, so use whatever you like.

Vases, Pencil Holders, and More

As you might have picked up on by now, you can alter so many different items to hold your favorite things. You might already be looking around your home or office to locate items you can alter or use as decoration on another project. That's great—keep it up! If you're not quite there yet, never fear. In this section, we'll take a look at a few more projects to jump-start your creativity and get you thinking about more things you can alter.

Altered Floral Vase

Flowers, whether fresh or silk, can brighten any room—or mood! Rather than using a plain glass vase, though, why not alter that plain vase into something as beautiful as the flowers it holds?

Scrapworks design team artist Denise DiTullio altered this glass vase to fill with flowers. The result is fun and playful, making it a fantastic addition to any home.

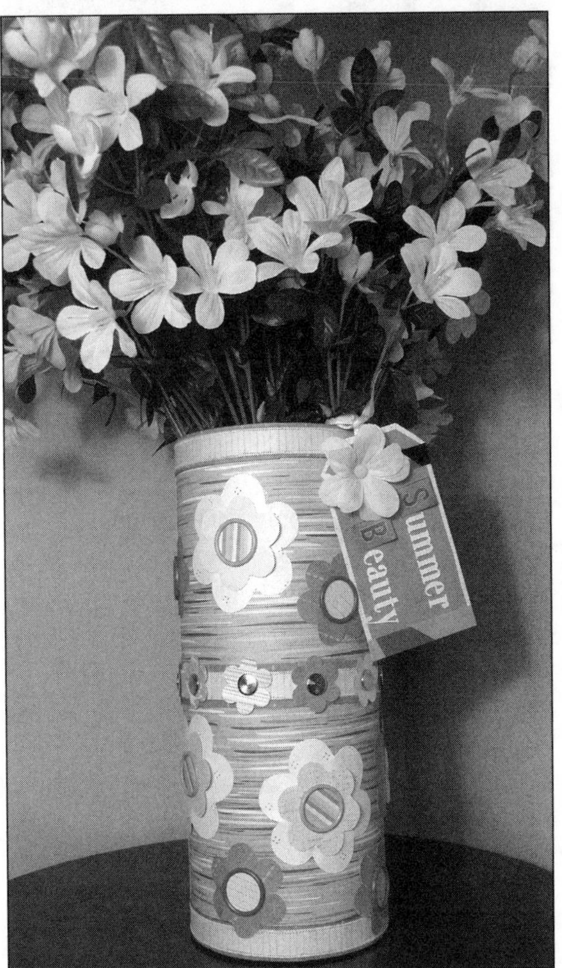

Denise's vase will instantly brighten any room.

To create your own altered vase, you'll need:

- Glass vase
- 3 sheets 12×12-inch coordinating patterned paper (Ethan Kate Evening Wear by Scrapworks)
- Alphabet and border stickers (Scrapworks)
- Silver studs, small circular frames (Scrapworks)
- Ribbon (Chatterbox)
- Gray inkpad
- Brad
- Silk flowers
- Decoupage glue
- Sewing machine and thread
- Decorative flower paper punch

With your supplies at the ready, it's time to begin altering your vase:

1. Cover the vase with patterned paper. Adhere with decoupage glue.
2. From a coordinating patterned paper, cut 3 (1½-inch-wide) strips of paper. From a second sheet of paper, cut 3 (¾-inch-wide) strips of paper.
3. Adhere 1 (¾-inch) strip to 1 (1½-inch) strip, centering the smaller strip on top of the larger one. Sew these together using a zigzag stitch on your sewing machine.
4. Repeat step 3 so you have three total strips to wrap around the vase.
5. Adhere one strip near the top of the vase and another near the bottom of the vase.
6. Use paper punch to punch flowers from patterned papers.
7. Attach punched flowers with conchos in the center of the third strip and then adhere the decorated third strip to the middle of the vase.

8. Scan the punched flower on your computer, and print it out enlarged in two different sizes. Cut out the flowers, and use them as templates to make additional flowers.
9. Add these additional flowers around rest of the vase.
10. Create a tag and add the words *Summer Beauty* with alphabet stickers. Add the tag to the vase using a small scrap of ribbon.

Creating an altered vase is a great way to liven up any room's décor. Next time you plan to give flowers as a gift, try presenting them to your recipient in a beautiful altered vase—a treasure that will last long after the flowers have wilted.

Picture This

Feeling a little nervous about using your sewing machine? Substitute rub-on stitches for real ones. Don't want to use your computer to make a flower template? Opt for precut floral shapes in a variety of sizes.

Altered Art Supply Can

Need a fun holder for all your art pens, paintbrushes, and tools lying around your desk? Look no further. This project helps you create the perfect storage solution.

This pen and tool holder looks great in any art room and keeps your art supplies organized.

(Supply can by Tara Daigle)

Tara created this supply holder from a can that was originally full of cashews. After enjoying the nuts, Tara cleaned out the can and grabbed a few extra supplies:

- Patterned paper and alphabet die-cut circle shapes (3 Bugs in a Rug)
- Alphabet rubber stamps (PSX)
- Ribbon (Li'l Davis Designs)
- Self-adhesive label

She then followed these steps to create her can:

1. Measure the patterned paper to fit the can. Cut the paper, and adhere it to the can. Let this dry completely.
2. Add alphabet die-cuts spelling *Art* to can.
3. Stamp the word *stuff* on self-adhesive label. Adhere the label to the can.
4. Adhere ribbon around the entire top edge of the can.

It's just that easy. Tara's can makes a great addition to any craft room. Try creating one of your own!

Clear Altered Cans

It's no secret that I love flowers. Real flowers, silk flowers, paper flowers—you name it. I especially love using flowers in my scrapbooking and altered art. So when Prima Marketing, Inc., introduced these clear cans full of flowers, I knew I was in heaven.

Of course, I purchased several cans right away and started using the flowers to my heart's content. What I failed to notice, however, was that the can itself had just as much potential as its contents! Michelle Van Etten, a design team member for Prima, was the first to realize that these cans had some serious potential for crafters and altered artists.

Notice how Michelle filled her can first with sand and then added seashells. She then added a pair of photographs embellished using patterned paper by My Mind's Eye, a wooden frame and some flowers by Prima, and even coastal netting. She finished off the piece by lining the exterior of the can and the handle with miniature shells. The end result is a priceless work of art that incorporates some of her favorite photographs, elements of nature, and art supplies.

The can comes full of high-quality faux flowers, with rickrack trim and gemstones to match.

This can has become the perfect showcase for these beach memories!

(Can by Michelle Van Etten)

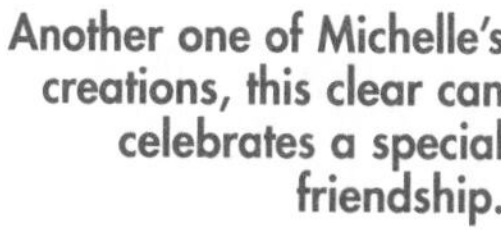

Another one of Michelle's creations, this clear can celebrates a special friendship.

(Can by Michelle Van Etten)

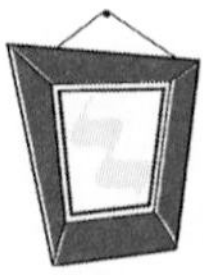

Picture This

Creating your own keepsake in a clear can is simple to do. Just add elements that reflect your style or the project's theme until the look is complete.

For her Best Friends can, Michelle created a miniature scrapbook page featuring a photograph and some journaling and then inserted it into the can. She added embellishments to the outside and inside of the can, and the result is priceless.

Try creating your own clear can design:

1. Design your can's background on a sheet of patterned paper or thin cardstock.
2. Add photographs, ephemera, or whatever else strikes your fancy.
3. Insert the sheet into the can.
4. Add embellishments, found objects, and accents to the can's interior and exterior.

These clear altered cans are one-of-a-kind keepsakes. And don't forget—you still get to keep and use all the fun treats that come inside the can!

The Least You Need to Know

- Altering metal tins can result in many personalized storage and gift options.
- Creating an altered wooden jewelry box is a fun way to express your personal style.
- Anything from a glass vase to a cashew can makes a great altered display for your flowers, art supplies, or anything else you want to showcase.
- By altering clear cans, you create a unique item to display your artwork.

In This Chapter

- Altering mirrors and photo frames
- Creating artist shadow boxes
- Making an altered puzzle

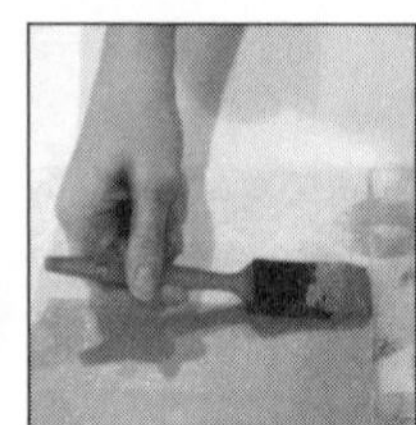

Chapter 18

On Display

If you've tried all or even a few of the projects in the earlier chapters of the book, altering items might be second nature to you by now. You've mastered all the basic skills and created some beautiful projects.

Whether you choose to create all these projects or adapt them to create your own new ideas, the results are sure to please.

Altering Framed Pieces

There's nothing quite like a beautiful frame. When I see a gorgeous frame, I am instantly struck by its possibilities—what photo I could put in it, where in my home I'd display it, etc.

Creating altered frames takes this concept even further. When you create an altered frame this beautiful, what goes inside is just the icing on the cake.

Notice how the patterned paper on this mirror reads "Shine"—perfect for this project!

(Mirror by Julie Ann Kelley)

Altered Framed Mirror

Altered mirrors are a blast to create. This framed mirror looks great in your home once you've altered it to your satisfaction. Plus, what goes inside really is the *real* art—your reflection. To get started, let's create this altered mirror, designed by Julie Ann Kelley.

To create an altered mirror of your own to dress up a favorite table or wall, gather these supplies:

- Unfinished wooden mirror (Julie found hers at Ikea.)
- 12×12-inch patterned papers (Urban Lily)
- "Smile" Woven tab label (Scrapworks Tailored Tabs)
- Cardstock
- Brads
- Decoupage glue/finish

Then, follow these steps to create your mirror:

1. Measure the dimensions of your mirror's surrounding frame, and cut the patterned paper to fit.
2. Adhere the patterned paper to frame with decoupage glue.
3. Cut circles from the patterned paper, and mount these on cardstock.

4. Coat all paper areas with decoupage glue.
5. Coat the circle embellishments with decoupage glue and set aside.
6. Allow all the pieces to dry completely.
7. Adhere the circle embellishments and the woven tab to the mirror frame.

You now have a beautiful and affirming mirror to display anywhere in your home, whether mounted on the wall or displayed on a tabletop.

Picture This

Altered mirrors are fantastic gifts for teenagers! Consider making a small altered mirror and adding a magnet on the back of the final product. Present to your favorite teen for a great school locker decoration!

Mermaid Frame

This beautiful project—perfect for a young girl's room or to complement the décor of anyone young at heart—was designed by Alecia Ackerman Grimm. Design this gorgeous frame to display a quote, as Alecia did, or to give a favorite photo center stage.

To create your own mermaid frame, you'll need these supplies:

- Unfinished photo frame
- 1 sheet 12×12-inch patterned paper (BasicGrey)
- Scrap of light brown textured paper
- Natural mix of small seashells and starfish (found at your local craft store)
- Mermaid paper doll (Mermaid Tears)
- Natural-colored raffia
- 1 sheet white cardstock (optional)
- Computer for journaling (optional)
- Decoupage glue/finish

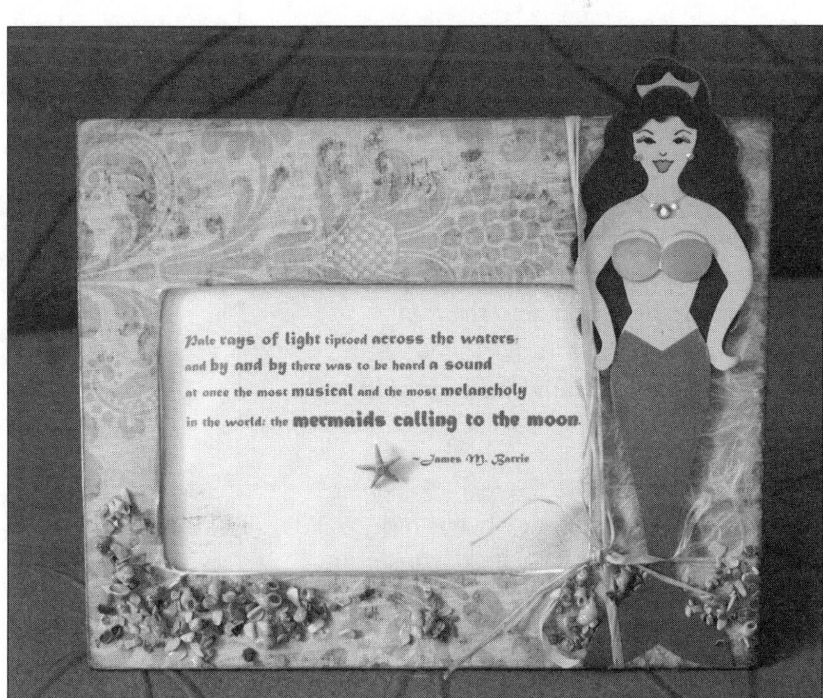

I love how the quote Alecia used in this frame really complements its design.

(Frame by Alecia Ackerman Grimm)

Follow these steps to create your altered frame:

1. Measure the dimensions of your frame, and cut patterned paper to fit.
2. Adhere the paper to the frame with decoupage glue. Let this dry completely.
3. Adhere the mulberry paper to the frame along right-hand side. Let this dry completely.
4. Adhere the mermaid paper doll on top of the mulberry paper.
5. Print this or another favorite quote on white cardstock:

   > Pale rays of light tiptoed across the waters; and by and by there was to be heard a sound at once the most musical and the most melancholy in the world: the mermaids calling to the moon.
   >
   > —J.M. Barrie

Unalterable Fact

Want to find the perfect quote for your own project? Try the Internet! Two of my favorite websites for quotes are www.quotationspage.com and www.goodquotes.com.

6. Cut the cardstock to fit the frame, and insert the quote in the frame.
7. Adhere the shell mix to the frame. Add the starfish to the cardstock piece.
8. Tie the raffia around the right side of the frame.

Whether you choose to create this exact frame design or create one of your own, you'll be so glad you did. Quotes make wonderful additions to frames and can provide a touch of inspiration to any room.

Shadow Boxes: Dimensional Framed Art

We got a little three-dimensional in Chapter 17, so let's do it some more by creating a *shadow box*. Shadow boxes are surprisingly easy to create. Creating a shadow box is much like creating an altered book page or scrapbook page, except you can frame the finished product without having to worry about whether the frame will smash the dimensional artwork you've created.

Transforming Talk

A **shadow box** is a framed piece of three-dimensional art with ample space between the art and the glass of the frame.

You can find shadow boxes at most art and hobby stores, as well as at specialty framing stores. You may also be able to find them at your local scrapbooking or stamping store. Shadow boxes come in a variety of sizes, colors, and styles. Select one that matches the tone and mood of the piece you plan to create.

Making a Shadow Box

With your shadow box frame selected, you're ready to get creative:

1. Measure a piece of background paper to fit your shadow box.
2. Embellish, alter, and decorate the paper to your heart's content. Consider adapting one of the projects from an earlier chapter if you're stuck for ideas.
3. Insert the decorated paper into your shadow box.

This shadow box makes a great addition to any little boy's room.

(Shadow box by Cheryl Baase)

Now hang your completed shadow box on a wall or display on a tabletop.

> **Picture This**
>
> By now, you've learned that just about anything can be altered! Don't forget that this includes the shadow box frame itself. Try any of the ideas in Chapter 17 to get started.

Triple-Panel Shadow Box

One of my favorite products to hit the market lately is the triple-panel shadow box, manufactured by EK Success' Maple Lane Studio imprint. These unique shadow boxes are 8 inches square, and 3 Plexiglas panels slide in and out of the shadow box. When all three panels are altered and inserted into the shadow box, the result is a dimensional, stunning piece of altered artwork.

My parents recently took a trip to Italy. When they returned home, they had hundreds of photographs to showcase their vacation. I asked my father to send me a few of his favorites, and this shadow box was born.

To create your own shadow box, round up these items:

- 3 to 6 favorite photographs
- 8-inch triple-panel shadow box (Maple Lane Studio by EK Success)
- Chipboard alphabet letters (Li'l Davis Designs)
- Rub-on decorative accents (Chatterbox)
- Rub-on numbers and alphabet (Scrapworks)
- Adhesive of your choice

This triple-panel shadow box features an Italian theme.

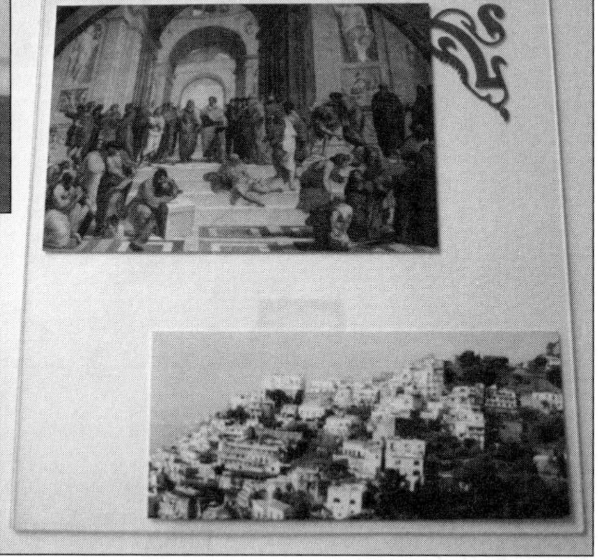

This back panel sets the foundation for the rest of the project.

This shadow box design can appear quite complicated at first, but that's really not the case! The key is to remember that the shadow box design is created in layers. Here's how to do it:

1. Remove the three Plexiglas panels from the box.
2. Start with the panel you plan to put in the far back of the shadow box. This is the bottom layer of your art piece.
3. Trim the photographs you want to use on the back panel to the desired sizes.
4. Adhere one photograph to the top-left corner of the panel.
5. Adhere a second photograph to the bottom-right corner of the panel.
6. Add a rub-on accent to the top-right corner of the panel.
7. Insert the finished panel into the back of the shadow box.

Picture This

You'll have plenty of empty space on this back panel, but don't worry! The holes will be filled in when you place all three panels into the shadow box.

The front panel provides key title and date information for the photos in the shadow box.

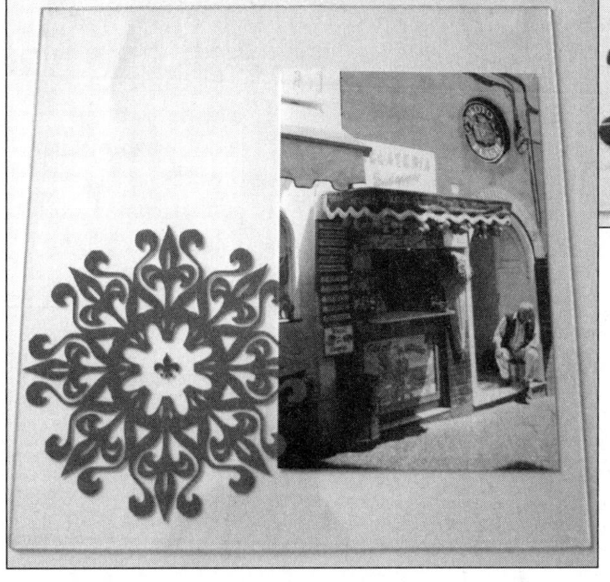

The middle panel features a beautiful design element as well as favorite photo.

To create the middle panel for your shadow box, follow these steps:

1. Adhere a vertically oriented photograph to the right side of the Plexiglas panel.
2. Add a large rub-on accent to the bottom-left corner of the panel.
3. Insert the finished panel into the middle of the shadow box.

It's time to create the final panel of your shadow box:

1. Trim a photo to a small size (so it won't completely cover the images on the two back panels), and adhere it to the bottom of the Plexiglas panel, slightly to the right of center.
2. Use rub-ons to apply the date to the top-right corner of the panel.
3. Add a title with chipboard letters along the left edge of the panel.
4. Insert the finished panel into the front of the shadow box.

Your shadow box is now complete, and you have a beautiful, multi-layered work of altered art that's ready for display.

Altered Puzzle

Puzzles can be great fun to alter. They are already so varied and unique—and can only become more so with your creative alterations. Try creating an altered puzzle as a stand-alone project, or alter just a piece or two and add it to existing artwork. Ready to get started? This beautiful altered puzzle project is an interesting piece of artwork and a fun addition to any room.

To create your own altered puzzle, gather the following supplies:

- Wooden puzzle
- Decoupage glue
- Sandpaper
- Paint in color of your choice
- Scraps of patterned paper, fabric pieces, and ephemera

Follow these steps to alter your puzzle:

1. Sand the puzzle surface so the original images are worn away.
2. Paint the puzzle edges in coordinating colors.
3. Trace each puzzle piece onto a scrap of patterned paper. Trim the paper to size, and it adhere to puzzle piece.
4. Coat each piece with a layer of decoupage glue.
5. Embellish the puzzle pieces with ephemera and fabric scraps.

Picture This

When looking for a puzzle to alter, look for a child's wooden or cardboard tray puzzle with 10 to 15 pieces. These are excellent for altering. There are no special things to consider when purchasing a puzzle—just select whatever puzzle happens to catch your eye. Flea markets and garage sales are a great place to find puzzles for altering!

This cute altered puzzle is fun and interactive, making it a great conversation starter.

(Puzzle by Mandy Collins)

Picture This

Don't have a puzzle you want to alter? Try altering any child's toy. Wooden blocks and board games are great choices.

Creating an altered puzzle is an exciting way to experiment with your artwork and create altered items that will always bring a smile to your face.

The Least You Need to Know

- An altered mirror or frame displays a favorite photograph or quote beautifully.
- A shadow box is a great way to display your multi-dimensional altered art creations.
- Altering a puzzle or other child's toy is a fun way to experiment artistically and create an interactive piece of altered art.

Appendix A

Transforming Talk Glossary

altered art The craft of taking a secondhand item, such as a book or old wooden box, and using creative techniques and tools to alter and change the item, giving it a new purpose and artistic meaning.

archival ink Ink that is permanent, waterproof, and lightfast. It's specifically designed to last for hundreds of years, ensuring that your artwork will last.

artist trading cards (ATCs) Miniature works of art, sized the same ($2\frac{1}{2} \times 3\frac{1}{2}$-inch) as traditional sports trading cards. They are usually one-of-a-kind originals and are created to be traded, never sold.

board books Small, sturdy books made from heavy-duty cardboard. They're typically made for very young children and feature bright, colorful designs.

bookbinding tape A self-adhesive cloth tape printers and bookbinders use to hold the covers and pages of a book together.

brayer A small roller with a handle, much like a miniature paint roller, that's used to evenly apply ink and paint to paper and other surfaces.

burnishing The act of rubbing the back of an image or element using a blunt edge. (A credit card works particularly well.) Images should be rubbed thoroughly and with a good amount of strength.

collage sheet An $8\frac{1}{2} \times 11$-inch page featuring small-scale reproductions of vintage art and ephemera.

emulsion A goolike coating of chemicals that lies in between the layers of Polaroid film that enables it to develop correctly.

emulsion lift The process of separating the emulsion coating from the image itself to perform an image transfer.

ephemera Printed material with little or no lasting value. Examples include memorabilia, junk mail, receipts, and maps.

gel medium A liquid gel that acts as an adhesive for altered art and collage, drying to a smooth finish. It's available in matte or glossy finish and can also be used to create a protective coating on top of your artwork, sealing out air and dust. Finally, it can be mixed with acrylic paint to extend drying time and add dimension to the dried paint.

gesso A primer commonly used by fine artists to prepare painting surfaces for decoration. It's generally white or black and can be applied like paint.

heat embossing The act of applying embossing powder to a stamped image and then heating the image. The heat melts the powder, resulting in a raised, fully metallic image.

image transfer The act of literally transferring an image from one surface to another, such as from a paper background to a clear Mylar background. Only the image, not the paper it's printed on, is transferred, creating a semi-transparent effect in the resulting image.

masking The act of covering one part of your design prior to applying ink or paint, allowing it to remain free of color to create contrast.

masking fluid A medium that, when used on your page, resists paint and ink in the area it's applied.

Microfleur A form of flower press that works in the microwave, yielding natural results in minutes.

niche A shallow opening in an altered book that can be filled with small dimensional items such as seashells, metal charms, and more.

sampler An altered book that contains pages and spreads decorated in all sorts of ways, without any real regard to whether or not they go together.

shadow box A framed piece of three-dimensional art, with ample space between the art and the glass of the frame.

Stampbord A specially designed stamping surface. It's similar to cardboard, but is thicker, stronger, and has a clay coating designed to hold ink and deliver amazing stamping impressions.

texture comb A small, triangle-shape object featuring various decorative edges. You rake the comb through wet paint, leaving decorative marks in the final painted design.

Victorian scrap A die-cut, embossed, lithograph printed image from the Victorian era, often featuring playful images of children or animals, and are usually brightly colored. Original Victorian scraps as well as reproductions are widely used in altered art.

walnut ink An ink traditionally made from walnuts, known for its thickness and deep color. Many manufacturers now mass-produce it synthetically as well as naturally.

Appendix B

Contributing Artists

I am so grateful that I've had the opportunity to work with such an amazing team of altered artists and scrapbookers from across the globe. All the following artists contributed to the projects in this book:

Alecia Ackerman Grimm
aleciagrimm.typepad.com

Alecia Grimm is a spirited artist who lives in downtown Atlanta, Georgia, but is originally from the frozen tundra of North Dakota. She is married and has four kids who keep her on her toes. She has been scrapbooking, painting, and creating art journals for almost 10 years. She is fascinated with photos and the process of narrating everyday life through art. She thrives on challenge and strives to be an innovative and design-driven mixed-media artist. Her work has previously appeared in numerous industry publications, including *The Complete Idiot's Guide to Scrapbook Projects Illustrated.*

Cheryl Baase
www.cropaddict.com/photopost/showgallery.php?cat=524

Cheryl is a scrapbook and altered artist residing in Lansing, Michigan. Her work has previously appeared in *Memory Makers*, *Legacy*, *Cantata*, *Paperkuts*, and *Jo-Ann's ScrapEssentials Volume 2.* She currently is on the design teams for Die Cuts With a View and Crop Addict.

Nancy Baumiller
nancybaumillersblog.blogspot.com
www.flickr.com/photos/nancys_vintage_freebies

Nancy is a mixed-media collage and altered artist residing in Fort Lawn, South Carolina. This publication is a first for her, and she's very excited have been included.

Jackie Baxted

Jackie was introduced to scrapbooking three years ago, and over the years, her interests have shifted to altered art. She loves the feeling she gets when creating something new by altering an object. Jackie says, "I like to think that by altering an object you are adding a piece of yourself to the new object." Her favorite projects are altered books and shrines.

Pam Callaghan

www.scrapbook.com/resumes/14619.html

Pam is an avid scrapbooker and currently lives in Ohio with her husband, Kevin, and son, Sean. In addition to contributing artwork to my first book, *The Complete Idiot's Guide to Scrapbook Projects Illustrated*, Pam's work has also appeared in several magazines, including *Scrapbooks Etc.*, *Creating Keepsakes*, *Scrapbook Trends*, *PaperART*, *Legacy*, and *Scrap and Stamp Arts*. Pam's work has also been featured in several major idea books, and she enjoys creating artwork for QVC and trade shows.

Chris Chapman

Chris Chapman has been paper crafting for about eight years. Although primarily a scrapbooker, she also enjoys altered arts, especially converting unusual and disgarded items into papercraft projects. She teaches classes and her work has been published in idea books from *Making Memories*, *Simple Scrapbooks*, and *Papercuts*. Chris resides in Southern California.

Mandy Collins

pearlmaple.blogspot.com

Mandy is a craftsperson currently living in Australia. She has a mixed background in art, quilt making, watercolor, and doll making. When her daughter took up scrapbooking six years ago, Mandy became more interested in paper arts—quickly jumping into mail art and altered books. Altered books are now her favorite because, as she says, it's the only way she can use all her skills in art, sewing, computer technology, and stamping all in the same piece and never look too overdone!

Lynn Anne Cutler

forum.scrapfriends.us/blog/lynnanne

Lynn Anne is a writer, teacher, and memory artist living in western New Jersey with her scrapbooker husband and two toddlers. Her work has previously appeared in *Scrapbook Answers*, *Legacy*, and *The Rubber Stamper*.

Tara Daigle

Tara Daigle has been scrapbooking for six years. She enjoys creating traditional scrapbook layouts as well as altered art. She currently resides in Mobile, Alabama, with her husband and their twin boys. Her work has been featured in idea books by Creating Keepsakes, Memory Makers, and Cantata books. Tara has also been featured in other publications, including *Paper Trends* magazine. She is a designer for Fiber Scraps and Scrapjazz.com.

April Derrick

www.ataleintime.com

April is a scrapbook designer and teacher currently residing in Perryville, Arkansas. She is the design team leader at www.memoryvilla.com. Her work has previously appeared in *The Complete Idiot's Guide to Scrapbook Projects Illustrated*, as well as Pine Cone Press books. April's magazine credits include *Memory Makers*, *Scrapbook Trends*, and *Creating Keepsakes*.

Diane DiTullio

www.scrapsubmit.com/Bio.php?B43

Diane is a scrapbook and altered artist currently residing in Hanover, Massachusetts. Her work has been published in *Simple Scrapbooks*, *Scrapbook Trends*, *Paper Crafts*, *Paper Art*, *Paper Trends*, and Cantata Books. Diane is also a design team member for Scrapworks and ACherryonTop.com. Diane enjoys teaching at her local scrapbook store, The Crop Shop.

Rachael Giallongo

www.rachaelgiallongo.com

A resident of Auburn, New Hampshire, Rachael has been scrapbooking since 1998 and says her greatest inspiration is preserving memories for her four children. Rachael was a featured artist in *The Complete Idiot's Guide to Scrapbook Projects Illustrated*, and her work has appeared in many other major publications, including *Creating Keepsakes*, *Memory Makers*, *Scrapbook Trends*, and several Pinecone Press publications.

Claudia Hafner

www.claudiahafner.com

Claudia is an altered artist based in London, United Kingdom. She works with a wide range of media, influenced by her education as a cultural anthropologist and her travels. Her art has been previously displayed at the House of Cards I Exhibition in Columbus, Ohio, and in Durham, United Kingdom. She has also been published in *Scrapbooking Ideas*. She is an active contributor to the UK altered art community and a member of the International Society of Altered Book Artists.

Julie Ann Kelley

www.scrapbookresumes.com/JulieAnnKelley

Julie is a digital and paper scrapbook and altered artist who lives in Massachusetts with her husband and two wonderful children. In addition to this project, she has been published by Cantata Books, Ready Set Create, and Scrapstreet.com. Although her children are her greatest creative inspiration for scrapbook pages, altering items for use as gifts and home decoration is something she has always enjoyed.

Diane Keys

groups.yahoo.com/group/friendlyfeline

Diane Keys is a mixed-media artist living in Elgin, Illinois. She has had artwork published in *The New Pliedes Anthology of Poetry*, *Somerset Studio*, the *Colorado Springs Gazette*, and the *Chicago Sun-Times*. She is a contributing artist for Art-O-Mat vending machines and will have artwork appearing soon in a Somerset Special Publication called "Altered Couture."

Jen Kinton-Bailey

www.jenkinton-bailey.com

Jen is a mixed-media collage artist living in Greensboro, North Carolina. She is a member of several art groups, and her work has been featured numerous places. Her work has even been included on a collage sheet for other artists to use in their own altered art projects. Jen loves to share her techniques with other artists and has written several classes on different altered art techniques for ARTchix Studio.

Carolyn Lontin

www.scrapbookresumes.com/CarolynLontin

Carolyn is an artist dabbling in all areas of paper crafting, from scrapbooking to altered arts, and she is rarely seen without her camera in hand. She resides in Colorado with her husband, son, and two dogs. Her work has recently appeared in many popular scrapbook and paper crafting magazines and idea books, as well as on QVC.

Wendy Malichio

wendymalichio.typepad.com/wendysway

Wendy is a scrapbook and altered artist currently residing in Connecticut. Her work has previously appeared in *Creating Keepsakes*, *Memory Makers*, *Paper Kuts*, *Scrapbook Trends*, *Legacy*, *Paper Crafts*, *Simple Scrapbooks*, *Scrapbook Premier/Brainiac Series*, *Scrapbook Retailer*, *Leisure Arts Idea Books (NanC and Co.)*, *Correspondence Art Magazine*, *MDW Splendor Idea Book*, *Cantata Books*, *My Life in a Scrapbook*, and *Scrapbooking Magazine.com*, along with several other publications and scrapbooking and paper crafting videos. She is also a contributing designer of *Cards! Fast and Fabulous*.

Mandy Rentmeester–van Goeije

www.beadsandart.com

Mandy is a self-taught artist from the Netherlands. She specializes in ATCs, altered art, digital photography, and jewelry with a distinct, fantasylike style. Initially a teacher, Mandy is now fully devoted to the artistic path. She finds inspiration in nature, art, distant cultures, and mysteries of the world.

Julie Richards

Julie was blessed with a heart for creating and discovered scrapbooking five years ago. When she's not shopping for the newest scrapbook supplies, she spends time with her husband and four children in Pflugerville, Texas. Her work has been published by *Creating Keepsakes*, *Memory Makers*, *Scrapbooks Etc.*, and Canata Publishing.

Robin Riley-Wright

Robin is a freelance graphic designer, living on the edge of the pine barrens in southern New Jersey. Robin loves paper and paper arts and enjoys working on both altered books and wheel-thrown pottery in her log home studio.

Kate Schaefer

kateschaefer.typepad.com

www.myspace.com/kisforkiddo

Kate Schaefer is an accomplished scrapbook artist and a newcomer to altered art. She lives with her husband in North Liberty, Iowa. Her work has previously appeared in *The Complete Idiot's Guide to Scrapbook Projects Illustrated.*

Belinda Spiwak

www.artdustbunnies.com

alteredbelly.blogspot.com

Belinda is a mixed media artist and teacher residing in Aurora, Illinois. Her artwork and various art-related articles have been published in *Legacy* and *Altered Arts* magazines, as well as in art zines such as *The Gleaner Zine*, *The Book Artist Zine*, *Art Echoes Zine*, and *The AB Zine*. Belinda also self-publishes her own art zines and owns several art-related Yahoo! groups.

Yvonne Thistle-Brewer

Yvonne Thistle-Brewer is an altered artist currently residing in Guelph, Ontario, Canada. She enjoys creating artist trading cards and sharing them with artists across the globe.

Michelle Van Etten

www.scrapbookresumes.com/MichelleVanEtten

Michelle Van Etten is a freelance designer residing in Pensacola, Florida. Her work has been featured in many publications, including *The Complete Idiot's Guide to Scrapbook Projects Illustrated.* She currently serves on a few manufacturer design teams, including Prima Marketing, Inc.

Sandy Wisneski

www.picturetrail.com/stampcat3

Stamping has been a love of Sandy's from the first time she saw embossing powder melt. She has been stamping for more than 12 years, but recently has pursued altered art as well as a variety of other art mediums. She has been published in *Vamp Stamp News*, *The Rubberstamper*, *CorrespondenceArt*, and *Paper Trends*. Several projects are published in a new book, *Beyond Scrapbooks: Using Your Scrapbook Supplies to Make Beautiful Cards, Gifts, Books, Journals, Home Decorations and More!* During the day, Sandy is a reading specialist at Ripon Middle School. Sandy and her husband enjoy golfing together as well as being with their grandson, Mason.

Appendix C

Materials Guide

Due to the nature of altered art, many projects in this book use items that are one-of-a-kind, ephemera, or aren't available commercially. When this is the case, it's nearly impossible to replicate a project exactly. Use your imagination or substitute a similar product. However, many projects in this book due use products from the scrapbooking and craft industry, which are indeed widely available. That's where this materials guide comes in.

When possible, this listing lets you know exactly what products were used to create each project in this book. If you notice a stamp or item on a project that you'd like to use in your own artwork, use this appendix to identify the manufacturer. Then, turn to Appendix D to learn how to contact that manufacturer to purchase your product.

Chapter 1

Blue Flower Girl
Victorian scrap image (Victorian Scrapworks), chipboard words (Magnetic Poetry), Permapaque pens (Sakura).

Dreams
Transparent floral image (Altered Pages), tweed flowers (Michael Miller Memories), sticker (Violette Stickers), stamps (100 Proof Press), rub-on letters (Scrapworks), chipboard arrow (Heidi Swapp), scrap piece of metallic mesh.

Go Fish
Mailbox letters (Making Memories), fish Victorians scraps (Victorian Scrapworks), chipboard arrow (Heidi Swapp).

Beach Collage
See Chapter 16 for complete instructions and supplies.

Artist Trading Cards
Collage sheet images (Teesha Moore—www.teeshamoore.com), Dymo labeler, additional images from greeting cards.

Chapter 2

Always Wish
Collage sheet images (Altered Pages), Victorian scrap images (Victorian Scrapworks), stamps (100 Proof Press), miniature clock (Li'l Davis Designs), key (Li'l Davis Designs).

Daddy's Girl
Patterned paper (Heidi Grace Designs), chipboard letter (Pressed Petals), sticker (Scrapworks), stamp (Catslife Press).

Chapter 3

Prom Journal
Paper doll (Mermaid Tears), flower (Mermaid Tears), chipboard letter (Making Memories), ribbon (Making Memories, May Arts, Bazzill Basics), floral journal.

Chapter 4

Carnival
Stickers (Violette Stickers), stamps (Technique Tuesday).

True Love
All products by Sweetwater Scrapbook.

Chapter 5

The Story of the Christmas Guest
Stamps (100 Proof Press, Catslife Press), stickers (Violette Stickers).

What Will the Girl Become?
Stamps (100 Proof Press, Catslife Press), collage sheet image (Altered Pages), ribbon (Strano Designs).

A Fairytale
Victorian scrap images, metallic trim (Victorian Scrapworks), stamp (Catslife Press), ribbon (Strano Designs).

Chapter 6

The Eyes Are the Window to the Soul
Stamp (Enchanted Ink), quote and word die cuts (K&Company).

Always Shine
Stamp (100 Proof Press).

Retro Cocktail Party
Stamps (100 Proof Press), fabric papers (Michael Miller Memories), ribbon (Strano Designs).

Chapter 7

Image
Stamps (100 Proof Press, Catslife Press), collage sheet images (Altered Pages).

A Wish for Happy
Stamps (Ma Vinci's Reliquary), collage sheet image (Altered Pages), Victorian Scrap (Victorian Scrapworks).

Chapter 8

Angels
Patterned paper (Karen Foster Design), chipboard letters (Making Memories).

Daydream
Frame (Heidi Swapp).

Chapter 10

Splash
Stamp (100 Proof Press), letter stickers (Chatterbox).

Chapter 12

That Night He Dreamt
Collage sheet images (Altered Pages).

Chapter 13

British Invasion
Patterned paper (Reminisce), quote die cut (K&Company), stamp (100 Proof Press), rub-on letters (Making Memories).

Pop
Patterned paper (CherryArte), word and phrase die cuts (K&Company), stamps (Enchanted Ink, Technique Tuesday).

Chapter 14

Love Letters Album
Patterned paper (Scenic Route Paper Co), bookplate (L'il Davis Designs), flower (Prima).

This Is What Happiness Looks Like
Patterned paper (Making Memories, Scenic Route Paper Co), vintage image (Memories in the Making), stamp (Catslife Press), date stamp.

Special Delivery
Stamps (Ma Vinci's Reliquary, Catslife Press).

Mom's Brag Book
Patterned paper (KI Memories), button (Junkitz).

Chapter 15

Cards Tin
Tin (Pinecone Press), patterned paper (Design Originals), ribbon (Offray), letters (Li'l Davis Designs).

Appendix D

Further Resources

You've mastered the basics of altered art, and now it's time to take your artwork a step further. Consult these great resources as you look to build your arsenal of skills and try even more mediums.

Books

These are some of my favorite books that are currently available to altered artists and crafters.

Artist Trading Cards: An Anthology of ATCs. Laguna Hills, CA: Stampington & Company, 2004.

Bantock, Nick. *Urgent 2nd Class: Creating Curious Collage, Dubious Documents, and Other Art from Ephemera.* San Francisco: Chronicle Books, 2004.

Berlin, Bernie. *Artist Trading Card Workshop.* Cincinnati: North Light Books, 2006.

Brazelton, Bev. *Altered Books Workshop.* Cincinnati: North Light Books, 2004.

Bright, Allyson. *Complete Idiot's Guide to Scrapbook Projects Illustrated, The.* Indianapolis: Alpha Books, 2006.

Curry, Nancy. *Texture Effects for Rubber Stamping.* Cincinnati: North Light Books, 2004.

Cyr, Gabe. *New Directions in Altered Books.* New York: Lark Books, 2006.

Finwall, Barbara, Nancy Javier, and Jerilyn Clements. *Let's Play Cards.* Little Rock: Leisure Arts, 2005.

———. *Let's Trade: Artist Trading Cards.* Little Rock: Leisure Arts, 2004.

Goodson, Laurie, and Betsy McLaughlin. *Altered Book Special Effects.* Fort Worth: Design Originals, 2003.

Harrison, Holly. *Altered Books, Collaborative Journals, and Other Adventures in Bookmaking.* Gloucester, MA: Rockport Publishers, 2003.

Harrison, Holly, and Paula Grasdal. *Collage for the Soul.* Gloucester, MA: Rockport Publishers, 2003.

Hellmuth, Claudine. *Collage Discovery Workshop.* Cincinnati: North Light Books, 2003.

———. *Collage Discovery Workshop: Beyond the Unexpected.* Cincinnati: North Light Books, 2005.

Mason, Jenn. *Pockets, Pullouts, and Hiding Places: Interactive Elements for Altered Books, Memory Art, and Collage.* Gloucester, MA: Quarry Books, 2005.

Matthiessen, Barbara. *Altered Book Collage.* New York: Sterling Publishing Company, 2005.

Meyer, Kim, and Susan Stover. *How to Paint with Jacquard.* Healdsburg, CA: Jacquard, 2005.

Michel, Karen. *The Complete Guide to Altered Imagery.* Gloucester, MA: Quarry Books, 2005.

Perella, Lynne. *Alphabetica: An A–Z Creativity Guide for Collage and Book Artists.* Gloucester, MA: Quarry Books, 2006.

———. *Artist Journals and Sketchbooks.* Gloucester, MA: Quarry Books, 2004.

Riley, Lesley. *Quilted Memories.* New York: Sterling Publishing Company, 2005.

Smiley, Jan Bode. *The Art of Fabric Books.* Lafayette, CA: C&T Publishing, 2005.

Sussman, Pam. *Fabric Art Journals.* Gloucester, MA: Quarry Books, 2005.

Taylor, Terry. *Altered Art.* New York: Lark Books, 2004.

———. *Artful Paper Dolls: New Ways to Play with a Traditional Form.* New York: Lark Books, 2006.

True Colors: A Palette of Collaborative Art Journals. Laguna Hills, CA: Stampington & Company, 2003.

Wingert, Carol, and Tena Sprenger. *Artful Memories.* Cincinnati: North Light Books, 2006.

Internet Resources

The Internet has a wealth of information available for the altered artist. Enjoy these websites, or try searching for additional resources on your own.

Manufacturers

You can find most of the products needed for projects in this book at your local art, craft, or scrapbooking store. If you need assistance obtaining a particular product, please visit the manufacturer's website so you can find stores that sell what you're looking for.

100 Proof Press
www.100proofpress.com

Altered Pages
www.alteredpages.com

American Crafts
www.americancrafts.com

Beacon Adhesives
www.beaconadhesives.com

Carolee's Creations
www.adornit.com

Catslife Press
www.catslifepress.com

Daisy D's Paper Company
www.daisydspaper.com

Daylab
www.daylab.com

Enchanted Ink
www.enchantedink.com

Fiber Scraps
www.fiberscraps.com

Jacquard
www.jacquardproducts.com

Lazar StudioWERX
www.lazarstudiowerxretail.com

Leisure Arts/Memories in the Making
www.leisurearts.com

Li'l Davis Designs
www.lildavisdesigns.com

Ma Vinci's Reliquary
reliquary.cyberstampers.com

Masquepen
www.masquepen.com

Michael Miller Memories
www.michaelmillermemories.com

Microfleur
www.microfleur.com.au

Sakura
www.gellyroll.com

Scenic Route Paper Company
www.scenicroutepaper.com

Stampord/Ampersand Art Supply
www.stampbord.com

Stewart Superior
www.stewartsuperior.com

Strano Designs
www.stranodesigns.com

Sweetwater Scrapbook
www.sweetwaterscrapbook.com

Technique Tuesday
www.techniquetuesday.com

Victorian Scrapworks
www.victorianscrapworks.com

Violette Stickers
www.violettestickers.com

Walnut Hollow
www.walnuthollow.com

Altered Art Communities

These websites enable you to connect with other altered artists in other parts of the nation and world:

Altered Art
groups.msn.com/altered art

The Altered Book
www.altered-book.com

Artist Trading Cards
www.atcards.com

The International Society of Altered Book Artists
www.alteredbookartists.com

Additional Resources

Turn to these sites for additional help and information:

Altered Arts Magazine
www.alteredarts.com

Copyright for Collage Artists
www.funnystrange.com/copyright

Index

A

B

C

D

E

F

G

H

I-J-K-L

M

S

T

U-V

W-X-Y-Z